Principle Based Enterprise Architecture

A SYSTEMATIC APPROACH TO ENTERPRISE ARCHITECTURE
AND GOVERNANCE

Ian Koenig

Technics Publications
BASKING RIDGE, NEW JERSEY

2 Lindsley Road
Basking Ridge, NJ 07920 USA
https://www.TechnicsPub.com

Cover design by Lorena Molinari

Edited by Lauren McCafferty

All rights reserved. No part of this book may be reproduced or transmitted in any form or by any means, electronic or mechanical, including photocopying, recording or by any information storage and retrieval system, without written permission from the publisher, except for the inclusion of brief quotations in a review.

The author and publisher have taken care in the preparation of this book, but make no expressed or implied warranty of any kind and assume no responsibility for errors or omissions. No liability is assumed for incidental or consequential damages in connection with or arising out of the use of the information or programs contained herein.

All trade and product names are trademarks, registered trademarks, or service marks of their respective companies and are the property of their respective holders and should be treated as such.

First Edition

First Printing 2019

Copyright © 2018 Ian Koenig

ISBN, print ed.	9781634624947
ISBN, Kindle ed.	9781634624954
ISBN, PDF ed.	9781634624978

Library of Congress Control Number: 2019933348

To my wife Nancy and my children Robert and Jonathan, who never understood what I did for a living, but always gave me the support I needed to do it.

To my mother Beverly, whose fortitude through difficult times helped make me the person I am today.

Contents

Acknowledgments _____ xi

Introduction _____ 1

PART I: The Principle Based Enterprise Architecture (PBEA) Method _____ 11

Chapter 1: Context _____ 13
    Objectives _____ 14
    Solutions _____ 14
    Placement of Function (PoF) _____ 15
    Environments _____ 16

Chapter 2: Assets _____ 19
    System assets _____ 20
    Data Assets _____ 27
    Software assets _____ 30
    Infrastructure assets _____ 31
    The art of versioning _____ 31

Chapter 3: Program Increments _____ 35

Chapter 4: Roles _____ 37
    Product owner _____ 37
    Business capability owner _____ 38
    Technology owner _____ 38
    Asset owner _____ 40
    Technical architect _____ 41
    Enterprise architect _____ 41
    Solution architect _____ 41

Chapter 5: An Example - vNews (Pronounced: Nu News) _____ 43

Chapter 6: Architecture Governance _____ 47
    Asset governance _____ 48
    API governance _____ 51
    Software asset governance _____ 53

Chapter 7: Architecture Metrics _____ 55
    The Asset Checklist _____ 55
    Technical debt and architecture debt _____ 61
    Outcomes and the 'body of evidence' _____ 63

Chapter 8: Best Practices and Processes _____ 65
Inventories and registries _____ 65
Patterns _____ 69
Architecture diagramming _____ 69
Architecting testable solutions _____ 70
Architecting secure and compliant solutions _____ 74
Architecting responsive solutions _____ 78
Operational practice _____ 82
Monitoring practice _____ 83
Graceful degradation of service _____ 84

Chapter 9: Change Management _____ 87
Golden rule evolution _____ 87
Root cause analysis (Why? Why? Why?) _____ 90
Technology standard evolution _____ 90

Chapter 10: Getting Started with PBEA _____ 93
Step 1 _____ 93
Step 2 _____ 93
Step 3 _____ 94
Step 4 _____ 94
Step 5 _____ 95
Step 6 _____ 95
Step 7 _____ 96
Step 8 _____ 97
Step 9 _____ 97
Step 10 _____ 98
Step 11 _____ 98
Step 12 _____ 99

PART II: PBEA Architecture Objectives, Principles, and Golden Rules _____ 101

Chapter 11: Architecture Principles _____ 103

Chapter 12: Architecture Golden Rules _____ 105

Chapter 13: Architecture Objectives for Systems _____ 107
Safe solutions _____ 107
Responsive solutions _____ 108
Effective solutions _____ 108

Chapter 14: Architecture Objectives for Data _____111
Safe solutions _____111
Responsive solutions _____111
Effective solutions _____112

Chapter 15: Asset Principles and Golden Rules _____113
Secure systems (safe solutions) _____113
Compliant systems and data (safe solutions) _____115
Scalable systems (responsive solutions) _____117
Manageable systems (responsive solutions) _____117
Reliable systems and data (responsive solutions) _____119
Simple systems (effective solutions) _____120
Modular systems and data (effective solutions) _____121
Maintainable systems (effective solutions) _____123
Mastered systems and data (effective solutions) _____124
Global systems and data (effective solutions) _____125

PART III: System Asset Golden Rules and Measures _____127

Chapter 16: Secure Systems – Golden Rules and Measures _____129
Protect end-user authentication secrets _____129
Control access to important systems and data _____131
Keep web traffic private _____132
Body of evidence _____133
Sanitize inputs from untrusted sources before use _____133
Do not let data become code. _____136
Minimize access to regulated data and protect it when used _____137
Do not place sensitive data in a URL _____140
Use third-party software safely _____140
Catch internet-facing security exposures before they are exploited _____144
Record and report important security related events _____145
Use standard authentication implementations _____147
Use standard encryption implementations _____149
Architect system assets to degrade gracefully when attacked _____150
Deploy system assets only into known safe environments _____151

Chapter 17: Compliant Systems – Golden Rules and Measures _____153
Protect the organization's intellectual property _____153
Use third-party Intellectual Property (IP) in accordance with its license _____154
Store Source code in a secure and managed repository _____156
Golden rule measures _____156

Ensure end-user interfaces are accessible _____ 157

Chapter 18: Scalable Systems – Golden Rules and Measures _____ 159
Deliver acceptable performance under anticipated load _____ 160
Optimize the cost of capacity _____ 161
Set appropriate limits on auto-scaling _____ 164

Chapter 19: Manageable Systems – Golden Rules and Measures _____ 167
Respond to standard control commands _____ 168
Publish appropriate operational events and error messages _____ 169
Publish performance and capacity data _____ 171
Maintain a complete inventory of all operational resources _____ 172

Chapter 20: Reliable Systems – Golden Rules and Measures _____ 175
Record all requests and measure adherence to your SLA _____ 176
Record all calls made to other assets and measure the dependent assets' adherence to their SLA _____ 177
Continue to meet SLA obligations in the event of a single failure _____ 179
Continue to meet SLA obligations in the event of a site failure _____ 181
Ensure that functional testing includes at least one test case covering each of the capabilities and features supported _____ 182
Handle unrecoverable failures and recoverable failures appropriately _____ 184
Ensure all production changes are repeatable and auditable _____ 185

Chapter 21: Simple Systems – Golden Rules and Measures _____ 187
Do not use unmaintained assets or deprecated APIs _____ 187
Do not couple an asset to an environment _____ 189
One asset, one team _____ 190
Follow Placement of Function (PoF) _____ 192
Package code to facilitate independent releases _____ 192
Minimize code duplication and complexity _____ 194

Chapter 22: Modular Systems – Golden Rules and Measures _____ 197
Expose and consume only well-defined external interfaces _____ 198
Manage and version control External Interfaces _____ 202
Do not couple External Interfaces to their implementation _____ 204
Handle retries appropriately _____ 205

Chapter 23: Maintainable Systems – Golden Rules and Measures _____ 207
Make interfaces directly callable without a proprietary library _____ 207
Trace requests and failures to their source _____ 209
Appropriately comment source code and interfaces _____ 211

Chapter 24: Mastered Systems – Golden Rules and Measures 213
Register the master system asset for every data asset 214
Keep data quality high 216
Encapsulate data 218
Trace data to its source 219
Do not connect end-user applications directly to data masters 220
Do not lose data 222

Chapter 25: Global Systems - Golden Rules and Measures 225
Handle data in a globalized way 226
Distinguish third-party translations from company translations 227
Adapt to the user's preferred locale 230

PART IV: Data Asset Golden Rules and Measures 233

Chapter 26: Compliant Data - Golden Rules and Measures 235
Classify and manage data according to the data classification 235
Retain data as required by the business and by legal and regulatory requirements, and destroy thereafter 237

Chapter 27: Reliable Data - Golden Rules and Measures 241
Data curation processes are designed and followed 241
Data schemas are designed and adhered to 243
Data is accurate 245
Data is complete 247
Data is timely 248
Data quality control processes are defined and followed 249

Chapter 28: Modular Data – Golden Rules and Measures 251
Databases and models are defined flexibly to support changing requirements 251
Meaning is defined separately from presentation and not inferred from presentation 253
Master data and product data evolve separately 255

Chapter 29: Mastered Data - Golden Rules and Measures 257
Each data asset is mastered by one and only one system asset 257
Master data assets are modeled 259
Data Enrichments are mastered 262

Chapter 30: Global Data – Golden Rules and Measures 265
Number-centric data is stored in a globalized way 265
Textual data is stored in a globalized way 267

Chapter 31: Technology Ownership and Operational Readiness 269

Chapter 32: Asset Ownership ___ 273

Chapter 33: Architecture Responsibilities ___ 275

Chapter 34: Software Development Responsibilities ___ 277

Chapter 35: Testing Responsibilities ___ 279

Chapter 36: Build-to-Deploy Responsibilities ___ 281

Chapter 37: Hosting & Operations Responsibilities ___ 283

Chapter 38: Hosting Security Responsibilities ___ 285
    Security processes ___ 285
    Cloud account management ___ 287

Chapter 39: End-User Computing Environment Responsibilities ___ 289

Appendices ___ 291

Appendix 1: Technology Owner Checklist ___ 293

Appendix 2: Additional Checklist for the Cloud ___ 295

Appendix 3: Golden Rules for Systems Quick Reference ___ 297

Appendix 4: Golden Rules for Data Quick Reference ___ 301

Index ___ 303

Acknowledgments

This work would not have been possible without the contributions of:

- Ted Hills
- Bill Kilgallon
- Bruce Maxfield
- Dean Myers
- Paul Rogers
- Gregory Saxton
- Jeff Seitter
- Laurel Shifrin
- Don Steiner
- Peter Shier

I would like to especially thank Peter Shier, who provided a technical review of this work prior to publishing. Peter has spent his career working at software companies, while I have spent mine at electronic publishers. His background was a nice complement to mine and his insights and guidance are much appreciated.

Introduction

The term **architecture**, as it applies to technology, is tough to define. It simultaneously imposes structure upon a set of systems and data while also describing the structure of the systems and datasets themselves. Let's begin with a few definitions:

- **Architecture**.[1] The structure of components, their relationships, and the principles and guidelines governing their design and evolution over time.

- **Enterprise Architecture**. An architecture whose scope is an entire organization.

- **Design**. A technological solution to a given business problem according to and constrained by an architecture.

- **Component**. An encapsulation of system functionality or data aligned to an implementation structure. Components are modular and replaceable. A component contains behavior, provides services, and makes them available through interfaces.

- **Component Behavior.** The functionality provided by the component. In other words, what benefit it provides the system of which it is a part. The functionality of the component is provided as one or more services through one or more interfaces.

- **Service.** The functionality of a component as provided through an interface.

- **Interface**.[2] the place at which independent and often unrelated systems meet and act on or communicate with each other; how interaction or communication is achieved.

Zooming in on the architecture of a system component and the data components it houses, we reveal greater and greater detail. As more detail is resolved, the scope of the architecture is narrowed to the point where we start talking about design rather than architecture. When we refer to an enterprise architecture, we mean the highest-level view of the technology and data landscape that makes sense to describe, as well as the methodology for producing that high-level view.

---

[1] Architecture – See https://bit.ly/1Ku1KFO.

[2] Interface – See https://bit.ly/2SfRDV8.

But why do we need an enterprise architecture? Can't we let the software engineers just get on with writing the code, without all this structure and process? CEOs and architects alike commonly ask this question. But before answering, let's ask a related question: *Before the invention of the GPS, why did we need highway maps?*

Imagine trying to drive from New York to Los Angeles using only the detailed street maps of all the cities in the United States. While you could certainly get there in the end, it would be neither easy nor quick. To solve the problem of driving from New York to Los Angeles, you simply don't need the granular detail provided by these street maps. In fact, the detail gets in the way of understanding the "big picture" (and probably takes up the whole back seat as well). What you need is a context map that abstracts away the unnecessary detail, providing just enough so that the entire picture can fit in your brain at once, and you can see how to get from Point-A to Point-B. In other words, you need a map with a wider view: A United States map.

Enterprise Architecture   System Architecture   System Design

In an enterprise the size of the United States, at the most abstract level, we have states, cities within states, and interstate highways connecting them. To complete the mission (driving from New York to Los Angeles), all we need to know is which states we want to go through, and which interstates we want to take to optimize time. This is an architectural approach.

At this level of abstraction, even though we know that the road systems within each city are different, that level of detail is not immediately important. If we stop in a city for fuel or to stay overnight, we can always refer to the detailed map for that city, knowing how it fits into the overall United States context map. Using this analogy, the enterprise architecture is like the highway map of the U.S. It lays out the high-level structure of how all the states (systems) and interstate highways (system-to-system interfaces) fit together, so that the more-detailed state maps (system level architectures and designs) have context.

The key point to recognize is that enterprise architecture gains perspective of the whole enterprise, abstracting away detail to draw higher-level relationships. System-level architecture, on the other hand, is about zooming in to shrink scope and increase detail. System design takes the system architecture and further reduces scope, increasing detail. We can imagine "zooming out" to the architecture level, moving to a different part of the map, and "zooming back in" again. Patterns then capture similarities between groups of elements within the architecture, preserving a basic understanding of what is happening at a more detailed level even as that detail is abstracted away.

The **Principle Based Enterprise Architecture (PBEA) Method** provides a systematic, objective, metrics-based approach to the practice of enterprise architecture. In the PBEA method, we decompose the enterprise technology landscape into individual building blocks called *assets*. There are two types of assets: *system assets* and *data assets*. We often treat system assets as the *houses* in which data assets live. However, system assets and data assets are independent and are equally important. An asset is a component. But *component* is a general term and is used at all levels of granularity. The term *asset* is used to indicate the level of granularity at which these components are inventoried, managed, and governed.

At its core, the PBEA is based on a set of business objectives and guiding principles. The principles are the mission statements for the building blocks (i.e. the assets) of the architecture. Each principle is further described by a set of what we call "golden rules," which define how to achieve the mission – and the consequences of deviation. These "golden rules" are the requirements for meeting the goal as defined by the architecture principles.

In order to maintain a governable architecture while avoiding the dreaded "death by governance," it is important to limit the golden rules to only those that are truly essential. This allows us to avoid the clutter caused by trying to enforce every good idea.

The **Principle Based Enterprise Architecture (PBEA) Method** defines the key roles and processes for creating the Enterprise (Technology and Data) Architecture.

Book outline

This book is organized into five Parts:

- Part 1 lays out the foundational concepts of the Principle Based Architecture (PBEA) Method and describes how the suggested approach helps an organization build and manage an enterprise architecture. It begins with a set of architecture objectives and links those technology-oriented objectives to concepts that matter to businesses. It then provides context, including how we build technology platforms from assets and measure something called *technical debt*. Part 1 also shares a set of best practices and organizational roles that interact to define, build, manage, and evolve the enterprise architecture.

- Part 2 defines the architecture principles and golden rules in more detail. It describes how the system and data building blocks (i.e. assets) are measured and how that measurement allows technical debt to be calculated across the entire landscape. Technical debt is measured using checklists and correlated to business risk as well as the cost to mediate said risk.

- Part 3 defines the golden rules and measures for *system* assets. Each golden rule is supported by a *body of evidence*. Through stories and the experiences of others, this evidence describes why the golden rule is worth following and what might go wrong if an asset does not follow the rule.

- Part 4 defines the golden rules and measures for *data* assets. The PBEA method treats data as an asset, meaning that data is a first-class citizen in the architecture. Even though data assets exist within system assets or as the payload of system interfaces (i.e. APIs), data is measured against a unique set of golden rules. Data that does not adhere to the golden rules adds to the overall technical debt.

- Part 5 elaborates the role of Technology Ownership. Appendix 1 is a checklist for technology ownership and operational readiness. While measuring each asset individually, to a great extent, measures the entire landscape of products built on platforms composed of system and data assets, this method does not tell the whole story. In addition to measuring the individual assets, one must understand the context in which they are integrated and operated. The role of technology ownership and the operational readiness checklist fill this purpose.

PBEA touches on several areas in the software lifecycle, operational lifecycle, data lifecycle or product lifecycle, that it must work in conjunction with, but are not enterprise architecture and therefore not part of PBEA. These areas are mentioned in the book as "out-of-scope."

Book audience

We intend for this book to be read by CTOs, CIOs, and architects who are looking for a coherent approach to implementing an enterprise-wide architecture practice across a medium- to large-sized technology organization. For a small startup, this book will provide some particularly useful guidelines, but the overall method will need to be adapted to avoid becoming too heavyweight. In other words, in describing the method, I have presumed certain role breakdowns which I find typical in medium to large-sized organizations. In a small startup, many of these roles may be the responsibility of a single person. In these cases, coordination and consensus building should be easier than when they are in large organizations.

If you have worked in a medium to large technology organization, and witnessed products and platforms collapsing under the burden of technical debt, then this book is for you. If you have seen technology organizations fail to learn from their mistakes, then this book is also for you. If you have been involved in the development of a product where version-two required a virtual rewrite of version-one or worked in a technology organization that spent an excessive portion of their budget on maintenance, then the PBEA method may provide both insight and benefit. If you are an enterprise architect and have seen one or more enterprise architecture functions get eliminated because they were seen as too distant from the realities of the business, then this book will provide you a concrete, fact-based approach to building an enterprise architecture function that is fully aligned with business objectives and that delivers real measurable benefit.

About the author

Ian Koenig has spent over 35 years in various technology roles, most recently as Chief Architect of three different companies earning more than $2 billion. The Principle Based Architecture (PBEA) method was built from those experiences and has been proven successful across multiple industries including the financial services industry, and the legal industry. The method has been applied to organizations providing the content that serves those industries.

Ian began his career as a software developer and was an early adopter of the Microsoft Windows Platform, beginning with early versions of Windows 1.0.[3] In 1994, Ian was one of seven individuals presented with the Windows Pioneer Award (https://en.wikipedia.org/wiki/Windows_Pioneers) recognizing each for their early contributions to the success of the Microsoft Windows platform.

---

[3] In 1985, the average PC had 640K (that's Kilobytes) of memory and the CPU was clocked at 8MHz (that's megahertz).

Why I authored this book

I began my career as a software developer. I wrote code. I was only responsible for the code that I wrote, not for the complete system and not for the work of others. As I advanced in my career, I became a team leader and then a software development manager. I became responsible for the work of others. That is when I first started to notice the difference in output from different developers. Some developers produced code 10 times or even 100 times as fast as others. I do not mean that they produced 10 times as much code in the same time period. I mean they produced 10 times as much functionality, sometimes with one-tenth as many lines of code. Some people's code was consistently the root cause of a software crash and other people's code rarely was. And strangely, the people who produced the most functionality the fastest also tended to be the ones seldom responsible for system crashes. And when they were the ones responsible, the underlying cause was often found and fixed quickly.

As I advanced further in my career, not only was I responsible for the output of a reasonably-sized team of software developers, but I was also the individual representing that team in larger company meetings. That was when I noticed there was something similar operating at the team level to what I had noticed at the individual level. Some teams' systems easily adapted to new business requirements and some did not, and this did not seem to be dependent on the type of requirement. It seemed to be related to the way the teams operated, and the architecture of the system(s).

Eventually, I moved out of software development into architecture. My responsibility shifted from delivering a single component of a system to making the entire system work better, faster, more efficiently, and more effectively. I evolved my thinking around why some systems just seemed of higher quality and were more adaptable to change than others. I also noticed for the first time how much duplicate work was being done. So much money was being wasted producing the same component multiple times and fixing the bugs multiple times. I was fairly educated about object-oriented methodologies and the benefits of reuse, so facilitating reuse across groups made a ton of sense. Why would a team want to build something new, costing valuable time and money, if another team had already solved that problem?

This is when I began thinking about organizational dynamics, human behavior, and this often-irrational belief under which many people operated: as long as they had ownership and control, everything would be fine – even if another group was clearly more proficient than they were.

This was when I learned of something called the *optimism bias*,[4] which can be summarized as follows. Take any arbitrary group of people and ask them an arbitrary set of questions where each person must rate themselves: below-average, average, or above average. Invariably, no matter the group, and no matter the questions, most of the group will rate themselves above-average, most of the time; of course, this cannot be true for everyone. Everyone cannot be *above average*.

I began to ask myself: *"How can we increase reuse if everybody thinks they are doing it better than the next person?"* The conclusion I reached is that there needed to be some unbiased assessment to prove a reusable component was of high quality. For people to feel comfortable reusing the work of somebody else, it would help to have sort of a good programming "seal of approval." There also had to be a mentality that incentivized groups to help one another, as well as an organizational environment where each group would realize they could not succeed by building everything alone.

Around this same time, I first read about the concept of technical debt,[5] as espoused by Ward Cunningham in 1992. My initial reaction was that it was absolutely brilliant. But the more I read on the subject, the more I realized that – as currently understood – technical debt was about poor coding practices or systems that were poorly maintained. It was not as much about bad architecture or design, nor was there a way to put a real dollar amount to the technical debt associated with any system in a larger platform architecture.

My experience with software development and systems architecture told me that the hardest problems to fix were often the initial architecture and design issues, not the outputs of a poor programmer. Sometimes these decisions were set in stone in the first week of a year-long project. There had to be some way of objectively guiding these early decisions. It was imperative to quantify bad architecture and design decisions with dollar amounts, since they require real investments of money to fix.

I had observed that when smart people argued about technical solutions, they were often arguing over some misunderstanding of the problem, rather than over the solution itself. Once they clarified terminology and meaning, so that they agreed on the problem they were discussing, they often agreed on the solution as well. I realized that if people were clear on terminology, definitions, and problem statements, and followed a few good rules, many bad architecture and design decisions could be avoided.

---

4   Optimism bias – See: https://bit.ly/1ILuJF9.

5   Technical debt – See: https://bit.ly/1nLoei8.

But life isn't perfect. The realities of software delivery (including the need to make short-term delivery dates, and a dependence on others) made some non-optimal decisions inevitable – even when everybody agreed in principle that with a bit more time and money, a different decision would have been made. Life is compromise, and so is architecture and software development.

We may not be able to avoid compromise, but at the very least, we can meticulously track our compromises. The concept of technical debt seemed like an efficient way to track not only what compromises had been made, but also how big each compromise was. The concept that debt incurs interest the longer it remains unpaid also perfectly fits this analogy. The more compromises made in the design and implementation of any software-based system, the more "brittle" (or inflexible) that system becomes, and the more expensive to maintain and operate. The additional maintenance and operational cost required for a brittle system was like paying interest on the original debt. The longer the principle remained unpaid (i.e. kept incurring technical debt), the more money was spent on interest over the lifetime of the system.

The first time I explained my methodology (of defining a set of agreed-upon rules and measuring architecture and technical debt) to a technology audience, it went extremely well. There were lots of questions about who got to make which decision and how to ensure the process didn't "get in the way" of getting the job done. But, in general, people understood.

The first time I explained my methodology to an executive business audience, it didn't go so well. They understood that some systems and groups could deliver new features quickly and others could not. They liked the idea of measuring technical debt in dollars, but the first question I was asked was, "Is that real money?" I assured them that it was, but I didn't have a very compelling way of explaining why or how. Most of the audience members had had the experience of technology groups demanding more time or more money to "do it right," only to deliver disappointing results.

For the tool to be useful, tech people had to use it to explain to their less tech-savvy counterparts (who often controlled the budget) why one technology decision might be better than another for a valid business reason. It had to have something to do with a measurable impact on either company reputation, revenue, cost, and/or the customer. Merely being a *"great technology idea – trust me, I'm an expert"* was not a winning argument.

I started to do some research. I sought real-world examples of businesses being significantly impacted by some technology problems that everybody was aware of, but nobody could explain well enough to prioritize and fix. At the time, I was working for an organization in the legal industry, so I used the term *body of evidence* to describe these evidentiary stories behind the "golden rules."

The next time I explained the methodology to an executive business audience, it went much better. I was able to use one of the key systems that everybody knew was important as an example. I pointed out a set of high-priority corrective actions that were required, how much was required to fix them, and why delaying the fixes would potentially lead to either revenue loss, increased cost, or unhappy customers. People understood that.

This work is the methodology for *enterprise architecture* and *architecture governance* that I developed over the course of my thirty-five-year career. I did not do this alone. I stood on the shoulders of others who came before me, and had the assistance of many smart, dedicated people with whom I have worked.

I hope this book will provide you with some useful tools and guidelines in your effort to be part of a great technology organization.

PBEA is a proven methodology

This incarnation of the PBEA methodology was implemented in a large company of more than 18,000 employees, of whom over 4,000 worked on technology in some capacity. The organization's primary product and platform had originally been built on a mainframe over 20 years prior and extended over the years to support an internet front end. The product supported 1.1 million users, averaging 450,000 searches per week. User population and search volume was growing 10% - 15% per year. Countless millions of lines of code supported the legacy platform, much of it written in mainframe assembler code. The people able to write mainframe assembler code were literally dying out.

Using the PBEA method, we determined that the cost of building out a new platform was less than the cost of closing out the debt, which was estimated at over $500 million. Essentially, after years of under-investment in technology the legacy platform had been allowed to "*collapse under the burden of debt.*" This analysis supported a business case for building a brand-new platform based on modern technology and the PBEA model. I was a member of the team that presented the business case to the board of directors. Even though it was the largest single technology investment ever proposed in the organization, the case was compelling enough that it was approved.

The new platform and its main product were built using the PBEA framework, allowing technical debt to be managed and maintained at a low level over the course of the project. I was involved in the project for nine years and can attest to the debt measurement during that period. This low level of debt was in stark contrast to that of the legacy system and other projects that did not follow the PBEA method.

While the technical debt was low, it was never actually zero. This is a crucial point. There were always compromises that needed to be made; the PBEA method allowed those compromises to be made intelligently, maximizing time-to-market while minimizing business risk and technical debt. The debt was tracked, and corrective actions were planned and implemented, as future investments were made.

A side benefit of using the PBEA process was the ability to quantify security technical debt and risk. Since security and compliance are both core principles of PBEA, the PBEA checklists helped turn long and tedious security audits of the technology platform and processes into painless checklist reviews. While I no longer work at the organization, I have checked back on several occasions; they continue to reap the benefits of building their new products and platforms using a sound architecture methodology.

It is both the immediate and the long-term impact of PBEA that compelled me to take the time to author this book. I hope that others may benefit both from my successes as well as from the failures from which I have learned.

Additional information on PBEA

This book has an adjunct website: http://pbea.iankoenig.com. Additional information on the PBEA method, as well as some downloadable content, is available from that site.

Typographic Conventions used in this book

Italic

> Indicates new terms and quotes from people.

> Best Practices are outlined and set apart from the main text of the book.

PART I

The Principle Based Enterprise Architecture (PBEA) Method

The PBEA method grew from the experience of watching how large technology organizations function (or do not function). How many times have you sat in meetings listening to people bemoan the mistakes other groups have made and now must live with? How many times have you been to a conference and heard people from different organizations tell similar stories of woe?

The PBEA method begins with those stories, sometimes called "technology war stories," presuming that if so many smart people are telling comparable tales, there must be a common pattern behind them. Usually these stories are about things that have gone painfully wrong, but sometimes they are about things that have gone surprisingly right. So, the method begins with the stories and assesses each story based on the outcome's *impact*. If the outcome has an impact on company reputation and could lead to company officers testifying in front of the senate, being jailed, or being fired, then the outcome is classified as *catastrophic impact*. If the outcome has a measurable impact on revenues, then the outcome is classified as *high impact*. If the outcome has a measurable impact on cost, then it could be either *high impact* or *medium impact* depending on the amount.

For each story, a root cause analysis is performed. Preventing the root cause then becomes a golden rule that ought to be followed. For example, if the outcome is something like *"Doctor, it hurts when I do this,"* the golden rule to follow might be *"Well, don't do that."*

Once the golden rule has been derived through root cause analysis, the stories are then organized so that all the stories of bad outcomes with the same root cause, which can be avoided by following the same golden rule, are collected together. These stories then supply the *body-of-evidence* that the rule is worth following. In addition, since the body-of-evidence is based on things that either impacted company reputation, revenues, costs, or customers, the reasons for following the rule should be recognizable by technology-savvy and lay folk alike.

Once an organization has identified a good set of golden rules with the associated body-of-evidence, then each rule is assessed a *likelihood*, based on the question, *"How likely is this bad outcome to happen, if the golden rule is not followed?"*

For example, if a system buried deep behind multiple firewalls leaves itself open to a SQL injection attack,[6] then while the impact may be high, the likelihood of the outcome might only be medium. But if a system that faces the Internet does not encrypt its traffic and sends passwords "in the clear," then both impact and likelihood are probably high.

The business risk associated with breaking a golden rule thus becomes the cross product of impact and likelihood, thus defining the severity associated with breaking a golden rule. The formula for translating impact and likelihood to severity may be found in Chapter 9 – Change Management.

---

[6] SQL Injection – See: https://bit.ly/1iqhW1m.

CHAPTER 1

Context

While enterprise architecture is often associated with achieving technical goals, the purpose of enterprise architecture is really to achieve business objectives. This book provides a systematic approach for using enterprise architecture to measure technical debt, aligning debt to business objectives, and producing actionable metrics that drive business insight.

We are taking for granted that an organization which would implement an enterprise architecture has technologists and that those technologists are grouped into one or more technology organizations. At the highest level of abstraction, we assume that the purpose of a technology organization is to produce solutions, which are supplied to end users. Solutions deliver business capabilities (or feature sets) to end users, through the integration of technology and data components (called assets) into a production environment, along with operational processes, business rules, and more.

Most organizations have a product management function responsible for defining business requirements and a technology organization responsible for building solutions that satisfy the requirements. There generally also exists a set of unstated requirements that are expected of all products, but not specified as business requirements. We call these *non-functional requirements*. A major focus of the PBEA method is ensuring that solutions deliver the non-functional requirements. For example, it is generally expected by the business and by senior management that all solutions are secure, but security is rarely defined as specific business requirements for a product, so the requirement is therefore implicit. PBEA makes these non-functional requirements explicit.

Objectives

The *business objectives* driving the PBEA Method are to assist organizations in producing:

1. *Safe* **Solutions**. Ensure systems and data are secure (limiting the attack surface and protecting privacy) and compliant with corporate policy and the law.

2. *Responsive* **Solutions**. Ensure that systems and data are highly available, reliable, and responsive to the end user.

3. *Effective* **Solutions**. Ensure that products can add new functionality quickly, so that the end user may benefit from innovations and investments as soon as possible. This demands that systems and data be versatile and flexible. It also demands that systems and data minimize total-cost-of-ownership and maximize time-to-market

The PBEA Architecture *principles* are defined as the mission statements to achieve these objectives. While the objectives apply equally to system assets and data assets, the principles and *golden rules* are individualized to the type of asset.

Solutions

Solutions deliver business capabilities and associated features through the integration of multiple *system* and *data* assets. A solution could either be used internally or externally to the organization. The term *product* is commonly used for a solution that is used externally, such as a product which is sold to customers.

A business capability is a coarse-grained[7] set of coherent features and functions that provide business benefit. Business capabilities are the building blocks of solutions and should be reusable across multiple solutions. Assets (which are defined in more detail below) are the building blocks of business capabilities and should be reusable across multiple capabilities. Of course, this method of building coarser-grained capabilities out of finer-grained capabilities can be repeated as many times as an organization feels it has the resources and ability to manage. However, the PBEA method only reaches the asset level as the finest-grained reusable building

---

[7] *Coarse-grained* here implies fewer, larger components than fine-grained. Business capabilities are coarse-grained, while features are fine-grained. For example, when a company's advertisement compares its product to a competitor's, checking off all the things its product can do that the competitor's product cannot, that's a capability. There could be 100 features making up that capability.

block that is managed across the enterprise. We have found that this level is usually sufficient and that attempting to manage more components at a deeper level of granularity adds more complexity to the process than it is worth.

Solutions are defined in terms of the business capabilities and features that satisfy end-user needs. Rarely, if ever, should each business capability become a single monolithic implementation. Instead, we should decompose each business capability into a set of technology and data building blocks (i.e. assets). Those assets that are common to several business capabilities should be built just once.

The process for this decomposition and mapping from business capability to technology and data building blocks is called *placement-of-function* (PoF).

Placement of Function (PoF)

Solutions are defined in terms of the capabilities and features that satisfy end-user needs. Assets are defined at a granularity which optimizes reusability, agility, and operational expense (OpEx). As such, there is not a one-to-one mapping between a user-oriented feature and the assets that deliver it. In fact, the integration of multiple assets is required to deliver any business capability or feature.

Placement of function (PoF) is the process by which we map feature-oriented business requirements, expressed as user stories to asset-oriented functional and non-functional requirements.

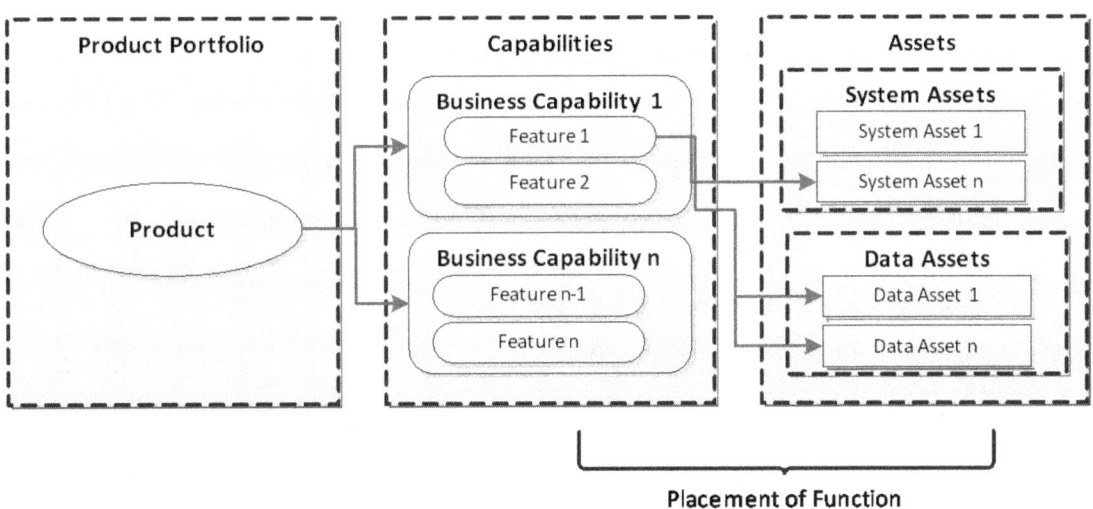

The placement-of-function (PoF) process enumerates:

- The impact matrix of assets affected by a new or modified capability or feature as well as the scope of the change and the cost

- New assets required (if any)

- Which combination of features and user stories will be implemented by which assets

- How those assets integrate to deliver the combination of features

- Risks, issues, and unknowns

Placement-of-function artifacts should be organized around coherent feature sets and not around random buckets of unrelated requirements. They should be versioned and maintained as a record of what needs drove which decisions, so that these are not lost in the sands of time.

It should be noted that while PBEA goes into detail about the construction and governance of assets, the management of business capabilities and features is generally considered out of scope.

> Organize placement-of-function (PoF) artifacts around feature sets. The PoF should make explicitly clear which features and user stories it is associated with. As new user stories are prioritized and implemented, delivering an enhanced feature, a new version of the PoF artifact should be produced, if it has changed as a result of the enhancement.

Environments

The implementation of a solution involves the integration of assets into an environment. The environment includes the integration of multiple system and data assets, with a single infrastructure asset, along with governing policies and procedures.

For example:

- A **production environment** serves actual end users. It contains production instances of each system asset integrated into a network backbone provided by the infrastructure asset. The network backbone implements security protocols that govern interactions among the various assets, among other things.

- A **test environment** is one that mimics the production environment well enough that versions of each asset may be tested for both functionality and performance prior to being released into production.

- A **development environment** is generally a scaled down test environment with enough segmentation that individual assets may be upgraded independently and in parallel in a manner that minimizes the impact of changes in one asset on another asset that may be changing in parallel.

- An **enterprise environment** is one that supports the employees in performing their job function. It usually includes the email asset, multiple internal system assets and in the case of software development, assets such as source-code-control.

While most PBEA processes are oriented around specific individual assets, it is important to recognize that no asset is an island, and the overall operation of a solution depends on each asset operating effectively. That implies the integrated environment of infrastructure, systems, data, end users, and operations all work effectively and efficiently. As such, a *technology ownership and operational readiness* checklist is provided in Appendix 1, which speaks to the final integrated solution, ensuring appropriate process and controls are clearly defined as well as ownership and responsibility.

CHAPTER 2

Assets

Assets are the technology and data "building blocks" of the product and the platform. A platform[8] is a group of technologies that are used as a base upon which other applications, processes, or technologies are developed. There are two basic types of assets: *system assets* and *data assets*. In a traditional *service-oriented architecture* (SOA), system asset interfaces are called services.

Assets are grouped into *domains*. A domain is a coherent grouping of assets that perform a similar function. Examples of some common domain groupings include: content systems, product systems, business systems, and operational systems.

PBEA expands on the traditional SOA model in two important ways:

1. An SOA is typically unclear about whether a *service* includes the implementation or just refers to the interface. In PBEA, a system asset always includes both interface and implementation.

2. An SOA typically treats data as *part-of* systems and interfaces. PBEA treats data as an asset. Data assets and system assets are treated as peers in the model, even though *data-at-rest*[9] exist within system assets, and *data-in-motion*[10] is intimately related to system interfaces and APIs.

As such, PBEA is a method for producing an *asset-oriented architecture* (AOA).

A single asset should be owned by a single team, but a single team may own multiple assets. The team is responsible[11] for all aspects of development, testing, deployment, performance,

---

[8] Platform – See: https://bit.ly/2sZMrHr.

[9] Data-at-rest - refers to data as it is persisted in databases and file systems.

[10] Data-in-motion - refers to data as it is carried between assets via system interfaces.

[11] When I use the term *responsible*, I always mean *accountable* and *responsible*. In my experience, when accountability and responsibility are misaligned, bad things happen.

security, and availability. They may delegate portions of this responsibility to other groups, but in the end, they are wholly responsible and accountable (i.e. no finger pointing). This is an important guiding principle in organizational design, especially in large organizations. The leader of the asset team is known as the *Asset Owner.* The asset owner is ultimately responsible for achieving the expected results of the asset, from an architecture, development, delivery, and operational perspective. This approach is also known as a Single Team Owned Service Architecture (STOSA).[12]

How many assets should there be in my enterprise? There is no specific answer to this question, other than to have the right balance. Having too few assets is akin to having monolithic applications (which is bad). A few exceptionally large assets become hard to change and often lead to more assets being created that partially overlap in functionality. On the other hand, having too many assets makes it hard to manage, hard to find what you are looking for, and hard to govern. Having assets that are trivially simple, makes it easier to duplicate the functionality of the asset than to reuse it. This also causes proliferation and complexity. The right balance of asset size and asset count depends on the size, maturity, and culture of the organization.

System assets

A *system asset* is a separately instantiated and separately managed set of software and computing resources used as a building block for applications, platforms, and solutions. There is no predefined concept of how big or small an asset should be. But as a rule of thumb, if two things must be released in lock step (in other words at the same time or not at all), then they are a single asset. If two things are completely encapsulated,[13] talk to each other via well-defined interfaces, can be released independently, and do not live on the same (virtual) machine, they are likely to be independent assets.

---

[12] See: Architecting for Scale: High Availability for Your Growing Applications, by Lee Atchison, 2006, ISBN: 9781491943397.

[13] Encapsulation – is used to hide the values or state of an asset, preventing unauthorized parties' direct access to them. Access to data or state is only allowed via public interfaces.

Commercial off-the-shelf (COTS) packages & third-party solutions are not considered system assets in themselves; they are *software assets*. Software assets are discussed below. However, the physical instantiation of a software asset may be considered a system asset.[14]

As such, the primary distinction between a system asset and a software asset is that a system asset includes its physical instantiation as an operational entity and a software asset does not. To take advantage of the functionality of a system asset, you call one of its service interfaces. To take advantage of the functionality of a software asset, you first must install it.

System assets are coarse-grained and perform one or more valuable services. Items of narrow scope or easily reimplemented are not significant enough to be considered system assets. In this context a service is defined as something functional and useful to the clients of the system asset. The clients access the service(s) provided by the system asset through well-defined service interfaces. When a system asset delivers exactly one service, it is classified as a *microservice*. Microservice based architectures are in-vogue as of the time of this writing. A microservice is a system asset that performs one very discrete function and is generally supported by a team of between three to eight people.[15] The PBEA method fully supports the production of microservices.

Some system assets present functionality through application programming interfaces (APIs). Some present functionality through human interfaces. When a system asset provides its functions via APIs to be consumed by other system assets, it is called a *service asset*. When a system asset provides functions directly consumable by end users through a human interface, it is called an *application asset*.

Technology innovations happen fairly quickly. As systems age, they tend to become more complex and costlier to operate. Eventually, most systems should either be migrated onto newer platforms or simply retired. The need to migrate or retire a system does not imply that it was badly architected or badly designed. It is just an inevitable chapter in the lifecycle of a technology system. As such, it is worthwhile to keep track of where a system is in its lifecycle.

One methodology for doing this is the Gartner TIME model.[16] In this model, systems are given one of four classifications:

---

[14] Business Systems, such as CRM or Billing rarely differentiate one company from another so are usually COTS packages that are purchased, customized, instantiated, integrated into the environment, and operated. The packaged software is itself a software asset, but the instantiation and operation of it is considered a system asset (and a whole bunch of data assets).

[15] A team of 3 – 8 people is sometimes called a two-pizza team.

[16] Gartner TIME model – See: https://bit.ly/2DWF9ck.

- **Tolerate**: Systems are high-quality, but low business value. These are not worth the time and effort required to migrate away.

- **Invest**: Systems are high-quality with a much higher business value. These systems are worth further investment to get better returns or reduce more cost.

- **Migrate**: Classifying a system as *migrate* is a bit more nuanced. While the system generally has high value, it is also costly to operate, maintain and/or enhance. Therefore, rather than continue the expense, these systems should be migrated onto more effective platforms. Often, this is confused with investing, but investment is taking a current application and improving upon it but migrating is looking to maintain value while reducing cost.

- **Eliminate**: Eliminate is an essential part of the software lifecycle but is rarely factored into the original business plan and often missed. Systems to eliminate are of low quality and low business value. Often, they are old, expensive to operate, or are supporting products whose revenue no longer justifies the cost of operation.

PBEA specifically recommends avoiding the term *legacy technology*, and instead using a system like the one above. The key is to focus on whether budget is best spent enhancing existing systems, migrating them onto new platforms, or decommissioning (i.e. eliminating) them.

A $1 billion company could easily have 500 to 1,500 system assets at any one time, two-thirds of which could be classified as *migrate* or *eliminate*. Why do many companies find it so difficult to just migrate or eliminate these systems? The simple answer is that most companies have a very poor understanding of cost, except at the highest level. While the company often knows what it costs to run all their technology, they rarely understand what it costs to operate a single system; this makes it is hard to justify spending money to either migrate or eliminate that system.

When the cost of an asset cannot be quantified, the savings associated with eliminating it cannot be quantified either. Therefore, if an asset is required by a product that has even one dollar of quantifiable revenue, that dollar of revenue can trump one thousand dollars of untracked cost. In other words, organizations that cannot attribute operational costs all the way to the revenue generating product, could spend 20+ years trying to retire unprofitable technology. As these assets age and receive less and less investment, they often reach a point where they are undermaintained, are unable to support increasing demand and are no longer able to support the current SLAs.

PBEA recommends keeping close track of the operational expense (OpEx) of every individual asset, as well as the investment strategy, so that when it is time to migrate the asset, or eliminate it, the business justification for doing so will be obvious to all involved.

System Asset SLA (Service-Level Agreement)

A system asset delivers one or more services through its interfaces. Either explicitly or implicitly, there is a service-level agreement (SLA) which defines the reliability, availability, and performance that a client of the service can expect. PBEA recommends that every asset has a well-defined, written SLA. The SLA defines the operational characteristics of the interface *contract* between service provider and consumer. The other two parts of the interface contract are: (1) the interface definition and how to call it, and (2) the version. More on the Service Interface Contract below.

SLAs are primarily about expectation management but may include financial implications and penalties as well. For example, the SLA that Amazon Web Services (AWS) provides on its EC2, EBS, and ECS services have a financial component if AWS does not meet its SLA. As of 1 Dec 2017, if the service has less than four nines [17] (99.99%) availability in a month but greater than two nines (99.0%), the consumer receives a 10% credit. If the service has less than 99.0% availability, the consumer receives a 30%

How does an SLA deal with scale?

A Service-Level-Agreement (SLA) is something the asset owner writes, so that an asset calling it knows what they can expect, and what they can measure. How exactly an asset scales to meet its performance SLA and how far it is expected to scale is not specifically defined by PBEA.

Experience has shown that expected load is generally a guess, at best. The product manager guesses and to avoid wrong, aims high. The asset owner then responds by doubling whatever the product manager said, to not be caught unprepared, especially if they have a long, involved budgeting cycle (see some of the body-of-evidence in the scalability rules in chapter 18). Then the Ops group adds another 50%, to give them time to respond to last minute upgrade requests. In the end, you have a system that averages 4% load (which I have seen many times).

In the PBEA method, the asset owner is effectively promising infinite scale, with best practice being auto-scaling up and down to stay just ahead of usage. While this may not always be possible, it is the right model. This measure aims to make it harder for an individual to avoid taking responsibility for a failure or a performance issue, and only promise performance up to some pre-defined maximum load.

---

[17] The term (four) nines, refers to the percentage of time that the service is available. For example, four nines means 99.99% availability, meaning 52 minutes of allowed down-time per year. "Five nines" means 5 minutes of allowed down-time per year.

credit. The SLA also defines how availability is measured and what a *credit* means.[18]

SLAs may be internal or external (i.e. provided to customers). They are especially useful for problem diagnosis when measured. An SLA should only contain terms that can be measured, monitored, and alarmed on (both by provider and consumer).

An SLA should, at a minimum, define guarantees for:

- **Response time**. How long does it take to process a request and return a response? This is almost always a variable defined as $x\%$ of requests will be returned in y seconds. 100% of requests will return in z seconds (i.e. the timeout value after which no response should be expected). For example: 95% of requests responded within 2 seconds; 99% of requests responded within 4 seconds; 100% of requests responded within 60 seconds (in which case the response will be an error code).

- **Availability**. How much time is the service is expected to be up? For example: 99.99% available 24x7x365 (also referred to as "four nines"). Note that when measuring availability, planned down-time is still down-time. It counts against the overall availability SLA.

- **Dependability**. How many failures are expected to be generated in the measurement period? Typically, a percentage, measured as the number of failed requests divided by the total number of requests. For example, 99.99% dependable.

- **Recovery Time Objective (RTO)**. In the event of an outage, how long is it expected to take to recover service?

- **Recovery Point Objective (RPO)**. In the event of an outage, how much data may be lost? Often this objective is internal and not published outside the organization.

Service Interfaces (APIs)

The *service(s)* provided by a system asset are consumed through *service interfaces*. A service interface is also known as an *application programming interface* (API). The most common approach to defining service interfaces on the Internet is called *Representational State Transfer* (REST).[19] PBEA assumes the use of REST (see sidebar below) for service interfaces but is easily adaptable to other models.

---

[18] SLA credit – See: See https://amzn.to/1IWDle9.

[19] *Representational State Transfer* (REST) – See: https://bit.ly/1JR7VCX.

One of the more important architecture decisions in the definition of a service interface is whether to make it open 'to the world' or keep it internal. Making an interface open creates an external dependency on the interface definition. An external dependency means that if you make a change, they are affected. This then creates the obligation to support and maintain the version of the API for an extended period. Therefore, extra care must be taken with the design and functionality of any interface before releasing it to the public.

An interface is classified as either internal or external as follows:

- **Internal**: The interface is not exposed outside the boundary of the asset; All Internal APIs are also known as *Closed APIs* (see below).

- **External**: The interface is callable across the asset boundary, allowing the world outside the asset either to retrieve data, write data, or to drive its behavior. Access to external APIs may be either open or closed.

Only external interfaces may be made accessible to third parties (i.e. open). An interface is classified as open or closed as follows:

> ## Representational State Transfer (REST)
>
> REST is an architectural style used for creating web services. Web services provide interoperability between computer systems through representations of web resources using a uniform set of stateless operations. In a RESTful web service, requests made to a resource's URI elicit a response with a payload formatted in either HTML, XML, JSON, or some other format. When HTTP is used, the typical operations available are:
>
> - **GET** – Retrieve a representation of the addressed resource, expressed in an appropriate media type.
> - **PUT** –Replace the addressed resource, and if it does not exist, create it.
> - **POST** – *Not generally used.*
> - **DELETE** – Remove the addressed resource.

- **Closed**: An external interface that is published for use only by assets within the enterprise, and possibly only within a domain.

- **Open**: An external interface that is published so that third parties can use it. Technically, these are like closed interfaces except that a business decision has been made to secure and publish them, as well as to document and support them. Open interfaces generally require authentication and authorization to be used.

> When creating an external interface, don't take shortcuts because they happen to be closed interfaces. Write them as if they are eventually going to be open interfaces. Your customers will thank you.

The Service Interface Contract

A service interface is a *contract* between service provider and service consumer. The contract has four main parts:

(1) **Interface Definition**. This includes how to call the interface and the meaning of each parameter, including *idempotency*[20] and *temporal ordering*[21] of calls and responses. Also, the data model of the request and/or response payload and the meaning of each element or attribute. Note: the request or response data model is often tied to a data asset as well as the system asset and the service interface.

(2) **Interface Version**. Interface definition can be as much an art as a science. The system asset is upgraded constantly; as the asset changes, so must its interfaces (to provide the new or enhanced functionality). But unless great care is taken in both the original definition of an interface and any changes, upgrades will cause service consumers to break resulting in an outage. Every interface should have a version composed of three parts: *major_version.minor_version.revision*. Every time the system asset changes, the revision number of the interface should be incremented. If the interface also changes, but in a backwards-compatible manner, then the minor version number is incremented. If the interface changes in a non-backwards-compatible manner, then the major version number is incremented. A backwards-compatible change means that a consumer of the interface will continue working unchanged when the new interface is released. Non-backwards-compatible changes therefore imply that a consumer needs to make some sort of modification to use the new interface. Given the havoc a non-backwards compatible change will wreak on a large system, it is strongly recommended that instead of making a non-backwards compatible change to an interface, a brand new interface be defined, and both old and new interface are supported for a (prolonged) period. This implies that the major version number is incorporated into the name of the interface (In a REST interface, this is the URI of the interface).

(3) **Limits**. These include how often the interface can be called by the same consumer, and the number of items which may be requested in a single call.

(4) **Operational Characteristics**. Characteristics such as availability, RPO, and RTO, are inherited from the system asset SLA. In other words, these operational characteristics for every service interface provided by the system asset are the same. Performance, on the other hand, could be different between service interfaces offered by the same asset.

---

[20] Idempotent – See: https://bit.ly/2BnTjl3.

[21] Temporal ordering – Time-based ordering.

Data Assets

A *data asset* is a collection of one or more data sets managed as a building block of platforms and products. There are several axes along which data assets may be categorized.

Data storage

What we usually refer to as storage structure is really storage *interface* structure; that is, the structure of data as it's presented to a data management system or as presented by that data management system to its users. A data management system may change the structure of the data internally in a variety of ways, some of which might involve dramatic restructuring. However, we wouldn't classify data by how a data management system stores it internally, since that is really an attribute of the data management system rather than of the data.

Structured data refers to data that is stored in a data management system that requires that certain aspects of the data structure be stipulated at or before the time of storage. Most *business data* (see next section) is treated as structured data.

Unstructured data refers to data that is stored in a data management system that does not require that the data structure be stipulated at or before the time of storage. The term is a bit of a misnomer, since almost all data has structure. Most *content* (see next section) is treated as unstructured data.

The nature of the data

- **Content** is defined as the information and experiences that are directed towards an end user or audience.[22] Content may be human-readable text with supporting graphics, video, and audio, or structured data such as tables.

- **Business data** is defined as data that is used to operate the business. This includes transactional data (e.g., orders, purchases, sales) and reference data supporting such transactional data (e.g., customers, products, accounts). Most business data is *structured data* (see above), but some business data, such as contracts, is *unstructured data*.

- **Operational data** is defined as data that is used to support availability, performance, incident response, and problem resolution. The most common form of operational data is a log file.

- **Reference data** is defined as data that is used in a read-only fashion in support of some other data. Unfortunately, this is a relative definition.

---

[22] Content - See: https://bit.ly/2HT7Cnf.

- **Entity master data** is data about real-world entities including people, organizations, and places. Much of entity master data is structured (e.g., name, address, date of graduation), but includes some unstructured data as well (e.g., biographical narrative).

- **Relationship data** is data that defines the logical interconnections between data items. Relationship data is often collected from multiple data assets, extracted, and stored in one place to discover relationships that are not evident in a single data asset. A common approach to storing relationship data is using n-tuples in a graph database.

Every data asset is *mastered*[23] *by* exactly one system asset but is often *used by* many other assets. One can then categorize data assets indirectly by the categorization of the system assets that manage them. For instance, one could have product data assets, content data assets, business data assets, and operational data assets.

Data classification

Data classification or *information classification*[24] may be performed for two reasons:

- **Data Protection.** To determine the type of data vis-à-vis its required protection (e.g., personally identifiable information, material non-public information, proprietary information)

- **Data Retention.** To determine the length of time data needs to be kept. For example, mortgage records need to be kept for seven years after the last transaction. So, for a 30-year mortgage, that's 37 years! At the other extreme, operational, non-security-related logs may only need to be kept for 30 days. Retention policy is set by law, regulation, and/or corporate policy.

There is no single globally-accepted data classification scheme. An organization needs to define its own policy in keeping with the various laws and regulations in operation across the industries and regions in which it operates. For example, the General Data Protection Regulation 2016/679 (GDPR) is a regulation in EU law on data protection and privacy for all individuals within the European Union and the European Economic Area. GDPR and regulations like it are linking data protection concerns to data retention concerns.

---

[23] Master Data Management – A methodology for managing data such that there is a "single version of the truth." https://bit.ly/23TXz24.

[24] Information Classification – See: https://bit.ly/2UMAyip.

Data Service Level Agreement (SLA)

As with system assets, a data asset SLA sets down certain factors that can be expected and measured. So, if the data asset is determined to be inconsistent with its SLA, then both data provider and data consumer immediately know that something is wrong and should be addressed. But for data, the operational attributes specified in the SLA are not related to availability or performance, but instead to timeliness, accuracy, and completeness.

A Data SLA includes target metrics for:
- Timeliness (e.g. acceptable latency through the curation process and delivery to end users)
- Accuracy (e.g. acceptable error counts)
- Completeness (e.g. geographic scope and data properties having values).

Data specification

A Data specification is a description of a data asset including:
- A description of the data asset's characteristics, purpose, and definitions
- A field-by-field definition along with business rules that may guide how the field is used
- An enumeration of logical data models, schemas, and physical data models.
- A list of primary sources[25] of the data
- Enrichment and formatting details
- Documentation of presentation formatting, conversion processes, and operational processes
- The state of the data along with known gaps
- Organizational or geopolitical scope
- Retention requirements, usage constraints, and revision maintenance
- Curation policies
- Legal constraints, including allowed usage or embargoes.
- Stakeholders and other important contacts.

This is not intended to be a complete list or even a prescriptive list but is intended to provide an idea of the scope of a data specification. It is like a *functional specification*, but for a data asset rather than a system asset or product. In software development, a functional specification is a formal document used to describe in detail, a product's intended capabilities, appearance, and interactions with users. The *data specification* does this, except for data.

---

[25] The Trust-level of different sources is not discussed here. PBEA treats data source trust as a dynamic value and its handling is outside the scope of this book.

The Data Specification is intended to locate all the important guiding principles for a data asset. While we do not necessarily need to compile all the information into one single document, we also don't want it buried in emails, or to be "tribal knowledge."

Software assets

A *software asset* is a software package that is incorporated into one or more system assets. Software assets are often from 3rd parties but may be developed internally as well. A software asset may be from a commercial vendor, in which case it is known as *commercial-off-the-shelf* software (or *COTS*). It may also be open source software, or even software produced internal to the enterprise and shared between groups, such as a reusable library or code module.

A software asset is never a system asset, although in the case of large CRM or ERP systems, the software asset may represent 90% to 95% of the system asset. The distinction lies in the creation of custom code, custom configuration, custom implementation, and live operations. It can be confusing how to treat externally hosted services that are un-customized and called via public interfaces (e.g. the Amazon Redshift service). Are these software assets or system assets? While there are arguments for each, PBEA defines these as *system assets*, but in an external *domain*. Any functionality consumed through interfaces, no matter who provides it, is a system asset.

For example, when we refer to a software asset, we mean just the software – which could be sitting in a box on a disk or downloadable. We do not mean a running implementation of that software. Google Docs is a system asset. You use it without having to install it on your system and configure it. Microsoft Word, on the other hand, is a software asset. You must install it on some hardware that you own to use it. Microsoft Word Online is a system asset.

Software assets are generally managed through a process known as Software Asset Management. The software asset management process is outside the scope of this book, but is extremely important, especially for large enterprises (who may be the target of software compliance litigation).

All software assets, commercial or open source, must define:

- **Ownership**. Who developed the software (e.g., a foundation, company, individual, or community)?
- **Licensing Terms and Conditions**. Which licensing model does the software impose?

- **Usage Rights**. How may the software be used and for what purpose?

- **Modification Rights**. May changes be made to the software? If changes are made, what licensing terms are triggered? For example, if open source software is distributed under a copyleft[26] license, then anything derived from it must also be distributed freely.

- **Redistribution Rights**. May the original software or a modification be further distributed?

Failure to follow the (often illogical and inscrutable) licensing terms of software assets may result in fines and other financial penalties.

Infrastructure assets

An infrastructure asset is a special kind of asset that is reserved for defining the network and security backbone into which all the system assets are connected. For example, a VPC (virtual private cloud) definition, with all the network groups, and security groups is an infrastructure asset. There is generally one per platform per environment.

In a cloud deployment or in an on-premises containerized deployment, infrastructure definition is code and should be treated and managed as such.

For on-premises hardware, in a traditional data center, infrastructure assets need to be managed as one or more physical assets. Perhaps there is configuration data that should be treated as code, perhaps not. But either way, the asset model proposed by PBEA should be used for infrastructure as well. The more reliance there is on humans rather than automation, the more important the complete identification of assets, along with ownership, and governance.

The art of versioning

We have talked about the importance of versioning. Versioning is one of those things that people either do rigorously or learn the hard way that they should have done rigorously.

---

[26] Copyleft- See: https://bit.ly/1O8kQrR.

Everything that is changed should be versioned. That includes code modules, system assets, data assets, interfaces, schema, and system images. PBEA recommends using a consistent scheme for versioning, which was discussed in the earlier section on interfaces. The scheme for versioning applies to everything that is changed in building and releasing software, data, and systems.

In general, every change – no matter how insignificant – constitutes a revision. If a revision has been made since the last release, then it constitutes a version change. If the version change is backwards-compatible with the prior version, then it is a minor version change. If it is not backwards-compatible, then it is a major version change. The versioning scheme may use numbers, it may use dates, or it may use a combination of these. Whatever model is used for tracking versions should be clearly defined and used consistently.

A version is used for two things. In the event of a problem, it is used to identify precisely which instance of the thing needs to be scrutinized. It also is used as part of the SLA and the interface contract to inform any users of changes to an asset or its interface(s).

Let's look a bit deeper into the use of versioning during problem resolution. PBEA recommends that all systems are built from system images. A system image is a read-only file-system image that contains all the software that will reside on a compute instance, including the operating system, the foundation software, your software, and every patch.[27] System images are prebuilt from manifests. The image manifest is the list of every component used to build the compute instance, along with its version number. The image itself, along with its manifest is also versioned. (See Chapter 8).

If a problem is found in a service, the problem resolution process begins by identifying which computing instance(s) had the problem. The system image version is used to retrieve the manifest. The manifest identifies which versions of which components are installed. Once the culprit has been found, its version is then used as a lookup into a source code control system to identify the source code version to be investigated.

Now let's look a bit deeper at the use of versioning as it relates to interfaces. As a consumer of a service interface, I pay very close attention to the version numbers of all the interfaces of all the assets that I call. If there is only a revision change to an interface I call, then I assume that the change is very minor and has no impact on me. In fact, I assume not that the definition of the interface I am calling has changed, but that the asset providing the interface has undergone a minor change. If there is a minor version change to an interface, then I assume that there may

---

[27] An Amazon Machine Image (AMI) is an example of a system image. See: https://bit.ly/2DXyhLM.

be new capabilities I could take advantage of, but if I don't need those, then I need not make a change.

If on the other hand, there is a major version change, then I know that eventually I will need to change my asset to adapt to the latest version. If the asset providing the interface has followed the rules, then they have provided the new interface with a new name and have maintained the existing interface, so as not to affect me. But eventually they will stop supporting the version of the interface I am calling, so I need to be prepared.

If everybody follows the rules and abides by the interface contract, systems can both adapt to change and not break because of it.

CHAPTER 3

Program Increments

Program Increments (also called *projects* in a waterfall model) are essentially funding envelopes that occur over a period and provide some business benefit at the end. They begin, and they end, but the assets that have been created or modified over the course of the program increment live on. As such, it is very convenient to track governance actions as user stories to be completed during the program increment, or as milestones to be completed during the project. In this way, we can fully assess the impact of the work done, on the overall technical debt, as well as any corrective actions that need to be tracked.

A program increment may impact a single asset or a group of assets. Placement of function (defined in Chapter 1) enumerates the impacted assets. For each asset requiring governance, the specific process appropriate for that asset is invoked.

As user stories are translated into tasks and executed during the program increment, technical debt may be added or subtracted. In an agile delivery model, PBEA recommends that architecture governance actions are initiated, as required, when new stories are evaluated and translated into tasks. As each user story is evaluated, we recommend that a quick assessment is done to determine if completing the tasks requires a change to the architecture. If it does, then an additional user story should be written to perform an architecture review. In this way, the governance action can be placed on the backlog and prioritized so that it takes place after the architecture changes have been made but before all the code has been written, and before the program increment is complete.

In a waterfall delivery model, we recommend that the architecture assessments are tied both to project initiation and to change control. In other words, as blocks of business requirements are approved and sized, a quick evaluation is done as to whether the implementation requires an architecture change. If it does, then an architecture review should be scheduled as a milestone in the project.

Some tasks are relatively cheap, and some can be quite expensive. When a task is sized, the *true cost* should be used. True cost involves four figures: (1) the cost to build, (2) the cost to operate,

(3) the cost to maintain, and (4) technical debt. Using this model, if a task pays off more technical debt than the implementation cost, it can actually be free.

If a change to placement-of-function is required, it is important to make the change as early as possible. This is because changes to placement-of-function or to external APIs can impact multiple assets – potentially with unintended consequences.

CHAPTER 4

Roles

There is no "right" way to organize architecture or to define architecture roles, but there are many "wrong" ways. There are many models in the industry and the model chosen for a corporation needs to adapt to that company's culture.

For the sake of consistency, PBEA assumes an *agile delivery model*[28] and adopts a specific model, when describing the interactions amongst architects and between architects and their stakeholders. In the PBEA method, three distinct architecture roles are defined: *enterprise architects* (EAs), *solution architects* (SAs), and *technical architects* (TAs).

PBEA tries not to presume any specific organizational model, but we need some definition of roles for the architecture to be precise.

Enterprise architects are assumed to be responsible for the enterprise, while technical architects are assumed to be responsible for the architecture of specific assets and engineering functions. Solution architects are presumed to handle the architecture of end-to-end solutions aligned either to products or business capabilities or both. These are role descriptions not job descriptions, which implies that a single individual may perform multiple roles.

Additional (non-architecture) roles are also defined to provide context.

Product owner

A product owner is the individual responsible for defining the business requirements of the product or solution that is sold to customers. Where those requirements constitute a capability or feature that is common to multiple products and solutions, the product owner is responsible for working with the appropriate business capability owner to ensure that this product's needs

---

[28] Agile delivery model – See https://bit.ly/1ENe7uX.

are accurately represented as well as unified with the needs of other products. The business capability owner endeavors to meet the needs of all products via a common capability, rationalizing away arbitrary differences in product requirements which supply no benefit to the end user.

Rarely, if ever, will a product release satisfy every business requirement at once. The product owner will work with their counterparts to negotiate the prioritization and timing of delivery across releases of business capabilities and assets.

The peer role to the product owner in the technology organization is the *technology owner*. A single product owner may interact with multiple technology owners and a single technology owner may interact with multiple product owners.

Business capability owner

The *business capability owner* is the peer role to an *asset owner*. The business capability owner is responsible for working across business units and product owners to determine where their needs are similar enough to be satisfied by a common reusable capability. By creating a single business capability serving the needs of multiple business units and products, technology production becomes cheaper and multiple products inherit a common look and feel for shared functionality, so that they look like they are members of a coordinated product portfolio from a single company serving its end users.

The largest part of the business capability owner's role is defining a common set of business requirements that satisfy the needs of multiple products, determining which businesses truly have different end-user requirements and which are simply interpreting their end-user requirements as unique. In addition, the business capability owner sets the priority for which requirements are needed first and which sets of requirements constitute a releasable unit.

Technology owner

For all the technology that supports the business, including both product systems and internal or enterprise systems, we need to know who is accountable and responsible. Clearly-defined ownership helps to ensure that the technology supporting end users and employees does not become orphaned as people change jobs and the organization shifts.

These responsibilities are clearly enumerated in checklists. While many technology owners report into the development or operations groups, many instead report directly into business units. A technology owner may delegate portions of their responsibilities within their organization (and in some cases to other organizations), but regardless of delegation, the technology owner is ultimately responsible and accountable. These accountabilities may include: end-user computing environments, solutions and assets.

The end user computing environment includes desktops, laptops, lab machines, desktop software, and shared applications.

Solutions and assets include the following functions:

- **Software Development**. Build-to-deploy, source code, quality, and licensing, which are often delegated to an asset owner.

- **Architecture**. Asset inventory and technical debt management, which are often delegated to a solution or technical architect.

- **Hosting and Operations**. Account management, SLAs, reliability, availability, performance, and incident response, which are often delegated to an asset owner.

- **Security**. Application security, infrastructure (or environment) security, platform security, secure practices, and data compliance, which are often delegated to a security contact.

There are several reasons why we need to specify technology owner roles:

- Somebody must be responsible for every aspect of the organization's technology, whether it was built internally or not. Technology supports the business, and success of the business pays everybody's salaries. That includes software development, live operations, security, and compliance.

- Technology spent in the business units counts against total company technology spend, so it should not be ignored by the technology organization.

- Sometimes non-technology experts want to own technology because they believe that makes things faster and cheaper. Sometimes it does, but we want to make sure all cost and time-to-market comparisons are based on the same rules.

By clearly defining the responsibilities of a technology owner, and measuring everybody against the same criteria, organizational reporting lines become less relevant. This will hopefully help reduce cross-organization bickering, or perhaps even avoid it altogether.

Asset owner

An Asset owner is the individual responsible for all aspects of an asset and all the services it provides. This responsibility ranges from architecture and design, through development and delivery to live operations.

In many enterprises, these functions often report into completely different organizations. But significant research and experience show that it is best practice that ultimate ownership for providing a service (from cradle to grave) is the responsibility of a single individual.

A data asset owner is the individual responsible for all aspects of a data asset. This role is equivalent to that of the system asset owner except for a data asset. The responsibility includes curation processes, data accuracy, quality, and timeliness. This responsibility ranges from data modeling and design, through delivery to live products.

In larger organizations, it is often practical to organize by a combination of business alignment, asset alignment, and skillset alignment. For example, it might be more efficient to have a database administrator (DBA) group, rather than have individual DBAs sprinkled throughout the asset groups.

But even in this kind of organization, it is important that accountability and responsibility remain explicitly clear. In other words, we still recommend that every asset have a single owner for all aspects of the service, even though some of the sub-functions may be delegated to other organizational units.

> An asset should be owned by a single individual. This includes full responsibility and accountability for all aspects of the asset lifecycle, beginning with ideation and ending with live operation.

Technical architect

Technical architects are primarily responsible for the architecture and high-level design of individual assets. For system assets, this includes technology architecture. For data assets, this includes data architecture and data modeling. Technical architects are also responsible for the architecture diagrams for assets, completing checklists, and interacting with enterprise architects in the governance process.

Enterprise architect

Enterprise architects are aligned to the enterprise, not to specific business units or products. Enterprise architects are ultimately responsible for steering the direction of the organization's technology architecture and for measuring how far along the path the implementation is.

EAs focus on enterprise-wide activities such as:

- Drawing together the overall technology strategy across various products and domains
- Driving disruptive change
- Performing *technical due-diligence* for Mergers & Acquisitions (M&A)
- Driving out complexity
- Leading *architecture guilds*[29] (membership including EAs, SAs, TAs, and engineers)
- Educating the engineering staff on "good architecture practice."

Solution architect

Solution architects (SAs) are aligned to solutions, business capabilities, and feature sets, including their delivery. Solution architects are responsible for placement-of-function and for defining how solutions are implemented by integrating assets across domain boundaries. This includes both system assets and data assets. Organizationally, SAs should be aligned to business initiatives and not domains. They could report into either product organizations or engineering organizations, aligned either with enterprise architecture or technical architecture.

---

[29] A Guild is a community of best practice in the agile methodology. Guilds operate alongside squads, chapters and tribes.

CHAPTER 5

An Example – νNews[30] (Pronounced: Nu News)

For the sake of simplicity, we will define an example organization's products at a very high level. In doing so, we may further explore how the roles defined in the last chapter interact.

The organization sells one product:

- **News Alerts** – The product provides search and alerts on news for markets and companies.

The product is built from two business capabilities:

- **Company News** – Provides news search, news story display, and alerts for companies.
- **Market News** – Provides news search, news story display, and alerts for markets.

The business capabilities are built from the following system assets:

- **News Display** – Provides headline and story display for news.
- **Search** – Provides search capability for all data assets.
- **Alerts** – Provides end-user alerts for new data meeting user-defined criteria.

And these data assets:

- **Company News** – News about companies, including press releases.
- **Market News** – News about markets, including economic events.

The business capabilities are created from system and data assets as follows:

Business Capabilities	System Assets	Data Assets
Company News	News Display, Search, Alerts	Company News (Data)
Market News	News Display, Search, Alerts	Market News

---

[30] "ν" may look like a "vee," but it's the Greek letter "nu."

- Each **product** is assigned a product owner and a solution architect
- Each **business capability** is assigned a business capability owner and a solution architect
- Each **system asset** is assigned an asset owner and a technical architect
- Each **data asset** is assigned an asset owner, and a technical architect (who is a Data Architect)

For an organization of this size, there might only be one technology owner and one enterprise architect.

This is how the PBEA defines the roles, business capabilities, and assets that manifest in vNews. Again, the PBEA roles are just one model for organizing responsibilities. This is not necessarily the only model that would work.

Suppose vNews was so successful that they add a second product to their portfolio which provides financial information about companies as well as associated news. This new product has some capabilities that are unique to it and some that are shared with the existing product. During the business requirements review, the solution architect completes a placement-of-function exercise, which identifies that one new business capability is needed. To create the new business capability, one new system asset and two new data assets are required. No modifications are required to the *Company News* capability, but if there were, they would have been identified during the placement-of-function exercise, as well as exactly which system and data assets had to be enhanced.

The company now sells two products:

- **Company Info** – The product provides financials and news about companies
- **News Alerts** – The product provides search and alerts on news for markets and companies.

The new Company Info product reuses the company news business capability and creates a new capability for displaying company financials. As such, the new product is composed of the following capabilities:

- **Company Financials** – Provides fundamentals and filings for companies (new business capability)
- **Company News** – Provides news search, news story display and alerts for companies (reused from the News Alerts product).

The new company financials business capability is built from the following new system asset:

- **Financials** - Provides retrieval and display for company fundamentals and filings.

And the following new data assets:

- **Company Fundamentals** – *As-reported*[31] and *standardized*[32] financial information about companies
- **Company Filings** – SEC filings.

The products in the portfolio are composed of business capabilities as follows:

Product	Business Capabilities
Company Info	Company Financials + Company News
News Alerts	Company News + Market News

The Business Capabilities are composed from system and data assets as follows:

Business Capabilities	System Assets	Data Assets
Company Financials	Financials	Fundamentals, Filings
Company News	News Display, Search, Alerts	Company News
Market News	News Display, Search, Alerts	Market News

---

[31] As-reported financial information is stored exactly as the company reported it in the public filing.

[32] Standardized financial information is normalized according to some accounting standard (e.g. US GAAP) so that one company's data may be compared to that of another company.

CHAPTER 6

Architecture Governance

An asset-oriented architecture (AOA) focuses on clearly delineating and enumerating each of the building blocks of the solutions in an enterprise. This approach facilitates increased re-use of systems and data and increased quality through hypervigilance on encapsulation and APIs. The enumeration of these building blocks that we call assets, provides the inventory that we use to track technical debt. Technical debt is the primary metric that we use to drive business insight through architecture.

As I mentioned earlier, enterprise architecture exists to provide business benefits. These business benefits are derived primarily from the increased reuse and measurability of the system and data assets comprising the AOA. Time-to-market, total-cost-of-ownership, and integration benefits all derive in some way from increasing reuse and measurability. As such, achieving the business goals of an AOA requires that we achieve reuse and measurability goals, and that requires governance. Architecture governance is not about policing the architecture. It is the process of measuring the adherence of the assets to the strategy and to the golden rules, so that *corrective actions* can be prioritized based on business impact and cost and thus influence future investment decisions.

Asset governance begins with people, who have well-defined decision rights and a clear escalation path in the case of conflict. Policies (which we call *principles* and *golden rules*) define what we are trying to achieve in a measurable way. *Golden rule measures* provide a checklist to quantify compliance with the rules. Golden rules do not define the functional requirements of products, but rather the non-functional requirements. As stated in Chapter 1, non-functional requirements are those aspects of the solution which are expected, but rarely stated explicitly. The asset governance process measures adherence of assets to the strategy and the golden rules thus producing metrics for compliance or deviation. The process iterates so that, over time, we achieve the right level of compliance with policy and strategy balancing investment and in new features with the investment required to pay-off technical debt and eliminate the associated business risk.

Asset governance is distinct from program and project management, which is another type of governance. Program increments, and projects are the funding envelopes initiated to deliver a business benefit through creating, changing, or decommissioning assets. They have financial goals, functional goals, and time-frame goals. But even after all the investment dollars have been spent, the assets live on, and they require operational support, maintenance, and basic enhancements.

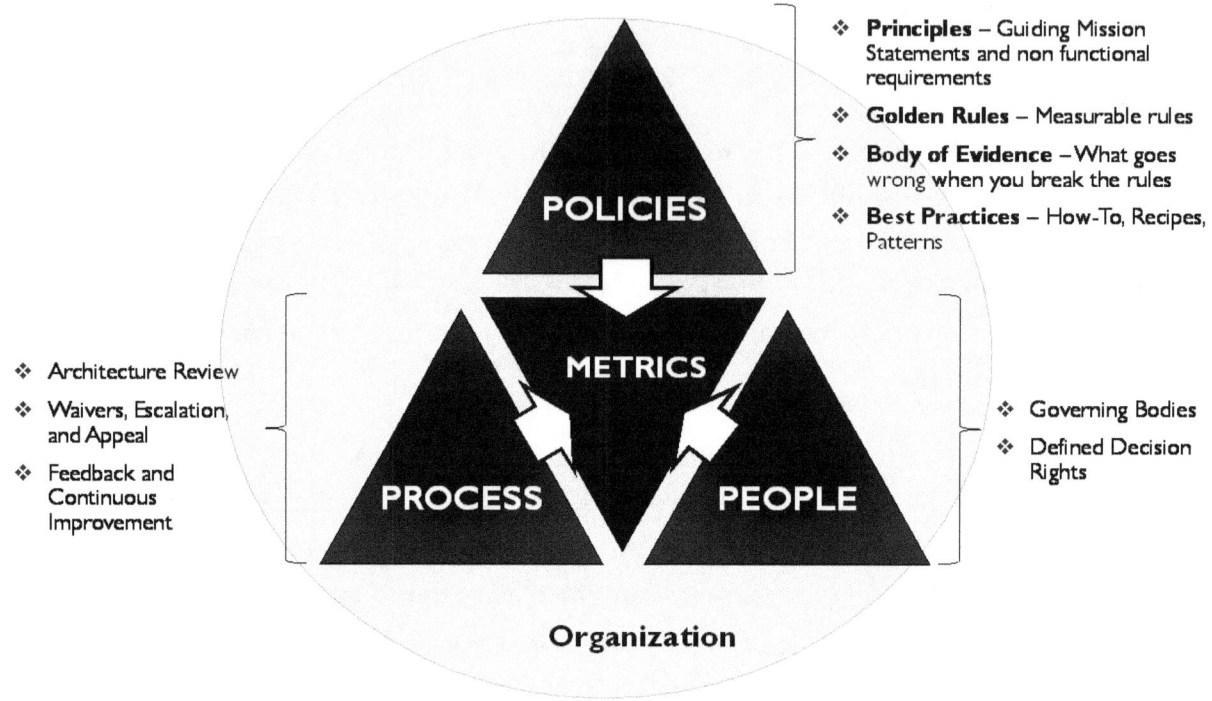

Asset governance

Enterprise architects (EAs), solution architects (SAs), and technical architects (TAs) work together in the governance process but each has a distinct and prescribed role.

System assets proceed through a series of reviews. This should be done early in the software development lifecycle so that rework may be kept to a minimum. The first review is called a "pre-implementation review." Ideally, this review occurs towards the beginning of a program increment, after systems architecture has reached an appropriate level of maturity and diagrams can be produced (See Chapter 3, above). In reality, coding sometimes begins first. There are also many systems developed long before a governance process existed, as well as systems that are acquired from other companies, where there may have been no governance at all. To address the need to govern these systems too, there are four different governance levels which an asset may follow (including Level 0: which means no architecture governance – i.e.

trusted). If the system asset exposes application programming interfaces (APIs), then an API review is scheduled sometime after an API design has sufficiently matured.

Before the system asset delivers into the production environment, the physical architecture should be completed, and a post-implementation review should be performed. The post-implementation review measures the operational characteristics of the asset, such as availability, disaster recovery, scalability, some aspects of security, and manageability.

The architecture review process begins with the production of diagramming artifacts. The review process may begin as soon as the first set of diagrams are produced and need not wait until everything is complete. It is usually best to iterate through the review, especially for complex systems. After the review is complete and solution architects, technical architects, and enterprise architects are satisfied that the architecture represents intent, an asset checklist is completed. This checklist is used as a scorecard for the asset. System assets and data assets are both assessed – system assets using the system asset checklist and data assets using the data asset checklist.

Governance levels for systems assets

It's important to know if systems are safe. Companies are frequently asked by prospects, customers, and of course regulators, to explain and affirm that security and compliance controls are in place. Through the architecture governance process, compliance and divergence with declared controls, standards, and technology best practices are measured and reported through a system asset dashboard. Architecture governance identifies, assesses, and provides input to leadership, to prioritize remediation of decisions inconsistent with company policies, as well as statutory and regulatory obligations.

There are four levels of governance (excluding level zero, which represents *trust* and no architecture governance). These are defined based on achieving specific business objectives. All systems that are built, licensed, installed, operated, or consumed through Software as a Service (SaaS), or consumed through Application Programming Interfaces (APIs, are subject to governance. The governance levels align closely to the PBEA Objectives:

0. **Trusted**. No golden rule measurement but often supported by a *security assessment* (as appropriate for a third party or an external system).

1. **Safe**. Metrics regarding whether the asset is secure, and compliant.

2. **Responsive**. Metrics regarding whether the asset is *safe*, and whether the system achieves desired performance, availability, and recovery objectives. Incidents and problems can be resolved quickly.

3. **Effective**. Metrics regarding whether the asset is *safe* and *responsive* and is designed to be upgraded easily and cost-effectively, avoiding entropy.

4. **Global**. Metrics regarding whether the asset can be localized for a new geography without performing "major surgery".

What makes governance arduous?

To participate in system asset governance, one must understand the golden rules and their associated diagramming guidelines. Mastery takes time. The challenge of finding time is difficult in any business environment. One must balance the investment of time required to learn and understand the PBEA method and golden rules with the pressure to deliver new software technology. Somebody just learning PBEA does not want to discover that projects they've already completed have broken the rules *(rules they didn't even know existed)*. That is quite frankly demoralizing. Let's face it, no one wakes up excited each day to do harm to the organization paying their salary, by wasting time, money, or creating security or compliance issues.

The challenge is that we can neither afford to waste time, nor take unnecessary risks associated with breaking the golden rules. These golden rules – and the policies, strategies, standards, and best practices they represent – eloquently capture decades of knowledge from hundreds of technologists across the industry.

Most of this knowledge is distilled into the checklist that is the key deliverable of the governance process. It is organized around the principles and golden rules, with Yes/No answers to identify compliance with, or divergence from, the rules themselves. Answering these questions provides meaningful metrics on both individual and aggregate scales. Examining a portfolio of asset metrics could identify patterns of exceptions that require funding to provide both training for staff and remediation to systems.

For example, if we see that several security golden rules are commonly broken across many assets in the portfolio, we have discovered a need for improved training in "writing secure code". Or if we see that systems are generally built without globalization in mind, not only might we have a training issue, but we also know that a requirement to localize a product for a new geography would also imply investment in globalizing the supporting systems as well.

Governance levels are practical strategies to govern most IT investments by calibrating the amount of metrics produced, proportional to the business objective. Even systems we choose not to govern should still be identified in the asset inventory and tracked. Prioritizing which systems to measure first does not need to be difficult.

What triggers asset governance?

As the business adapts to ever-changing market conditions, we not only deal with the ramifications of past decisions, but also try to make the best decisions for the future. The biggest decisions often involve allocation of limited resources.

Asset governance is triggered by an investment in an asset, the creation of a new asset, changes in technology solutions, and mergers and acquisitions. Triggers related to asset and technology are generally the result of a *software development lifecycle* (SDLC).

Governance is a process with checks and balances implemented by people. Tasks may initiate governance, but architecture governance measures assets, not programs of effort. There are often lots of tasks taking place at any one time, but only tasks that manifest in an architecture change need initiate an architecture governance action. If any of the following criteria is true, then it's likely the asset has changed significantly; as such, it is subject to review:

- The asset is new or was acquired through merger or acquisition.

- The asset has undergone an architecturally significant change. For example:
    - Components have changed.
    - External APIs have changed.
    - Data models have changed.
    - COTS software has changed.

Remember, governing is about *measuring*, not *policing*.

API governance

API governance occurs as a stage in the system asset governance process. We manage how system assets are expressed across boundaries by ensuring the right API specifications and implementations are built. By governing both boundaries and interfaces we produce a loose federation of services that are broadly reusable, consumable, and agile.

Reuse is achieved by:
- Modeling services with the appropriate granularity (so there are neither too many nor too few).

- Making services available over a broadly interoperable and scalable protocol.

- Registering, maintaining, and sharing interface descriptions and the artifacts used to describe them (*e.g.,* media types and schemas) across the enterprise.

Consume-ability is achieved by:
- Adopting a uniform resource centric design, where each document takes the form of a resource representation built according to the principles and constraints of REST.
- Establishing patterns that standardize solutions and drive consistency and cohesion.
- Building an enterprise-wide canonical data model used to name and define the document media types exchanged using APIs and the schemas they employ.

Agility is achieved by:
- Enforcing clear separation between interface specification and service implementation.
- Making use of content negotiation to allow clients and servers to extend support for different document (resource) representations and formats such as XML and JSON, over time while maintaining backward compatibility.
- Enforcing clear *separation-of-concerns (SoC)* between business capabilities, assets, non-functional requirements, and policy enforcement.
- Adopting a comprehensive and consistent model for versioning.
- Encapsulating choice of technology within the asset implementation and not exposing it through APIs.

Public APIs are generally offered to authenticated users in the context of revenue generating access models like a subscription. As such they ought to enforce run-time policies. These include:
- Monitoring to gather performance and usage metrics.
- Gathering metrics and analytics to determine usage patterns.
- Throttling, shaping, and blocking traffic to manage workloads and threats.
- Protecting all API entry points against security vulnerabilities.

> *Separation of concerns*[33] (SoC) is a design principle for separating software into distinct sections, such that each section addresses a separate concern. A concern is a set of information that affects the code of a computer program and defines a *bounded context*.[34]

---

[33] Separation of concerns – See: https://bit.ly/2nyAc24.

[34] Bounded content – See: https://bit.ly/2thC7vJ.

> A *loosely coupled*[35] system is one in which each of its components has little or no knowledge of the definitions of other components. In a loosely-coupled system, services that communicate with each other via interfaces may change independently and in any order.

Software asset governance

Historically, developers would discover a software product, fall in love with it, and then implement it within the context of their product or system, assuming the pressure to deliver imbued them with the right to choose whatever software made that possible. Some companies, especially those with strong centralized technology groups over-enthusiastically ended these actions by implementing and enforcing *corporate standards*, often including an arduous, bureaucratic approach to adopting a new standard and often no process for removing an old one. Both approaches are seriously flawed.

As with all PBEA governance processes, the recommended approach revolves around:

- Change is inevitable and good, so make it easy.
- Long-term accountability ultimately resides with product owners and technology owners and not central bodies.
- The best way to avoid solving the same problem multiple times is to make pre-existing solutions accessible and easy to reuse.
- Governance doesn't exist to say "No." It exists to make the real cost and real benefit measurable so that a good business decision can be made.

The business benefits of software asset governance process (known in the industry as *Software Asset Management*) are:

- **Compliance.** Effective management of the technology portfolio of 3rd-party commercial off-the-shelf (COTS) software allows tracking of licenses so that potentially huge fines may be avoided.
- **Optimization.** When common technology solutions are used for similar technology problems, costs may be optimized, implementation patterns reused, and economies of scale realized.

---

35   Loose coupling – See: https://bit.ly/2HV1aft.

- **Operation.** Applying standard solutions to solve similar problems avoids waste in every facet of the software development lifecycle (SDLC) and IT operations. This optimizes skills across the organization and therefore reduces overall cost of ownership.

- **Security.** Eventually vulnerabilities stemming from use of third-party technology will occur. Only through an accurate inventory of these third-party technologies and a map to the systems they employ, may associated security vulnerabilities be dealt with effectively.[36]

- **Evolution.** Use new technology and versions appropriately. All software has a limited shelf life.

The recommended software asset governance process:

1. Identifies the *problem being solved*. In other words, each registered technology standard is associated with one or more clearly defined technology or business problems.

2. Identifies which asset(s) the technology is associated with.

3. Identifies the major version that is being implemented.

4. Identifies whether this is a new solution to an existing problem or a solution to a new problem.

5. The process should be a registration process, not an approval gateway. Maintaining an accurate inventory of what technology is in use, and what version, is crucial, and much more important than having some central body, not involved in actual software development, pontificate as to whether a specific technology should be used or not.[37]

---

[36]. We can be pretty sure the CEO of Equifax in 2017, Richard Smith, did not realize the threat to both the organization and his position from a system patch that was missed, ultimately leading to a breach affecting 145 million customers (An example of body-of-evidence).

[37] Software Asset Governance is about reducing overall business risk, which requires an accurate software inventory. As such, we do not want to design processes that encourage development groups to ignore them to get their work done.

CHAPTER 7

Architecture Metrics

Architecture metrics are the informative facts created from governance processes, which measure the fitness of the technology investments that have been made. *Enterprise architecture governance* measures compliance, convergence, and deviation from strategy. Measures are aligned to business objectives through governance levels for systems and data. A dashboard presents these metrics in a way that can be understood by decision makers.

The production of actionable metrics is one of the key differentiators of PBEA from other enterprise architecture methodologies. The metrics are actionable because they identify where teams have made trade-off decisions to achieve release goals. While the *asset owner* has delegated decision making authority to their teams, the asset owner is accountable, and therefore must periodically review the metrics and make the conscious decision to manage business risks working with the *product owners* and/or *business capability owners* to prioritize the corrective actions.

The Asset Checklist

Each Business Objective is supported by several architecture principles. Architecture principles are then decomposed into golden rules, such that complying with the golden rule implies that the asset is adhering to the architecture principle and thus achieving the business objective. To take the subjectivity out of determining whether an asset adheres to the intent of the golden rule, each rule has several precise measures assigned. Golden rule measures are always "yes/no" questions. There are no essay questions. Therefore, we call it a checklist.[38] The questions are also worded so that "yes" is the answer which has no associated technical debt. If the answer is "no," then the checklist entry is associated with a *corrective action*, which is a description of what it will take to correct the defect. Since multiple defects may be corrected

---

[38] See https://bit.ly/2I5neE2 for an example system asset checklist.

through the same action, we allow multiple golden rule measures that have "no" answers to be associated with the same corrective action, to avoid double counting.

Enterprise architects, solution architects, and technical architects collaborate on the process to ensure that the overall scoring is fair and properly captures both business risk and debt. It is unfortunately very easy to get bogged down in the governance process itself and lose sight of the ultimate goal, which is to measure business risk associated with technology and to recommend and prioritize investments that reduce the most risk for the least cost. In other words, if the defect does not present too significant a risk, and you would never recommend spending the money to correct it, then take that into consideration when filling out the checklist and defining the corrective actions. We are not looking for perfection. We are looking for balance.

To create a *Technology Health and Business Risk* dashboard, the architecture collaboration first responds to each golden rule measure with a yes/no answer as described above. Since each golden rule has a set of measures, adherence with the underlying measures determine the adherence to the golden rule. In other words, if all the measures have answered yes because the asset complies with the measure, then clearly the asset also complies with the golden rule. If on the other hand, the asset complies with some of the golden rule measures but not all, there is a discussion required to determine whether the asset complies with the golden rule or not. This is a business risk assessment only. Regardless of whether the overall golden rule is considered compliant (i.e. minimal business risk), if there is a non-adherent measure and an associated corrective action, then there is debt. As such, the scores for the golden rules quantify business risk, while the cost of the corrective actions quantifies debt.

In the same way that we roll-up the scores for golden rule measures to score the golden rule, we also roll-up the scores for the golden rules to score the architecture principle. We roll-up architecture principle scores to score the business objective and we present the scores for each business objective along with associated technical debt on a dashboard for all to see. Asset scores and associated debt can be further rolled-up to domains, platforms and solutions as required. The purpose of the dashboard is to drive business insight and future investment decisions. So, it should be organized in a way that best serves that purpose given the way the organization operates and makes decisions.

As the health of each asset is rolled up to domain, platform and solution, the dashboard presents an assessment of the overall health of the technology and data landscape across the organization. When the dashboard is organized by domain, it is a technology alignment. When it is organized by technology owner or product owner, it is an ownership alignment. When the dashboard is organized by business capability and solution, it is a business alignment. In many organizations, all three alignment models are required to drive investment decisions, but as stated above, this depends on the culture of the organization. While the technology alignment is often the most logical view of business risk and technical debt, it is often the ownership-oriented view which gets the most action. Nobody likes to see a dashboard with their name next to a high risk or warning indicator.

Each individual checklist also contains which golden rules have been broken by which assets along with corrective actions. Each corrective action has an associated technical debt, which is the estimated cost for implementing the fix. Each golden rule has an associated business impact and a likelihood which when combined defines associated business risk.

As such, when the governance process is complete, not only does it yield a dashboard of business risk associated with technology and provide a measure for the overall technical debt, but it also provides a prioritized list of corrective actions, across the platforms, which can be fed back into the business' investment review process.

The purpose of asset governance is to create a public, easily understood view of the technology, and data landscape. The architecture debt associated with that asset and the detailed breakdown of what has contributed to the debt feeds into the portfolio planning process so that debt may be paid off *in the fullness of time*.

The architecture community, through the interactions associated with asset governance, works as a body to ensure that all the various assets (systems and data) make sense as a whole. If the "big picture" doesn't quite add up, they adjust the evolving technology strategy accordingly. They also harvest the best practices of one group and evangelize them to other groups.

Filling out an asset checklist

Each asset has an associated individual who is responsible for the system's architecture (i.e. the technical architect). Technical architects assess their own assets, since they are the ones most familiar with them. Enterprise architects, solutions architects, and technical architect's review the individual scores on each golden rule measure and perform the roll-up from golden rule measures to golden rules to principles to business objectives and finally to assets, as described above.

The technical architect begins by filling out the high-level metadata for the asset. This includes the name of the asset, a summary of what the asset does, the names of the various architects and owners.

The next step is to select the correct profiles for the asset. A profile is a behavior of the asset that determines whether golden rules are appropriate or not. For example, one type of behavior is whether the asset is a data master or not. If it exhibits this behavior, then the golden rules associated with data mastering need to be measured. If it does not exhibit this behavior, they do not. Another type of behavior is whether the asset exposes a human interface. Asset behaviors and associated profiles are intended to be flexible and tuned over time. The point of creating profiles is to eliminate the tendency for individual architects deciding inconsistently which rules apply to their asset and which do not. "N/A" or not-applicable may not be used as a response to a golden rule measure on the checklist.

After the profiles are set, defining the behavior of the asset, the technical architect goes through the checklist, answering yes or no as to whether the asset complies with each of the rules and measures that are presented.

For each measure, one of four responses is possible:

1. **Yes**. The asset materially meets the spirit of this rule. A "yes" answer does not require perfection, but it does carry accountability. So, if the answer is "yes," the technical architect is indicating that she knows enough to know the answer, and everything known leads to the conclusion that the answer should be yes. Many rules begin with an "If" statement. For example: "If you do *this* in your asset, then you should also do *that*." When the If-clause does not apply, because the asset doesn't do that, then the answer is still "Yes," because "Yes" implies compliance. For example, the measure might be: "If the asset exposes sensitive data through its API, then that data must be encrypted." If the asset does not expose sensitive data through its API, the response will be yes, since it complies.

2. **No**. The asset does not materially comply with the spirit of the golden rule measure. A "No" answer does not imply there isn't partial compliance and it doesn't necessarily imply a business risk. It means there isn't full compliance. A description of what doesn't comply, and a corrective action, along with an associated debt is captured.

3. **T-WVR**. This is a temporary waiver. It means the asset isn't compliant now, usually because of some external dependency that the asset owner has no control over. Please note that lack of budget, lack of time, or lack of talent are not external-dependencies even though they may be out of your control. Even if a T-WVR is requested, the corrective action should still be defined, and the associated debt assessed. For example, suppose you are forced to call an unmaintained asset for access to some data. The strategic asset that you would like to use has not yet been released and you cannot afford to wait. The debt captured is the cost of using the new asset after it becomes available. That cost may very well be zero.

4. **P-WVR**: This is a permanent waiver. It is typically used as an answer because a rule is not relevant and scoring it or assigning it debt is just a distraction, since there is neither intent nor need to take any action to resolve the issue. Granting permanent waivers is rare. In general, they exist because the asset behavior has not been properly captured by a profile. When the enterprise architecture group sees a permanent waiver being granted, it is generally an indicator that a new profile needs to be defined.

For rules which may not be complied with currently, but which can be followed without allocating additional budget, there is no debt – even though the rule is broken and there may be a corrective action and/or a business risk. Debt is not the same risk, although the two are correlated. When a corrective action has debt, the assumption is that prioritization and investment is required. This is a very important point. Debt represents the <u>additional</u> budget required to eliminate the business risk. While the debt remains unpaid and the corrective action remains open, the risk exists.

Additionally, when you identify corrective actions, you should not blindly define one for each broken rule. You want to write the corrective actions to be what you would recommend doing to close out the debt. For example, no matter how bad an implementation may be, you do not want to show millions of dollars of debt against something that could be rewritten for one thousand dollars. Debt should be a realistic representation of the cost to eliminate the business risk, the way you would recommend doing it. If replacement is the cheapest way to eliminate the debt, then there should be one corrective action, which is to migrate the asset. If the debt can be eliminated by simply retiring the asset, then that is the corrective action. But while the asset is running, then each broken rule represents a potential business risk.

Data assets are scored against the golden rules for data using the same process as that used for system assets. A benchmark of the data quality is established through the review process. Enterprise architects work with solutions architects and others within the business units and software development groups to establish operational governance over the data assets. Operational governance is carried out by the teams responsible for the development and maintenance of the data and the data management systems.

Enterprise architects work to ensure that all the various assets (i.e., systems and data) being developed make sense as a whole, and to adjust the evolving technology strategy accordingly. Enterprise architects also try to harvest the innovations of one group and evangelize them to other groups. These practices apply equally to system assets, and data assets. The principles and golden rules for each type of asset may be different and the people are different, but the process is essentially the same.

Guidelines for sizing corrective actions (i.e. calculating debt)

The architecture debt associated with a corrective action is basically the cost (usually measured in time, money, or story points) that it would take to resolve the issue, comply with the golden rule measure, and eliminate the business risk. It is determined in the same manner as the standard sizing process.

For data assets, the estimate should be based on how much it would take to correct the deviation as a one-time effort without ongoing maintenance (assuming ongoing maintenance is part of the operational process). In other words, estimate one pass through the data to correct the anomaly and one pass through the operational processes to correct the process, if necessary. Assume that after the data has been corrected, the newly corrected operational processes will keep the data correct.

Even though PBEA treats correcting a deviation as a one-time cost, the longer the deviation remains uncorrected, and the longer the business risk remains, the more *interest* accrues on the debt, making it costlier to correct. Technology generally becomes bigger, more complex, and harder to fix as it ages. This is the source of the *interest* on the debt.

"True" cost

To make good business decisions (which are essentially cost/benefit decisions), the true cost of the decision must be understood. This would seem an obvious statement to make, except that true cost is rarely well understood. Technology decisions typically only consider the build cost, and usually only the *initial* build cost. According to a Gartner study, initial build cost is generally between 2% and 10% of total lifecycle cost and rarely more than 15%. This means most of the cost of a decision is often not factored into the decision-making process.

So, what do we mean by "cost"? There are four 'factors':

- **The cost to build**. This is the cost to satisfy the desired functional requirements as well as non-functional requirements with software.

- **The cost to operate (OpEx)**. This is the cost to run the system including all compute, storage, and network costs. OpEx also includes any ongoing software license costs. OpEx is an ongoing cost. It must be paid every year for as long as the system is running.

- **The cost to maintain**. This is the cost to fix bugs and upgrade software as new versions come out. Maintenance cost is usually 5%-15% of the initial build cost. Additionally, maintenance is an annual cost not a one-time cost. In other words, you pay maintenance for as long as the asset is operational.

- **Technical debt.** This is the cost to implement all the corrective actions that have been identified for the asset. Rarely is an asset fully compliant with every golden rule. In other words, it rarely implements all the non-functional requirements and almost always carries a bit of debt.

The PBEA method for architecture governance is based on the premise that governance exists to *measure* the system and data assets which make up the organization's solutions, providing business insight and driving investment decisions. By using data to make decisions (and by understanding as much of the data as possible), better decisions will be made and there will be fewer disagreements between individuals and groups. True cost, including technical debt, is the data that most organizations are missing.

Technical debt and architecture debt

Both on an individual and a national scale, debt imprisons. – Tom Hodgkinson

Architecture debt is a key component of technical debt. The other key component is known as maintenance debt.

Technical debt = architecture debt + maintenance debt

Architecture debt is the key metric that comes from the asset governance process. Maintenance debt is the amount of money that was underspent on maintenance. For example, if we calculated that an asset required 5% of the initial build cost for year-on-year maintenance, and we only spent 2% year-on-year, then we are building up maintenance debt.

Therefore, technical debt is the difference between what we have spent on technology and what we should have spent. The architecture debt component is the cost to make the asset fully compliant with policy, strategy, and the golden rules. The maintenance debt component is the cost for the asset to be properly maintained, including fixing bugs and applying patches. Technical debt is essentially an obligation for future investment; one that may never be fully paid off, but which collects interest, and correlates to business risk for as long as it remains outstanding.

Carrying a bit of architecture debt is not intrinsically bad. Almost all assets carry some debt.[39] Managing debt means ensuring that we don't collapse under the burden of debt. If debt is managed appropriately (which entails mitigating the business risks associated with non-

---

[39] One could argue that an asset with zero technical debt has been over-engineered. Perhaps it could have been delivered sooner by choosing to carry a bit of debt for a while.

compliance of policy), then carrying the debt and paying it off over time is a natural part of the technology lifecycle. The architecture governance dashboard gives a global view of the debt being carried by the assets under governance and is a tool for managing the debt, and associated business risk.

There are several reasons that debt is usually incurred. These include: commercial decisions, IT planning and execution decisions, and financial planning decisions.

Commercial decisions

Commercial decisions may result in architecture debt. For example, when the decision is made to build out technology which should be migrated, rather than executing the migration, then technical debt is being added. Generally, the decision to do so is made as a trade-off by product and commercial decision makers with their IT counterparts.

When the choice is made to build-out existing assets instead of migrating them onto new technology platforms first, the following must be factored into the decision:

- The existing asset must eventually be migrated onto new technology. Migration costs generally increase as the number of interconnections between assets increase and/or the number of users accessing the asset increase. Cost also increase exponentially with complexity.

- The same functionality must also be built into the migrated asset. Hence, we will be spending twice to achieve the same end-user benefit.

- The existing technology must be maintained year on year (YoY) and that maintenance increases with age and amount of investment. The migrated asset must also be maintained, so once we begin the migration effort, we will be double spending on maintenance until the migration is complete.

Another commercial decision which tends to generate technical debt is the decision to release software and/or data before its ready. By ready, we don't mean that it has zero debt. We mean that it has been sufficiently architected, designed, implemented, and tested so that true cost and business benefit are balanced. Time-to-market (i.e. delivering quickly) almost always trumps long-term cost, so short-term decisions will inevitably be made. We expect that. PBEA provides the necessary tools so that the true cost of these decisions may be understood at the time the decision is made and a better cost / benefit balance can be achieved.

IT planning and execution decisions

IT Planning and execution decisions may also result in technical debt. For example, when an asset releases prior to complying with the architecture golden rules. Generally, this decision is made due to challenges or trade-offs in the software development lifecycle.

The primary driver for delivering before complying with the golden rules is time-to-market, and so is intimately tied to commercial decisions as stated above. Secondary drivers include unfunded or delayed dependencies. Provided business risks are mitigated, and the debt is eventually paid off, this iterative model works very well. Debt may be paid off by either fixing the underlying issues, or by migrating or retiring the asset. As such, if an asset is badly architected, badly implemented, and/or just old and under-maintained, the architecture debt can be used as a factor in the business justification to build a new asset and decommission the old.

Financial planning and analysis decisions

The financial planning and analysis function drives leadership decisions regarding the diversification of budgets for global functions and business units. Thus, technical debt may result from the choice to underinvest in annual maintenance after the initial release of a product or asset. Maintenance is an ongoing investment that is required to fix bugs and address non-discretionary (e.g. compliance related) software changes and patches. By not allocating enough ongoing funding to support live systems, maintenance debt increases. Technical debt is the sum of maintenance debt and architecture debt.

Outcomes and the 'body of evidence'

A major component of the work of enterprise architecture is to govern the evolving architecture of system and data assets with the goal of maximizing their value to the enterprise. This governance is not based on arbitrary rules, but on rules derived from extensive experience. PBEA includes a collection of stories of situations that went wrong in the past, that have cost money in redundant investment or lost revenue, that reduced competitiveness, upset end users, and increased business risk.

We call this collection of stories the body-of-evidence. The body-of-evidence provides business justification for the PBEA principles and golden rules.

The *stories* providing the body-of-evidence for the golden rules are generally *negative outcomes*. Such stories describe bad things that have happened applying technology in the past, which we would not want to accidentally repeat.

Once a negative outcome has been identified, it is assigned an impact measuring how bad the outcome was, and a likelihood that the bad outcome will happen. The combination of impact and likelihood defines how important it is to follow the golden rule (i.e. the rule's severity).

While golden rules can exist to promote *positive outcomes* as well as prevent *negative* ones, most of the stories making up the body-of-evidence avoid a negative outcome rather than promote a positive one. Several stories compare how one organization did better than another. In other words, the positive outcome is described in the context of one organization avoiding a negative outcome that another organization experienced.

CHAPTER **8**

Best Practices and Processes

A best practice is a method or technique that has consistently shown results superior to those achieved with other means. Best practices are not mandatory. An enterprise best practice is optional but following it will likely ensure your path is a happy one. PBEA best practices are primarily driven by evidence-based decision making and the use of actionable metrics. In this book, examples of best practices are set aside from the main body of text in boxes.

Inventories and registries

The first and most important of the recommended best practices by the PBEA method is the creation and maintenance of accurate inventories. The main examples of inventories and registries crucial to a well-organized enterprise architecture are:

- **Asset Inventory.** System assets and data assets grouped into domains.

- **Placement-of-function (PoF) inventory.** A complete list of placement-of-function artifacts organized by feature set and version.

- **API Inventory.** Interfaces exposed, and interfaces called by each system asset, as well as the data assets exposed through the system asset interfaces.

- **Technology Standards Registry.** Third-party technologies in use (including open source) mapped to the assets using them.

- **Data Asset Host Inventory.** Relates a data asset to the system asset which is the master for the data asset. The PGUID[40] namespace given to each data asset is also identified. A

---

[40] A PGUID is a Permanent Globally Unique Identifier. It is non-mnemonic and opaque and is used as the primary identifier for a data item. That fact that the identifier is permanent implies that it is allocated once, and once allocated is never changed and never reused.

data asset is mastered by exactly one system asset. A system asset may be the master for zero or more data assets.

- **Operational Instance Inventory**. Physical or virtual instances (e.g., computing instances, databases, and network devices) are mapped to the assets to which they belong. Instances are not shared. They are part of the asset's implementation.

The difference between an inventory and a registry is small. An inventory assumes completion, and usually involves a project to create the initial inventory, with well-defined processes for maintaining completeness. A registry, on the other hand, strives for completeness, but achieves it incrementally.

Asset inventory

The asset inventory is a list of all system and data assets, what each does, the results of its checklist (including how much debt is associated), and its ownership such as technology owner and asset owner. Additional metadata is defined for each asset to support security and compliance. For example, if the asset sends external email, it is flagged, since these types of assets are often the target of spambot[41] attacks. If the asset is subject to specific regulations (e.g. SOX[42] compliance, or HIPPA[43] compliance), this is flagged as well.

Placement of Function (PoF) inventory

The PoF inventory is the list of all PoF artifacts, which includes the mapping of assets to the *feature sets* and *business capabilities* supported. As such, the PoF inventory will usually depend on whatever tool the organization is using to manage *epics*, *features*, and *user stories*. The purpose of a PoF artifact is defined in Chapter 1.

API inventory

The API Inventory is composed of two primary lists:

- **Interfaces exposed by assets**. For each interface exposed by an asset to other assets, the interface specification, version, and a reference to the proper documentation is maintained
- **Interfaces consumed by assets**. For each asset, maintain a list of the interfaces provided by other assets which the asset calls. These lists should be updated regularly, so that a full dependency map can be produced on demand.

---

[41] Spambot attack – See: https://bit.ly/2ScY0Z3.

[42] Sarbanes-Oxley Act (SOX) – See: https://bit.ly/1Jhbio3.

[43] Health Insurance Portability and Accountability Act (HIPPA) – See: https://bit.ly/1PaH2Qr.

Technology standards registry

The technology standards inventory consists of three main pieces:

1. **Registry of Technology and Business Problems.** The problem registry is structured hierarchically so that common problems are grouped together.

2. **Registry of Technology Solutions.** The solution registry lists the internal or third-party technology, which problem(s) it is the solution for, and the *classification* of the solution. For third-party software, the vendor, the version number, and a reference to the license terms (which is critically important in the case of open source) are also identified. Where possible, subject matter experts should be identified, who may provide advice to first time implementers of the technology.

3. **Map of Technology Solutions to Assets.** Which assets use which technologies and vice versa.

Once a solution is used to solve a problem it sets a precedent and becomes the standard. The next person who comes along should try to reuse the solution or *provide a compelling reason* why a different solution makes business sense. The *burden of proof* is on choosing to do something different. This is the essence of how standardization is balanced with the adoption of emerging technology.

Each technology in the registry is given one of the following classifications:

- **Emerging.** This is a technology (version) which is not yet the standard, but which should be watched because within the next 6–18 months it will likely become the standard.

- **Standard.** This major version of this technology should be used for solving the defined problem today.

- **Deprecated.** This technology version was once a standard but has been replaced. It should no longer be used for new software solutions but should continue to be used where it has already been implemented.

- **Prohibited.** This technology version may not be used. It either has a known licensing issue or security vulnerability, or it is no longer being supplied security patches by the vendor. If it is in use, a project should be initiated to replace it.

Data asset host inventory

The data asset host inventory relates the system asset that masters a data asset to the data asset(s) that it masters. For each data asset, there is a PGUID namespace defined. The PGUID namespace is prepended to each PGUID for the data asset. This process supports both uniqueness and identification.

Operational instance inventory

The inventory of physical and virtual instances is perhaps the most critical inventory to keep 100% complete and accurate. Sadly, for many large companies, this is also the inventory whose accuracy is lacking.

In a traditional data center, holding the physical instance inventory is the job of the *configuration management database* (CMDB). I have seen many large projects focused on producing a complete CMDB, but I have rarely seen one succeed in creating a CMDB that is better than 90%, or more likely 80% complete and accurate.[44] In addition, once created, their accuracy often decays over time due to insufficient process control and too little automation. In the cloud, the provider's CMDB is the basis of your bill, so it is almost guaranteed to be complete and accurate. Nevertheless, it is a good idea to maintain your own inventory and use it to reconcile the bill.

The operational instance inventory is more than just the list of servers, databases, and network devices. A proper inventory also requires each physical or virtual device to be mapped to a single asset, so that Operational Expense (OpEx) can be fully attributed. In other words, we want to take the bill we get every month for running our data centers and allocate every cost item to exactly one asset. When we talk about assets not sharing infrastructure, this is what we really mean. An asset is a completely encapsulated thing that interacts with other assets only through well-defined interfaces. That way, when (not "if") something fails in the production environment, we can quickly map the device to an asset owner and discover who is responsible for resolving the problem.

PBEA expects that each server (or computing instance) in the inventory uses automation to pre-build *system images*[45] from system manifests. A system manifest is a list of every component installed on the server, along with its precise version and patch level, and where it is installed from. This includes operating system components, foundation software components, and every module of your code that is installed. When image creation is automated in this fashion, the system manifest is guaranteed to be correct.

---

[44] I am sure there are large companies out there who have complete and accurate CMDBs. I've just never met one, so I don't know if they achieved this feat through automation, which would be good, or through a process that slows down the release process and stifles innovation, which would be bad.

[45] In the Amazon Web Services cloud, this is known as an Amazon Machine Image (AMI). https://amzn.to/2oo4AtG.

In case of a security breach, for example, knowing the version number and patch level of a component can be the difference between blocking the attack early, or ending up in court later. The system manifest provides this information.

> Maintain accurate inventories of assets, APIs, technology standards, and data asset hosts (at a minimum). If the process for creating an accurate inventory is too onerous to implement, then at least create a registry with some easy way for people to self-maintain it.

> Maintain an inventory of every operational instance, which is as close to 100% complete and accurate as possible. Map every operational instance to a single asset and accurately measure the Operational Expense (OpEx) for each asset.

> Automate the creation of system images from system manifests. All servers (computing instances) are built from known, locked down system images.

Patterns

A pattern is a template for capturing a specific way of solving a commonly recurring problem. There are both architecture patterns and implementation patterns. The PBEA method presumes that central groups like enterprise architecture groups are not well positioned to invent patterns, but they are very well positioned to identify good implementations by one group, refine those into reusable patterns and evangelize their use to other groups. A collection of patterns is called a *Cookbook*.

Architecture diagramming

PBEA encourages organizations to adopt a common diagramming methodology. The PBEA Diagramming guidelines are outside the scope of this book. A reference for the guidelines may be found at: http://pbea.iankoenig.com.

For diagramming data models, PBEA recommends the Concept and Object Modeling Notation (COMN),[46] as defined in NoSQL and SQL Data Modeling, by Ted Hills, 2016.

Architecting testable solutions

For systems to be maintainable and reliable, they must be both testable and tested. Testability does not come for free. It must be architected and designed in. There are many fine works on how to test large software systems, and the PBEA method does not claim to add any value in this area. Nevertheless, architecting great solutions requires that they be testable, so we provide a few definitions and guidelines.

- **Testability.** The ability of an asset to enable test code that exercises code paths which may not be testable via functional or integration testing without creating highly convoluted and impractical tests. There are often many code paths that only execute in complex situations but are critical to proper function. A testable system often exposes internal-use-only[47] interfaces to invoke these hard-to-access code paths.

- **Functional Testing.** Testing the exposed functions of a system from an end-user perspective. In general, functional test development starts with business requirements and user stories and creates test cases that ensure the system delivers what the end user expects.

- **Unit Testing.** Testing the individual components of a system in isolation to ensure they function as-designed. Unit testing is often hierarchical, since the definition of a unit is quite flexible. A unit test case could cover a single method of a single object in a single module. These can then be aggregated into a set of unit tests for a module, which can be aggregated into a set of unit tests for an asset.

- **Integration Testing.** Testing the components of the system in the context of other components to ensure they function properly as a group.

- **Destructive Testing.** Testing that components of the system continue to work when other components fail. Destructive testing is used to find points of failure in an integrated system. Components are intentionally made to fail, to check the robustness of the integrated system.

---

[46] Concept and Object Modeling Notation (COMN) - See https://bit.ly/2tclKxv.

[47] A testable system exposes internal-use-only interfaces that exercise hard to access code and a secure system ensures these same interfaces are not misused. For example, they may be disabled in production.

- **Security Testing**. Uncovers security vulnerabilities of the system that might expose its data and resources to possible intruders.

> Design asset *unit-tests*[48] according to placement-of-function. Ensure that every asset that contributes to the delivery of a business requirement has at least one unit-test ensuring the asset performs as expected. This applies to data assets as well as system assets.

Unit testing

The fundamental building block of a solution is an asset. A system asset is a fully encapsulated aggregate of code, data, and systems. The only way in or out is through an API, and each API has an SLA providing a precise definition of how it is called, what it returns, and how it behaves. As such, each asset is an *autonomous computing entity*.[49]

The fact that each asset is autonomous implies that much of the functionality of the asset can be tested in isolation via unit testing using a test harness. A test harness is a set of programs which provide simple predictable responses for all interfaces to and from other assets. This isolates the component being tested from changes and idiosyncrasies in other assets. Well-architected test harnesses are almost as critical to producing reliable solutions as well architected systems.

> Build test harnesses for every system asset which simulate the interface of every asset that is called. Use that asset's SLA as a guide. Make the test harnesses configurable to simulate how a called asset is supposed to behave under normal operating conditions, as well as when it is under stress. Make test harnesses configurable to test how your asset behaves when the called asset meets its SLA and when it fails to meet its SLA. Being able to test how a system responds under load, as performance is degrading, is an important factor in testability.

> Build test harnesses that exercise every API exposed by an asset. Make the test harnesses configurable to simulate how a well-behaved client will use each API, as well as how an ill-behaved client may use each API.

Code path analysis should be performed to ensure that the unit test plan covers as much of the code as possible. It is not always possible to cover every code path, even with a perfectly defined unit test plan. For code paths that cannot easily be tested through calling an asset's

---

[48] Unit testing - See Chapter 8 – Architecting Testable Solutions.

[49] Autonomous computing – See: https://bit.ly/2GbJZ7H.

exposed interfaces, *testing hooks*[50] should be inserted in the code to enable testing these hard-to-reach code paths. When these *hooks* are inserted, it is critical that they be disabled in production environments to avoid them being used as an attack vector.

During unit testing, resource usage should be monitored to ensure that resources are both allocated and de-allocated when appropriate. In other words, there are no resource leaks and no resource hogging. Resources that require monitoring include, but are not limited to: memory, disk space, and network connections.

In addition to not using up all available resources, the unit should be tested to ensure it properly handles an out-of-resource condition. For example, what happens if it runs out of disk space and can no longer write to its log file?

If each asset has well designed test harnesses enabling semi-complete unit testing, small enclaves of assets can be tested together by integrating those assets together in a test environment, and only using the test harnesses that impersonate the assets not present in the enclave. This type of testing can be viewed as a type of *integration testing* (see below) or as another form of unit testing, where the definition of the unit is a small integration of assets.

Integration testing

Even though PBEA places significant importance on unit testing of assets, we do not mean to imply that unit testing is more important than integration testing. Each type of testing has its place and in fact, the unanticipated idiosyncratic behavior of other assets is a key cause of problems in production environments. Integration testing should aim to root out these problems before software is released.

While a significant portion of the code can be tested using these methods, for a solution to be reliable, performance testing, security testing, and functional testing must be performed in an environment that mimics production. This environment must include the system being tested as well as all other assets that may reasonably affect security, performance, reliability, or functionality.

Destructive testing

Part of creating a highly available architecture is to perform what is called *destructive-testing*. A well-known technology company (Netflix) has a tool called the *chaos-monkey*[51] to assist testing for unexpected failures. Chaos-monkey randomly causes disruptions to the applications and

---

[50] A *testing hook* is defined as an internal, private interface that is intended only to be used only by the development or test group and only during the test phase. It should be disabled at all other times.

[51] Chaos Monkey – See: https://bit.ly/1qkqDxZ.

underlying infrastructure. All assets are supposed to handle single-points-of-failure, so they should continue to meet their SLA obligations even given these random failures. This controlled chaos increases the hardness, or robustness, of that company's technology solutions in ways that, without chaos-monkey, would only be tested in a real emergency.

Another form of destructive testing is disaster-recovery rehearsal / testing. In this test, entire clusters and entire data centers are rebooted to ensure that the product adheres to its SLA under these conditions.

This is when the *recovery time* (RTO) and *recovery point* (RPO) objectives of the SLA are tested. In other words, when a cluster or data center fails, how long does it take to come back up and how much data was lost in the process?

Security testing

Security testing tools can be split into the following broad categories:

1. **Host malware scanning**. Tools that run on the host and look for files that match known malware.

2. **Vulnerability scanning**. Tools that look for network listener signatures that match known vulnerable protocols.

3. **Automated penetration testing**. Automated tools that exercise a live web application to find evidence of security defects that can be exploited.

4. **Source code scanning**. Automated tools that analyze the source code of an application to find evidence of security defects that can be exploited.

5. **White hat penetration testing**. A practiced human being takes a step back and employs all possible means to penetrate a system and escalate access. This can include social engineering of people, compromise of other systems to create new vectors, use of unpublished vulnerabilities or attacks, compromise of physical security controls – anything and everything.

All these security testing approaches offer different values for different situations and come at different costs.

At a minimum, we have found that performing a collection of automated penetration tests (several tools applied by a knowledgeable tester) periodically has a very high return on investment for security.

Educating software engineers in secure-software-practice also has a high return on investment. While many newly hired software engineers may be uneducated in secure-software-practice, once taught how to remediate a security defect, they generally do not repeat the same mistake. This result holds for reasonably stable teams, reasonably skilled coders, and assets that are under governance. The PBEA golden rules ask specific questions that are very likely to highlight whether secure coding practices are in use.

There is no way to quantify a "right answer" for the proper amount of security testing. Each organization must choose the frequency, type, and degree of testing based on their own unique circumstances. These security testing protocols should be mindfully built then monitored over time for effectiveness and held to a standard of producing actual and actionable reductions in risk.

Architecting secure and compliant solutions

Security architecture is generally concerned with managing and mitigating risk, while keeping the organization as free as possible to deliver groundbreaking new products to happy users. Compliance architecture, on the other hand, is concerned with adhering to legal and regulatory requirements as well as contractual obligations. Security issues can be exponentially cheaper to address when considered early in the architecture and design process.

PBEA prefers security exercises over compliance exercises. Security testing is an area that highlights the slight overlap but significant differences between compliance driven exercises and security driven exercises.

There are two inappropriate extremes that security exercises often degrade into if companies are not careful to avoid them.

In the first extreme, optimism rules, and common-sense security measures are not considered or implemented until after things have already been built and after things have already gone wrong. This makes even simple security improvements difficult and expensive. Retrofitting a security control is generally much more expensive than including it in the initial design.

The opposite extreme can be even worse. When organizations blindly apply security controls and policies without considering overall risk and alternative mitigations, it virtually guarantees an experience that will make the majority of their (few remaining) users frustrated and angry. A frustrated or angry user will either stop using the product or try to circumvent the controls (which generally represents a much larger threat than the one the controls were supposed to be addressing in the first place).

Security ≠ Compliance

It is important to distinguish between the security aspects of an effort and the compliance aspects. They are distinct.

A security exercise is designed to make a product more resistant to specifically defined anti-use cases (i.e. threats). A compliance exercise is often framed as a security discussion, but realistically focuses on the auditability and repeatability of a specific and highly prescriptive set of controls. All too often, these prescriptive implementations are overly general and map poorly to realizable risk reductions. The result is that a lot of time and money may be spent solving problems that no one can clearly articulate, may no longer exist, or in the worst-case scenario are both costly and ineffective.

PBEA defines security architecture in a way that balances cost and impact with the threat to the organization. Compliance architecture, on the other hand, is based on the regulatory environment which is often a lawyers' interpretation of the aggregate threat to the industry. It may bear little resemblance to the actual threat experienced today. Technology moves quickly. The law rarely keeps up and can lag the real threat by months or even years.

Consider the hypothetical example of two companies (call them Company A and Company B), each of whom had 10 systems that handled unmasked credit card numbers. When the PCI (Payment Card Industry) requirements were updated following the Target credit card breach, each organization estimated that the compliance remediation would cost $1M per system for a total of $10M. Company A quickly prioritized the compliance issue, siphoning the $10M in funds from other projects, since compliance was treated as a top priority.

Company B, on the other hand, looked at the problem from a security perspective first, realizing that it was not a good idea for 10 individual systems to have complete access to such sensitive data. Instead of blindly making each system compliant with the new regulations, Company B chose one system as the master file of the unmasked credit card numbers and created a new interface, so that the other systems could use opaque tokens rather than raw credit card numbers. Company B was able to complete the project in half the time at one fifth the cost, ending up with a better architecture and lower overall risk. Company B was even happier with their decision, when the PCI rules changed again. Company B's architecture was able to quickly adapt to the unforeseen change. Company A, however had another compliance issue on their hands.

Some compliance exercises are inevitable and necessary. Even in the credit card system example above, there was still one system that did have to become completely PCI compliant, meaning it had to implement the security controls and generate the necessary auditable artifacts required by the PCI rules without consideration of the actual security benefits.

Compliance exercises do have a place. History has shown that without automated processes that include frequent audit and review (compliance type activities), most organizations will struggle to maintain reliable controls. Compliance should be used as a tool, and not allowed to grow blindly until it consumes a disproportionate level of available resources.

Placement of the security function

In many organizations, security architecture is executed from a *security organization*. While this "outside in" approach creates easily understood processes and results in organizations creating many easy-to-audit artifacts, the most reliable aspect of it is the degree to which it is consistently expensive. This approach to security frequently degrades into a compliance exercise, where we are dictating controls rather than reliably reducing risk.

PBEA, recommends that security architecture be the responsibility of every architect, and writing secure code be the responsibility of every developer. The alternative approach of having a small number of security experts in an operational security group is neither scalable, repeatable, nor reliable.

Security controls should be usable by those needing them, and sustainable for the long term within available funding and business models. For this reason, PBEA distills security controls (and compliance controls) into golden rules that are measured for every asset under governance. In the PBEA model, the central security group is responsible for operational security and is mostly involved in run-time governance, finding issues, and performing root cause analysis. The root causes of those issues' worth solving are then translated into golden rules and measures.

Security incidents and strategy implications

For legal reasons, detailed and specific security incidents are not generally published. However, incidents within the industry are critical to understand and should inform an organization's security strategy. Following are a few examples of typical threats and attack vectors:

- **Cryptolocker**. Rather than trying to exfiltrate stolen data, this malware simply encrypts the data it finds locally on whatever system it compromised. It then "ransoms" the keys necessary to decrypt the data. When this happens, if you don't have off-device backups, you either lose the data or you pay the ransom (and possibly lose the data anyway). If the infected system has *write-access* to product repositories, the infection can manifest as a product outage. Even if the data has no value to the attacker, they can monetize it because the data has value to those being attacked. The strategic implications include:

- o The external perimeter complicates attacks, but it does not prevent them.
- o The spread of a successful attack can be limited by changing review controls, putting limits on access, segmenting production systems and networks, and separating production systems from desktop systems.
- o It's hard to find data or systems that aren't valuable enough to be attacked. Some just take more work and creativity for an attacker.
- o Off-line and off-site backups are both important and valuable.
- o Minor vulnerabilities can become major problems.
- o Automation is important, so automation designs should include "anti-use" cases.

- **Poorly-managed servers**. Suppose a poorly-managed sever has failed to get anti-malware updates for some time, but nobody recognized it. Suppose it was also used not just as a production server, but also to browse the internet. The wrong link was clicked, or the wrong plugin was installed, and what should have been a minor issue of nuisance malware (easily stopped by anti-virus software) has become a compromised production server. Perhaps you have an old production server that is internet-facing, and a team of developers leave it running even after it no longer hosts applications. Maybe the system has a single administrative password that is shared amongst the team members. People join the team and get the shared admin password. People leave the team and don't immediately forget the password. It's not a real production server, so patches may or may not get applied. Five years later, something... odd... is happening with the server. Is it an attacker? Is it a business-critical process? Who set it up? Who can say if should be patched or shut down? You have no idea who did what and why. The strategic implications include:

  - o Unmanaged servers don't have all the controls necessary to manage risk, so they can account for very high risk – especially if nobody is responsible for them.
  - o Unmanaged servers are an "unknown unknown." They don't show up on your reports, because reports are often generated from agents installed on managed servers.

- **Social engineering amplified attacks**. One might think an interface that tells a customer how much they owe on their bill this month doesn't need a lot of protection. It's not like attackers are rushing to pay other people's bills. But what if the attacker used that interface to get the invoice for a real customer of yours, then modified it slightly to divert the payment of the invoice, sending it on to the real customer by pretending to come from your company? In that case, when the customer does pay the bill, they might actually pay the attacker instead of you. The strategic implications include:

- o Social engineering will likely be a key part of many attacks and will likely make them worse than they would have been otherwise.

- o An attack may transpire directly between the attacker and your customer. You may not even see it – even though it was your lack of security control that was the initial attack vector.

Architecting responsive solutions

Responsive solutions meet Service Level Agreements (SLAs). They facilitate identification and resolution of problems quickly and long before end users complain.

SLAs define measurable quantities that a client may expect from a service. There are slight differences between SLAs written for end users of products vs. clients of service interfaces, but in general, all SLAs are fundamentally similar

A system asset SLA defines what a client may expect for: response time, latency, availability, and dependability, during normal operations as well as how long it will take to recover in the event of a failure.

Architecting responsive solutions ensure that every asset defines an SLA for its consumers, measures its adherence to its defined SLA, and sends an *operational alarm*[52] when an SLA metric is not met. In exceptionally large systems, it is often prudent for each asset to measure its own SLA as well as the SLAs of all assets upon which it depends.

Responsive solutions not only meet SLA obligations when everything is running smoothly. They also meet SLA obligations in failure scenarios. Responsive solutions have no single points of failure. In other words, no single device failure (not even a database failure) should cause the service to fail to meet its SLA.

---

[52] Alarm Handling, and error handling, in general is a huge topic, that ought to have a uniform architecture and design in an enterprise but is often (unfortunately) left up to individual developers to do what they think is best.

In addition, failure of an entire site may cause a momentary blip but should not cause service outage (i.e. SLA failure). For example, on Tuesday, February 28, 2017, failure of Amazon's S3 service brought many websites and online applications to their knees. Netflix, on the other hand, maintained service to its consumers. The Netflix architecture spanned twelve Amazon Web Services *regions*[53] globally, each with multiple *availability zones*.[54] Each zone has at least one data center along with associated power, networking, and connectivity. Because these zones are connected to each other, Netflix was able to design their cloud infrastructure, so their applications switch between zones automatically when failures occur, avoiding service disruptions.

> Every asset should define an SLA, measure its own adherence to its defined SLA, and for each asset that is called, measure that asset's adherence to its defined SLA. An operational alarm should be raised whenever there is an SLA violation. The severity of the violation should map to the severity of the alarm.

Measuring performance

Performance treated properly, should be defined as a business requirement, since it has everything to do with end-user expectations and in some cases, beating the competition. Unfortunately, it is generally treated as a non-functional requirement, which puts the onus of achieving high performance on the technology team. Very often higher response-time performance can be achieved by 'throwing hardware at the problem,' but latency is almost always determined by the underlying architecture of the platform and the individual system assets comprising the platform. And since cost is always a factor, the performance testing regimen should be adapted to this reality.

Measuring performance means measuring both response-time and latency. Both factors should be measured prior to a software release as well as during live operation. In each case the performance SLA is used as the gauge of success or failure. Throughput, on the other hand, is seldom an independent SLA metric, but is instead part of the response-time and latency metrics. In other words, response time and latency are measured under varying system load scenarios. Increasing throughput is one of the ways that load is placed on a system.

---

[53] Region – A region is a geographical area of one or more availability zones. In general regions are geographically diverse enough that no two regions are likely to be affected by the same disaster. In addition, all the data centers in a single region should be close enough, that a system in one data center can synchronously write to a database in another data center in the same region.

[54] Availability Zone - A zone is a group of resources distributed amongst one or more physical sites (or data centers). The fact that there may be multiple sites in a zone is opaque to the end user, so it is best to consider a zone to be a single site (even if it isn't). All the zones in a region are connected by high speed, low latency networks.

Performance testing,[55] at a minimum, certifies that the system, under normal load, meets its performance SLAs. For example, let's say the SLA requires that 95% of all data requests are returned in one second. A performance testing environment will then add load to the servers (often by adding additional data requestors, increasing the number of update events, and/or simulating typical operational events that might affect performance), and measure how long it takes for an individual request to be answered (response-time) as well as how long it takes for a data update to be applied (latency). If the system is handling what is considered normal load, and meets both performance SLAs, it is said to have 'passed.'

But performance testing done properly does not stop here. Instead, the 'load' should be continuously increased until the test fails. When performance is charted versus load, the graph often looks like a hockey stick. In other words, there is often very little impact in response-time or latency under low load, but at some point, performance decrease becomes super linear to load increase. That point should be noted and used during live operations to indicate when additional capacity might be demanded.

Measuring reliability and availability

Reliability and availability are often conflated, but availability simply means that the system is "up" and capable of handling end-user requests, while reliability includes factors like low error rates and ensuring data is not stale. When measuring availability, the performance SLA is often used as the gauge. In other words, if a request can be responded-to with an acceptable performance, the system is said to be "up."

Mature technology organizations maintain different SLAs for normal operations and for one or more failure scenarios. Their systems are architected specifically to meet these SLAs (which are driven by business requirements). For example, an SLA may allow for reduced functionality and/or performance in case of a disaster.

> Define SLAs for normal operations and under the most common failure scenarios. Make measurement objective by defining how to interpret as many common scenarios as feasible.

Failure scenarios

There are many types of failures. We will discuss the most common ones here:

- **Single Resource Failure**. A single resource failure indicates that one thing failed, usually a server or a disk or a network device. In general, platforms and assets should

---

[55] The environment used to measure performance is expected to be a fair duplicate of the production environment. While it may not be an exact replica, it is expected to replicate enough of the production environment that anything that may reasonably affect performance as measured is represented.

be architected with no single points of failure, meaning that there should never be an SLA violation or service outage in the event of a single resource failure. Components such as disk drives have moveable parts that eventually wear down and eventually fail. Component failure is nearly guaranteed to happen in any modern system, given the sheer magnitude of components making up any modern architecture.

- **Asset Instance Failure.** If there are multiple, simultaneous, single resource failures then an asset instance may fail. By asset instance, we mean the complete set of components making up an asset in a single site (i.e. data center or availability zone). Highly available architectures, having no single points of failure, protect against this event by spreading the operational implementation of the asset across more than one site. In other words, each site has a complete asset instance, so that the loss of one complete asset instance will not cause an SLA violation.

- **Site Failure.** A site failure is defined as all the asset instances located in a single site (i.e. data center or availability zone) failing at the same time. As with a single asset instance failure, a physical implementation that spans sites should be at least partially resilient to a site failure. The level of resilience depends on how much money was spent on capacity. For example, let's say that a system is architected so that its servers are spread across three sites with 1/3 of the capacity in each site. If one of the sites becomes unavailable, then only 2/3 of the capacity remains to service end users. If that capacity is enough to meet performance SLAs, then there will be no loss of service. But if, under high load, performance SLAs are not met, then the service will enter either a *brownout* situation (responses are slower than normal) or a *blackout* situation (requests get no response). A site failure is often considered a disaster scenario.

- **Region Failure.** Data centers and availability zones are regionalized. A region is loosely defined as a geographic area where systems in one data center within the region can synchronously write to databases and file systems located in another data center in the region. This is a loose definition, but it usually works. If all the data centers and availability zones in a region become unavailable at the same time, it is said to be a region failure.

- **Disaster Recovery.** The terms: 'disaster,' and disaster recovery evolved in the days before the cloud when companies generally had one or two data centers in a region. So, if one data center became completely unavailable, due to a power grid failure, that is a 'disaster.' Disaster Recovery (D/R) is the process of recovering service after a disaster. The most common architecture resilient to a disaster, is one that duplicates each asset instance in more than one site and tests to ensure that if a site becomes unavailable, services continues.

- **Business Continuity.** Business continuity means the continuation of business operations in case of a disaster. This includes everything that disaster recovery includes as well as ensuring that all functions of the business continue to function (such as sales, marketing, finance, software development, etc., etc.).

- **Brownouts.** A brownout is a term loosely defined as a service being partially operational. A product is composed of multiple individual services, not all of which are the same utility to each end user. For example, if I am using a product that allows me to trade stocks, the product will also include a news service and a way for me to set my personal preferences. If there is a failure scenario which allows me to continue trading, but does not allow me to change my preferences, the product still functions, but is not 100% operational. This is an example of a brownout. If what I consider to be a core function of the product, like either trading or news in the above example continues to function, but outside the performance SLA (i.e. it is slow), then again, the product is still functioning, but not 100%, so is in a brownout situation. Another type of brownout is when the product is working, but not fully meeting its performance SLA. Brownouts affect the reliability SLA, but do not affect the availability SLA.

- **Blackouts.** A blackout means that one or more core services of the product are unavailable. As such, the product is effectively not functional, even if one or more ancillary services are still working. The length of time that the blackout is in effect is used to measure service availability. But since a product is an amalgamation of individual services, determining whether the product is available or not requires that each service of the product be individually classified as critical to product operation or not. Because these classifications may differ depending on end-user profile, classifying an outage as a blackout and measuring availability and reliability may be subjective. Mature companies define all these factors in advance, so the metric is objective.

Operational practice

Operational practices help to keep systems running and achieving their SLA guarantees. While this is not a book about how to run a data center or a DevOps organization, the whole point of a great systems architecture is to deliver a great service. As such, following are a few rules of thumb:

- Do not perform manual operations on production systems for repeatable actions. If feasible, lock out all human access to production systems (allowing only automated processes). Therefore, the architecture of the system must account for automating operational processes to the greatest extent possible.

- Ensure all production changes are repeatable and auditable.

- Test all production changes in a staging environment (that mimics production) before applying them.

- Make changes to a single server, or some minimal set of servers, and verify the change works before applying the change to the rest of the servers in the scaling group. This implies that the system architecture and design tolerate a single server group running different versions of software.

- When making a rolling upgrade to a production scaling group, add servers to the group with the new change first so that if two servers fail during the upgrade process, SLAs continue to be met. Even if you are just upgrading the software on an existing set of servers, PBEA recommends this is done by first installing the new software on a new server and adding it to the group. Then each server in the group is temporarily taken down, upgraded, and added back into the group.

- Regularly check that all servers in a scaling group have identical version of the software and identical configurations (especially after an upgrade).

Monitoring practice

Systems must be monitored to ensure they are maintaining SLA guarantees. Anomalous behavior should fire an appropriate alarm, so that on-call staff can get ahead of any impending failure. To achieve this, well architected systems are built with failure in mind and have a clear understanding of the difference between anomalous behavior and normal behavior. They also do not flood operational staff with so many alarms that the staff cannot tell the difference between something requiring action versus something to watch versus something to ignore. Following are a few "rules of thumb":

- Monitor servers and compute instances to ensure they are operating properly. In a cloud environment, this often requires additional capability than what the cloud provider can do at the hypervisor level. At a minimum, CPU load, network load, free memory and free storage should be monitored. Memory should be monitored over time so that potential memory leaks can be spotted early. Free storage should be monitored to ensure that files (especially log files) do not overflow.

- Monitor configuration changes to determine whether and when changes to the infrastructure impact assets.

- Provide application performance monitoring to look inside the asset in the event of a failure or an impending failure.

- Monitor your dependencies' adherence to their SLA as well as what is normal behavior. Alarm when it is out of bounds.

- Monitor adherence to your own SLA as well as what is normal behavior. Alarm when it is out of bounds.

- Inject synthetic transactions into the request flow to measure how the capability is performing from the end user's perspective.

- Monitor the behavior of your end users. Algorithms that throttle requests and deny requests for an inappropriate amount of data will not only protect you from accidental misuse, but from bugs in your customer's application and malicious attacks as well.

- When monitoring load, monitor average load (on each compute instance) as well as one-minute peaks and sustained peaks (i.e. peaks greater than 10 minutes).

Graceful degradation of service

Good architectures account for the fact that eventually the load placed on a service will overtake the amount of available capacity and the service will fail. This understanding applies both to the system asset providing a service and to an asset that depends on the service provided. A service should not simply "do the best it can until it crashes." A proper architecture gracefully degrades service as load increases beyond the breaking point and recovers quickly when load goes back down (which it eventually always does). The load placed on any system asset tends to be "peaky." Systems should never crash.

Graceful degradation implies that the service (provided by a system asset) reduces the work it accomplishes in proportion to its overload condition. Graceful degradation applies both to end-user-facing services as well as to internal services.

One best practice for graceful degradation of end-user-facing services is to throttle requests from each user, using an exponential back-off algorithm. For example, an end-user-facing asset could allocate *request tokens* to each end user. The end user starts with say, 300 tokens (300 is just an example. The actual number of tokens granted is completely dependent on the nature of the application and the behavior of the average user). Every request uses one token decreasing the total number of requests the user may make by one. Tokens are replenished at some constant rate, say, one token per minute, back up to the maximum of 300.

> Throttle requests from each end user and use an exponential back-off algorithm in the event of an overload.

For example, a single end user starts the day at 9:00 AM by making 150 requests. Ten minutes later they make 150 more. Ten minutes later they make 150 more. What happens?

Time	Tokens available	Requests made	Tokens remaining
9:00	300	150	150
9:10	160	150	10
9:20	20	150	0

When the token count reaches zero, each request made will return an error code indicating that the request has been throttled. The application may queue the end user's request and retry when tokens are available or return a failure to the end user indicating that she should try again later.

If an asset providing a service is overloaded and begins to degrade its service, by throttling back requests, what should the calling asset do? The calling asset would not want to have the same error reoccur constantly. It would also want to handle the error quickly and gracefully without waiting for a timeout. In this case, one of the best practices is to use the circuit-breaker design pattern.[56] A circuit breaker goes into effect when the calling asset detects a failure (e.g. a performance SLA violation). The circuit breaker stops the calling asset from performing an action that is doomed to fail over and over. The circuit breaker retains the state of the called service over a series of requests (measured against the service's response-time SLA). The state machine within the circuit breaker operates concurrently with the requests passing through it, recording the state of the external service. Before the external service is called, the state of the service is verified. If the service is in a failure state and has not recovered, the request is queued. Requests are then made using an exponential back-off algorithm.

> In the event of failure, or overload condition, use the circuit-breaker design pattern to avoid making API calls that are almost guaranteed to fail and firing unnecessary operational alarms.

---

56 Circuit-breaker design pattern – See: https://bit.ly/1NU1sgW.

CHAPTER 9

Change Management

From personnel to company policies and everything in between, change is a fact of life. We are usually far better off embracing it and making the most of it rather than resisting. The PBEA method recommends specific approaches for managing change to PBEA objectives, artifacts, and processes.

Golden rule evolution

The golden rules can be updated based on the needs of the organization. They are not set in stone and can be changed to meet business directional changes or industry standard changes. A process should exist for introducing, approving, and deploying new changes to golden rules and the corresponding golden rule measures. In the organizational role model elaborated in Chapter 2, enterprise architects are the keepers of the golden rules and the associated measures. A new golden rule should only be defined either to avoid a negative-outcome or to support a positive-outcome, whose impact and likelihood make it worth the extra effort of supporting the new rule. Avoiding a bad negative outcome is the primary use case for creating a golden rule.

We recommend starting off with a small set of **golden rules** and then adding new rules as negative outcomes are identified that are worth preventing. In fact, the first step in implementing the PBEA method, is to go through the body-of-evidence stories enumerated in this book and decide which among them apply to your organization and systems. If the story applies, then verify that the impact/likelihood is appropriate as well. Incorporate all rules that have at least medium severity.

Golden rules evolve for several reasons:

- Through feedback from architecture reviews, and code reviews we learn that rules need clarifying, elaborating, or eliminating.

- Technology and the business changes and the rules must change with them.
- A negative outcome is experienced that was not caught by the existing set of rules, and that outcome is sufficiently severe that a new rule is required to avoid it in the future.

The following step-wise process is recommended, both for determining the initial set of golden rules as well as adding, clarifying, or deleting a rule.

1. Start with either a negative outcome that should be avoided in the future, or a positive outcome[57] that should be continued.

2. Assess the impact of the outcome using the *Assessing Impact* table below.

3. Perform root cause analysis on the outcome to determine why it occurred. Be very careful to identify the actual root cause and not the trigger. For example, human error is rarely the root cause of a negative outcome, but it is often the trigger.

4. Write a rule, that if followed, would prevent the negative outcome from occurring.

5. Determine whether the rule can be applied to the architecture, design, or implementation of a single asset. If the rule only applies to a group of assets, or an environment or an operational process and not a single asset, then you should consider making it the responsibility of a technology owner (see Part 5: Technology Ownership), rather than a golden rule.

6. Once the rule is written, determine how likely the negative outcome is to happen if the rule is broken. Likelihood may be high, medium, or low.

7. Determine the severity of the rule based on the *Translating impact/likelihood to severity* table below.

8. If following the rule avoids a severe negative outcome, then continue. If the negative outcome is not considered severe enough based on impact/likelihood, then stop.

9. Determine how you will measure whether an asset is following the rule or not. Write one or more measures for the rule for which the response to *"Does it comply?"* is a "Yes" or "No" answer.[58] Do not write rule measures which require an essay response. Word all rule measures so that answering "Yes" implies there is no debt.

---

[57] Usually, the golden rules exist to avoid negative outcomes rather than promote positive ones. But there is no reason that the process could not be used to promote positive outcomes. The text above is written from the "avoiding a negative outcome" point of view, so for a rule that promotes a positive outcome, some translation is required by the reader.

[58] Please note that some measures are conditional. For example, a measure may be written: "If highly-regulated (SPII) data is used, then it is masked." The assumption is that if the asset doesn't have any highly-regulated SPII data, then the response will be "yes" (i.e. It complies and there is no debt).

10. Read through each of the measures and determine how hard it will be for a person sufficiently knowledgeable to answer whether the asset complies with the measure or not. If answering the question requires archaeology or talking to 100 different people, you might want to reconsider whether the measure is appropriate or not.

11. Once the measures are written, assuming there is at least one measure that is considered "measurable,"[59] then you have written a new golden rule. Congratulations! Organize the rule under the appropriate architecture principle.

Assessing Impact	
Outcome	Impact
Affects company reputation or leads to an organization officer being found guilty of breaking the law	Catastrophic
Has a measurable effect on revenue	High
Has a large[60] measurable effect on cost	High
Has a moderate effect on cost	Medium
Otherwise	Low

Translating Impact/Likelihood to Severity			
Impact	Likelihood		
	High	Medium	Low
Catastrophic	Severity:1	Severity:1	Severity:1
High	Severity:1	Severity:2	Severity:2
Medium	Severity:2	Severity:3	
Low	Severity:3		

A rule is not immediately published once it is written. We assume there is some cadence to publishing a new asset checklist and that all the new or modified rules since the last checklist update are published together (along with guidance for the technology architect). When new rules are published, the story of the negative outcome event should also be published as the body-of-evidence for the rule.

---

[59] Ask the individuals who are tasked with answering the question how easy the outcome will be to objectively measure. I ran an exercise about five years into my last implementation of PBEA where we asked the technology architects to rate the quantifiability of each measure on a scale of 1 to 10. As a result of the exercise, we removed two dozen measures and clarified two dozen more.

[60] While the difference between a large effect and a moderate effect is not defined explicitly by PBEA, we recommend that any organization implementing PBEA sets actual value ranges for these, rather than leaving it to the interpretation of each individual.

Root cause analysis (Why? Why? Why?)

Given a problem, *root cause analysis*[61] is an iterative approach to problem-solving, by asking "Why?" again, and again, until you find the underlying reason that the problem occurred. Human error is rarely the root cause. For example:

Problem: There was a product outage.

Why was there an outage?	Human Error. An operator typed in the wrong command.
Why did the operator need to act?	Because a server ran out of memory and the operator was supposed to type in a command to reboot it but typed the command incorrectly.
Why was that operator responsibility?	Because we have not yet implemented auto-scaling and auto-correction, which would have automatically added a new server to the scaling group and removed the failed server.

Solution: Implement autoscaling and autocorrection. Oh, and by the way also fix the memory leak in the server, since that was one of the triggers. The operator typing in the wrong command was the second trigger. Operators likely need additional training and predefined scripts to run. Fix that too.

Note: It is common for problems that are not caught during testing, only to be found in production systems to have more than one trigger.

Technology standard evolution

Technology standards are temporary. The technology standards (software asset governance) process provides the means for new problems to be defined as well as new solutions. New solutions may apply either to a new problem or to an existing one. As new solutions are identified, old solutions are deprecated.

---

[61] The 5 whys – See: https://bit.ly/1hJIyt0.

Software Asset Management (SAM)[62] and security teams should be the watching for any 3rd party technology in use which exhibits a vulnerability, or which is no longer supported by its vendor. Projects should be initiated by these groups to replace the non-compliant technology early enough that it can all be replaced before the vulnerability ends in a breach. The length of time this takes will differ organization by organization (but don't be surprised if three years is a typical timeframe).

The following step-wise process is recommended:

1. Begin with a statement of the problem being solved not the technology you want to use to solve it. In other words, don't start with "I want to use Amazon Redshift." Start with "I need a fast, scalable cloud-based data warehouse or data lake that supports machine learning, parallel query execution, and columnar storage."

2. Scan through the existing Technology Standards Registry to see if that problem has already been solved and what the standard solution is. If the problem has already been solved using a different technology solution than the one you wanted, then consider using that solution rather than a new solution.

3. If the problem has never been solved before then add the new problem and solution to the registry. Classify the Technology solution according to the table below.

4. If the problem has been solved before, then decide whether the new solution you desire is better than the one already in use and why. If it is sufficiently better that you would recommend all future solvers of this problem to use the new solution, then the old solution should be deprecated (see table below). If on the other hand, this is just an alternative solution that is sufficiently inexpensive that there is no harm in having two competing standard solutions, then add the new solution to the registry as an alternate standard for the existing problem.

---

[62] A good Software Asset Management (SAM) process is a very important part of managing security exposure and overall financial risk for an enterprise. Implementing a good process, while very important, is outside the scope of this book. The following link: https://gtnr.it/2F0maMD is a Gartner review of SAM tools on the market as of 2018, but please be aware that implementing a tool is only a small part of doing Software Asset Management correctly.

Technology Solution Classification Methodology	
Classification	Description
Emerging	This is a technology and major version which is not yet the standard, but which should be watched because within the next 6–18 months it might become the standard. Use of emerging technology should be reviewed by the DevOps team targeted to support it.
Standard	This technology and major version should be used for solving the defined problem today and for the next 12 months at a minimum.
Deprecated	This technology's major version was once a standard but has been replaced. If an asset has already implemented it, the asset may continue to use it, but a new asset should defer to using the new standard.
Prohibited	This technology and major version may not be used under any circumstances. If it is in use, architecture debt should be assigned to any asset using the prohibited technology. In addition, there should be an active project to replace the technology across the entire enterprise.

CHAPTER 10

Getting Started with PBEA

Assuming you like the PBEA approach to enterprise architecture, you will probably start thinking about how to implement this in your organization, inevitably leading to the question "Where do I begin?" Follow these twelve steps.

Step 1

The first step in implementing PBEA is to clarify architecture roles. PBEA defines three distinct architecture roles, but as described in chapter four, roles do not translate one-to-one into job descriptions. To review, the three architecture roles are:

- **Technical architects.** *Technical architects* are aligned to individual assets. They are primarily responsible for architecture and high-level design. Technical architects are also responsible for producing architecture diagrams, completing checklists, and interacting with enterprise architects in the governance process.

- **Solution architects.** *Solution architects* are aligned to solutions and program increments. They are primarily responsible for *placement-of-function* and working across the assets that integrate to deliver the solution.

- **Enterprise architects.** *Enterprise architects* are aligned to the organization. They are primarily responsible for technology strategy and governance.

Step 2

Create an inventory of system and data assets. Eventually this inventory needs to be complete. But it doesn't need to be complete to get started. It is more important to have correct information for each asset in the inventory, than to have a mostly complete inventory with data that nobody trusts. At a minimum, each asset in the inventory needs to include the asset's name, description, lifecycle stage, and ownership.

By lifecycle stage, we mean whether the asset is to be *tolerated, invested-in, migrated,* or *retired* as defined in Chapter 2.

By ownership, we mean: technology owner, asset owner and technology architect. All three are required. These are roles. They can all be filled by the same individual if that makes sense. If not covered by assigning the asset owner, then we also need to define the operations owner and security point-of-contact.

Create an inventory of solutions and a list of active programs of effort along with the solution owner and solution architect. Look at the people assigned as architects across the technology and data landscape. Verify that there are no gaps and that individuals are not overloaded.

Step 3

The next step in implementing PBEA is to decide which rules matter. Read the rest of the book. Then go through each golden rule in Part III and in Part IV, focusing on the body-of-evidence stories. For each story, decide whether the story applies to you. Double-check that you agree with the associated impact and likelihood as it applies to your organization. If it does, great! If not, then modify accordingly. Double-check the severity of the rule. If it matters to your organization, then you have decided on your first rule. Do this for the rest of the rules.

Step 4

Once you have a baseline set of rules, the next step is to gather any other stories that your organization has experienced which will motivate people (both technologists and especially non-technologists). Follow the process defined in Chapter 9, section: golden rule evolution. Add body-of-evidence stories to the rules you already have decided on, where following the rule avoids the negative outcome. If the negative outcome cannot be avoided by an existing rule, write a new rule. Collect all the rules that matter, organized by principle and business objectives into a single document. Include all the body-of-evidence stories.

Step 5

Once you have an initial draft of the golden rules with associated body-of-evidence, you need to get buy-in, particularly from the individuals that will need to do the work. If your organization already has an *architecture council*, that is likely the correct body to start with. If not, then you will have to draw from people around the organization that you consider to be thought leaders. You want the people who will have to fill out the checklists to agree the rules are worth governing. You will want the people who decide what efforts are worth spending time on to agree as well. You want the people best placed to convince others to also agree. The best way to get buy-in is generally to do two things: (1) Make sure you have a few body-of-evidence stories that each stakeholder will identify with and agree would never want to happen (again). (2) Make sure that doing the right thing is also an easy thing to do. In other words, don't start with too many rules and make sure the ones you do start with can be answered by a sufficiently knowledgeable person without performing archaeology.[63]

Choose the appropriate governance level. You may want to start with just the level-one rules, but if you can get buy-in for level-four governance, especially for a brand-new asset, then do that. (More on the *governance levels* in Chapter 5).

Step 6

Now that you have agreement from thought leaders in the technology organization, find a sponsor outside the technology organization. Often, the easiest place to start is with *information security*. Many CISO's feel that they have little control over the software delivery organization, but their careers depend on good software with good security architecture. On the other hand, most software engineers find security policies both voluminous and inscrutable. Most executives immediately recognize the business value of good security and compliance, but they depend on the technology function to *do the right thing*.

That is why principle #1 and principle #2 are about security and compliance. These are not the sexiest areas of the technology landscape and are likely not the blogs software engineers are reading in their spare time, which is why they often need the most help.

---

[63] I have used the term "performing archaeology" regarding answering certain questions. My use of the term has to do with the fact that many companies are running systems that are so old, that nobody left in the organization was involved in either their design or initial implementation. As such, the reasoning behind certain decisions has been lost "to the sands of time" and figuring out why something was done the way it was done may require digging through reams of old documentation, if the answer exists at all.

Step 7

You are ready to do your first review. Which asset should you review first? Follow the money. Pick something that is actively being invested in or is just about to get an infusion of investment.[64] It helps if the technical architect that owns the architecture of the asset is already bought in to the process. It also helps if the asset being reviewed is integrated into one or more solutions where the solutions architect is bought-in as well.

Start by reviewing diagrams of the asset. If you follow PBEA diagramming guidelines, then start with the perspective view and continue through the system views. Review a few of the key sequence diagrams.

Fill out a checklist for the asset, being very careful to capture the corrective actions and associated technical debt. Roll up the scores for golden rule measures all the way to business objectives. You do not need a single score for the asset. Each asset should have a score for each business objective independently as well as the total debt associated with each objective.

Review both the overall score, the list of corrective actions sorted by severity, and the amount of debt for each corrective action. Ask yourselves the question: "Does this tell the right story about the asset and is it believable? Do the corrective actions represent the ordered list of architectural fixes that I would recommend?" If they do, great! If not, then go back through the checklist and figure out why not.

It's critically important for any new program of effort to have a quick win. If you can use the checklist to explain the most important actions to take and use the body-of-evidence stories to explain why each corrective action matters to the business, then you likely have a winning argument. Once you get agreement to invest in closing out technical debt, then you have a "quick win."[65]

Take your "quick wins" on the road. Tell the story of how the new process will help the organization and show off your successes. Success breeds success. Buy-in breeds more buy-in. There will always be a few individuals who will never buy-in. Don't waste your time trying to convince them. You don't need 100% buy-in to be successful. This is not meant to imply formal

---

[64] You might consider starting with something that has high risk rather than high investment. But getting a program like this one going requires an initial success. That means the people involved in the project must be amenable to finding and fixing any problems identified. This is generally easier to do when something has ongoing investment vs. something that does not.

[65] A "quick win" is something that: (a) every agrees we must do (b) everybody agrees is a priority (c) can be finished quickly enough to be taken on the road show.

presentations to multiple groups. It can be as simple as a hallway conversation, or just spreading the word, either in person or through internal collaboration tools.

Step 8

Do a few more reviews. Scan through the checklists, the summary scores, and the corrective actions. Verify they tell the right story.

Collect the individuals together who went through the process and review their experience. Was it easy or hard? Were there a lot of rules that required clarification? Were there a lot of rules that did not apply to the assets being reviewed? This is the starting point for the definition of asset profiles. You want to define the asset profiles so that the architect filling out the checklist never feels like the answer should be "N/A." (More on asset profiles in Part III).

Find a way for architects to share their experiences with other architects. Include guidance as to how others have answered a golden rule measure when there is ambiguity. Include guidance as to how to roll up scores from measures to rules to principles to business objectives. If the organization has an internal wiki, that is often a great way to share this kind of experience and guidance. Possibly create an email alias where people can ask questions, where the responses go into a searchable archive. You do not want all the valuable experiences and guidance to be buried in one-to-one emails.

Create a "review of reviews" process that regularly goes through finalized checklists with the enterprise architects, so that the community of architects start to achieve consistency as to how rules are scored and rolled up.

Use the asset review process to initiate the software asset governance process. In other words, as you are reviewing the asset, be sure to collect all the third-party software incorporated into the asset and get it into the technology standards registry.

Step 9

Review how your organization specifies and reviews business requirements. Pay particular attention to how requirements translate into architecture, design, and implementation. Insert a formal placement-of-function process into the loop. Generally, placement-of-function is done by solution architects. You want everybody who does placement-of-function to follow the same methodology and create similar artifacts, that are preserved and 'versioned.'

Step 10

If you already have an operational readiness checklist, then you are ahead of the game. If not, start with the checklist in Appendix 1. If you have an organization that spreads technology ownership across both business and technology groups, then get your house in order first, before reaching out to the technology owners in other groups.

This author has seen multiple occasions where a CTO and a business unit leader have argued about who a technology group should report to, especially after an acquisition. Once the business unit leader is presented with the checklist of technology owner responsibilities, the response is often *"You take it,"* rather than *"Mine!"*

Create the inventory of operational instances. Map each operational instance to the one and only one asset it supports. Verify that the technology owner of the asset feels ownership of the operational instances. Verify that each operational instance is owned and there are no gaps.

Create a list of all development, test and production environments. Ensure each environment has a technology owner who feels responsible and accountable.

Step 11

As the review process takes hold and a body of checklists, business risk scores, corrective actions, and technical debt get accumulated, aggregate the data into an overall dashboard that is placed somewhere anybody in the organization can see. When technology owners see low risk and low technical debt amounts next to their name, it reinforces a behavior. When technology owners see high risk, or high technical debt amounts next to their name, it reinforces a different behavior. Accolades and recognition are strong motivators. So are guilt and shame.

Step 12

Regularly take the pulse of the organization. Don't assume that because the process started off well, that it is continuing well. This is especially true as new thought-leaders, new architects, and new technology owners join the organization. Just because the previous technology owner was a staunch supporter of the architecture processes you have put in place, don't assume her replacement will automatically be bought-in as well.

PART II

PBEA Architecture Objectives, Principles, and Golden Rules

Now that the reader has been given an overview of the Principle-Based Architecture Method, it is time to be introduced to the meat of the approach, which are the golden rules and guiding principles.

The goal of the method is to provide an objective approach for both measuring and managing a medium to large technology environment as well as to guide an organization towards working collaboratively with its business partners towards making better technology decisions and tradeoffs.

When compromises have been made, they should be captured. Any risk to the business associated with those trade-offs should also be captured in a manner that can educate and guide future investment decisions.

This section discusses the architecture principles behind the Principle-Based Architecture method, how these principles support the business objectives of the method and how they organize the golden rules.

To review, the business goals of the method are to facilitate delivery of solutions that are: *safe, responsive,* and *effective.*

CHAPTER 11

Architecture Principles

The PBEA governance practice measures alignment with its core principles. (See Chapter 15). These architecture principles organize the non-functional (i.e. non-feature) requirements for the system and data assets in the architecture.

Principles are the architecture mission statements of what we want to achieve for end users and are not limited to a single division or product. In fact, the PBEA architecture principles and associated golden rules specifically capture the non-functional requirements that every product needs to adhere to, but which business requirements often presume.

Each principle is further elaborated as a set of golden rules, which define how to achieve the mission, and the consequences of deviation. Golden rules read like the requirements statements for meeting the mission statement of the principles. A golden rule exists to either promote one or more positive outcomes or prevent one or more negative outcomes. Often, we are preventing negative outcomes rather than promoting positive ones.

To make the (positive or negative) outcome tangible, it is framed in the context of a set of *stories* in which the outcome was the result of the actions taken by the individuals or groups who were actors in the story. In the case of a negative outcome, you would want to take different actions, so that you may avoid the negative outcome. The golden rule is the statement of *what you ought to d*o to avoid the negative outcome. The stories of what went wrong and why, provides the body-of-evidence that supports the golden rule. Golden rules are further elaborated into a set of *measures*, which are "yes/no" questions whose answers determine whether the golden rule has been followed.

Each outcome is assigned an *impact* (i.e. how bad is the negative outcome) and is also assessed a *likelihood* (i.e. how likely is it that the negative outcome occurs if the golden rule is not adhered to). The combination of impact and likelihood yields a *severity level* for breaking the golden rule. If a golden rule is broken, architecture debt is calculated as the cost to fix the issue and adhere to the golden rule.

Carrying architecture debt is not inherently bad. Everybody carries around a bit of debt. In fact, if an asset has zero debt, one could argue that the developers of the system were overly cautious and could have released sooner. The point is to measure architecture debt, track it and pay it off in the fullness of time, prioritizing the closure of the highest severity debt first.

To achieve the goal of a governable architecture, and to avoid the dreaded "death by governance," it is essential that the golden rules be limited to the rules that matter, avoiding the clutter caused by trying to govern every good idea. In other words, the negative outcomes that a golden rule exists to prevent must be worth preventing. Life is balance. So is technology architecture. Governance exists to measure the balance and keep it in line.

As no two companies are precisely alike, no two enterprise architectures will be precisely alike, and no two sets of core golden rules will be precisely alike, but you would be surprised (or maybe not) how often the principles are the same in every company that has achieved the technological maturity level to which we all aspire.

Companies who fail in this endeavor do so because they either think too narrowly or try to bite off too much at once. It is essential to marry the rigor of the process to the maturity of the organization and therefore to start off small (i.e. with a small set of Golden rules) and build out to larger set based on shared experiences. Through root cause analysis, we build golden rules from the body-of-evidence (i.e. stories of negative outcomes caused by architecture and design errors that have impeded business progress or caused end-user pain).

Principles (and the golden rules derived from them) impose constraints on technology. When properly applied, these constraints form the foundation both of architecture governance and of technology innovation. This may sound counterintuitive, as freedom is generally thought to drive innovation. But we need the freedom to explore innovative solutions to those things that differentiate us, while constraining those things that do not. Innovation on the Internet exploded once everybody agreed to standardize on HTTP over TCP/IP as a protocol, so they could focus on building end-user applications. Putting constraints on the more mundane factors and decisions allowed the real process of innovation to transpire.

> *The more constraints one imposes, the more one frees one's self. And the arbitrariness of the constraint serves only to obtain precision of execution.*
>
> -- Igor Stravinsky

CHAPTER **12**

Architecture Golden Rules

What is an architecture golden rule? It's a rule that when broken is likely to lead to a negative outcome for the end user or the business. But nothing is perfect, and rules will be broken, thus accumulating architecture debt. The PBEA checklists and dashboards are designed to measure and tracks these deviations, so that risk, cost, and time may be balanced. Breaking a rule is not necessarily bad – provided the deviation is transparent, measured, and tracked.

Adherence to the architectural golden rules lead to higher long-term value. The golden rules and the principles that organize them are not limited to a single division or product or company. In fact, the architecture principles and associated golden rules specifically capture the non-functional requirements that apply to almost every product and almost every company, but which business requirements often assume rather than specify.

Each golden rule is supported by a *body-of-evidence*, which provides the *proof* that the golden rule is not just some ivory tower nicety. These are the stories yielding negative outcomes that have happened through poor choices. Given the body-of-evidence, golden rules are defined through root-cause-analysis, to avoid these negative outcomes in the future. Adherence to golden rules has a direct correlation to customer satisfaction. Golden rules and the asset governance process are designed to catch issues early and share key insight across the architecture, development, and business communities.

The architecture principles for systems (and the golden rules derived from them) impose constraints on the system assets and their use of technology infrastructure. Constraints properly applied are both the foundation of architecture governance and of technology innovation.

The *golden rules for data* are distinct from those that apply to system assets, even though there is an obvious relationship between the two, and they serve the same business objectives.

The architecture principles are organized into four governance levels based on their alignment to business objectives.

CHAPTER **13**

Architecture Objectives for Systems

The primary objectives of the architecture should be organized around measurable business goals. These are, for solutions to be *safe*, *responsive*, and *effective*. These objectives are elaborated in the sections below. Having innovative solutions is usually a business goals as well, but we have yet to figure out how to precisely measure that. So, while it is a goal, measuring whether solutions are innovative is left as an exercise for the future.

Safe solutions

Safe solutions protect the brand and reputation of the organization. The impact of failing to be safe transcends any single product. A security breach in any product taints every product produced by that company in the eyes of the end user.

A compliance failure can result in large fines and in some cases jail. These principles apply not only to the code that is written, but also to the COTS technology that is bought, or licensed, or used and the way it is used. Safe solutions are secure and compliant

1. **Secure Systems**: Secure systems are consistent with the level of risk the organization has accepted. They protect and preserve access to proprietary services and confidential information in the organization's systems. They transport information in a secure manner as necessary for the class of information.

2. **Compliant Systems**: Compliant systems uphold the law and follow regulations. They adhere to the provisions of the organization's contractual obligations. They protect the intellectual property of the corporation and do not infringe the intellectual property of others.

Responsive solutions

Responsive solutions define service level agreements (SLAs) and meet them. They facilitate identification and resolution of problems quickly and long before end users complain. This includes the ability to react to demand by increasing (or decreasing) capacity in a manner that meets utilization needs (measured by performance SLAs). Having dramatically more capacity than is required may meet SLAs but is not cost effective. Responsive solutions are scalable, manageable, and reliable.

3. **Scalable Systems**: Scalable systems support load increases via a proportional increase in resources in a cost-effective manner.

4. **Manageable Systems**: Manageable systems have hooks to monitor, measure, and modify operational behavior. These systems know if something is going wrong before end users start experiencing problems. Issues are resolved before they become issues.

5. **Reliable Systems**: Reliable systems perform as expected, when expected. They provide measurable service in terms of responsiveness, availability, and dependability during normal operation, as well as in failure scenarios and in the event of a disaster.

Effective solutions

Effective solutions minimize time-to-market and optimize *total cost of ownership* (TCO). This requires systems to combat the tendency toward entropy and complexity and facilitate releasing new software in an agile, affordable, and predictable manner. Software tends to follow the *law of entropy*.[66] It becomes more disordered and therefore more complex over time. As software increases in complexity, it becomes harder and harder to change, which drags the release cycle, increasing time-to-market (which is bad) and increasing the cost of proper maintenance (which is also bad).

There are three aspects to total cost of ownership (TCO). Cost effective solutions minimize the one-time cost of bringing new solutions to market. They minimize the year-on-year cost of running and maintaining these solutions. Finally, they have just enough capacity (usually requiring just-in-time scalability) to achieve desired Service Levels without waste.

---

[66] Software Entropy – See: https://bit.ly/1NtVj7f.

Effective solutions are simple, modular, maintainable, mastered, and global.

6. **Simple Systems**: Simple systems have clear responsibilities with little or no overlap. They tessellate.[67] They are *"as simple as possible and no simpler."* They have proper placement-of-function, duplicate as little as possible and follow well-defined patterns and blueprints.

7. **Modular Systems**: Modular systems employ separation-of-concerns.[68] They divide labor among encapsulated components that are loosely-coupled via well-defined interfaces, and data models. They do not share computing resources.

8. **Maintainable Systems**: Maintainable systems are easily supported and easily modified. They can be extended into adjacent functional areas with minimal surgery.

9. **Mastered Systems**: Data (e.g., business data, content, and operational data) is handled rigorously. Data items are mastered, and their transit through systems and way-points are carefully managed. Values, names, mnemonics, identifiers, classifiers, and other descriptors (metadata) are handled with the utmost care.

10. **Global Systems**: Global systems can be easily localized for use in a specific geography, including but not limited to: language, script, culture, currency, color conventions, holidays, and sort-order.

---

[67] Tesselate – See: https://bit.ly/23a7orM.

[68] Separation of Concerns – See: https://bit.ly/2nyAc24.

CHAPTER 14

Architecture Objectives for Data

Data is an asset in the PBEA model. Data assets are peers to system assets, even though system assets supply the house in which data assets live. The architecture objectives for data serve the same business goals as for systems. These are: for solutions to be *safe, responsive,* and *effective*. These objectives are elaborated in the sections below.

Safe solutions

Safe solutions manage data in compliance with laws, regulations, corporate policies, and contractual obligations. Data is *intellectual property*.[69]

1. **Compliant Data**: Access to data is controlled to protect its value for generating revenue and to avoid improper use and exposure to liability. For example, regulated data is only present in specific systems and accessible only to authorized individuals. Data is managed and protected in compliance with laws, regulations, and corporate policies

Responsive solutions

Responsive solutions manage data in a well-controlled manner, so that users can rely on the data's structure and values. Data value is protected from its point of origin onward by preserving its accuracy, completeness, and timeliness.

---

[69] Intellectual property (IP) is a category of property that includes intangible creations of the human intellect. See: https://bit.ly/1Z2RUVQ.

2. **Reliable Data**: Reliable data is controlled and consistent everywhere it is presented so that the values can be trusted.

Effective solutions

Effective solutions minimize time-to-market, requiring that data be flexible and global (as appropriate). Data is flexible, reliable, well-managed and well-structured so that it may be used in as many products as possible without duplication.

3. **Modular Data**: Modular data is structured so that it can be used in many products, repeatedly enriched for ever-increasing value, and reformatted for multiple uses in online and print products at the lowest possible cost. Data represents a significant investment of curation, operations, fabrication, and storage resources.

4. **Mastered Data**: Mastered data has an authoritative "single source of truth" that avoids data redundancy. Since it is meant to displace lower quality sources of the same data and can be used in many places, standards for its definition are higher.

5. **Global Data:** Global Data supports rich diversity by following the globalization and localization rules. Global companies operate in many countries. Each country has its own languages, scripts, time zones, currencies, and customs for formatting text.

CHAPTER 15

Asset Principles and Golden Rules

While all PBEA objectives apply to both systems and data assets, how these objectives manifest as principles and golden rules are different. There are 10 core architecture principles, five of which apply both to systems and to data. The golden rules associated with each principle are further elaborated in parts three and four.

Secure systems (*safe* solutions)

Trust, but verify. – Ronald Reagan

Security is mostly a superstition. It does not exist in nature, nor do the children of men as a whole experience it. – Helen Keller

Safe solutions are **secure**. Throughout the entire product lifecycle and in every corner of the product, careful consideration must be given to securing the application from accidental and malicious operations (both from within and without). In the architecture, key functions and checkpoints should be identified to serve as secure boundaries. Access to resources across the secure boundary is both authenticated and authorized. By authenticated, we mean that the individual or system requesting the resource has been verified. By authorized, we mean that the requester, which has been verified by authentication, is allowed access to the requested resource.

Secure system assets are architected to balance cost and risk per company strategy. They protect and preserve access to proprietary services and confidential information in the organization's systems. They transport information in a secure manner appropriate for the class of information.

Information that crosses a secure boundary should follow the rules associated with the classification of said information. There may be a change in security level crossing from one side of the boundary to the other. Depending on how different the security levels are on each side of the boundary, different classes of data may be affected differently. For example, if customer personal information is moved from a core network (the most secure zone) to a DMZ[70] (less secure zone) across a core firewall, golden rules define the level of encryption demanded by that class of content.

Different classes of information may have different rules applied when the information is at rest, such as in a repository, or in motion, such as when it is being sent in a message and crossing a secure boundary from a zone with Security level "x" to a zone with security level "y." For example: billing information (and other information that affect the financials of an organization) needs to be secured against malicious intrusion and all but authorized access, according to the rules associated with that classification of the data. Different classes of data have different requirements for confidentiality and trust and access when in motion and at rest.

System designers need to ensure that their implementations guard against attack scenarios and provide necessary access controls that are required for the type of system. Reducing the *attack surface* is of paramount importance. It is difficult enough to guard the expected access points, it is almost impossible to guard against wide open access or unnecessary access points. By default, all firewall ports should be closed unless they need to be open. By default, no feature is installed and/or made accessible unless a legitimate need arises. The operating systems for production systems should be installed in a minimal locked-down configuration. All known vulnerabilities should be checked regularly. A mechanism should exist for applying security patches to all production systems automatically. Security is not only a function of narrow, deep expertise but also a collaborative process of multiple subject matter experts each looking at the problem from their own angle.

All inputs to systems (via APIs) must be sanitized and inspected to ensure the incoming data is appropriate. Failing to sanitize inputs is the root cause of SQL injection attacks. Treat all external input as untrusted until proven otherwise. There should be a complete inventory of every production system and its configuration, including every third-party software title installed, every process that is supposed to be running, and how every system operates under normal circumstances.

Any vulnerability that seems insignificant is worth examining closely. Alarm bells should ring if you hear phrases like "nobody would ever do that" or "how would anybody discover that?" It's almost certain that someone will prove you wrong. If the rewards are great enough, people

---

[70] In network architecture, the DMZ or demilitarized zone is a network layer that protects internal systems from external systems. It generally comprises a firewall facing externally and another facing internally, with a proxy in between. Only the proxy may connect across the internal firewall, thus preventing direct connection between internal systems and the Internet.

will go to great lengths to find a way into a system and exploit it. Where security is concerned, paranoia should be the norm.

	Secure Systems
1.1	Protect end-user authentication secrets.
1.2	Control access to important systems and data.
1.3	Keep web traffic private.
1.4	Sanitize inputs from untrusted sources before use.
1.5	Do not let data become code.
1.6	Minimize access to regulated data and protect it when used.
1.7	Do not place sensitive data in a URL.
1.8	Use third-party software safely.
1.9	Catch internet-facing security exposures before they are exploited.
1.10	Record and report on important security related events.
1.11	Use standard authentication implementations.
1.12	Use standard encryption implementations.
1.13	Architect system assets to degrade gracefully when attacked.
1.14	Deploy system assets only into known safe environments.

Compliant systems and data (*safe* solutions)

Intellectual Property has the shelf life of a banana – Bill Gates

It's a major milestone. … I am personally committed to full compliance. We are committed to being a responsible industry leader. – Bill Gates

Resistance is futile. – The Borg

Whether you believe the current controversy surrounding intellectual property protection in the software industry is a good thing or a bad thing, it would be naive to ignore it. Every company should clearly state a position, which is best governed through the architecture process.

Even seemingly altruistic efforts like *open source* have subversive elements. There are several cases of companies paying "undisclosed sums" out of court to settle cases where unsuspecting developers used open source software in a manner inconsistent with its license.

While enterprise architects are certainly not lawyers, they often find themselves in the position of needing to understand the difference between: patents, copyrights, trademarks, company secrets as well as what constitutes an invention and what does not. Some companies choose to patent everything, even those things they license for free. Other companies file no patents at all. Still others act more subtly and subversively.

Managing the intellectual property coming from the technology base of the organization and ensuring that other companies' intellectual property and licensing restrictions are not infringed is part of any well-governed enterprise architecture.

Most architectures and infrastructures incorporate data and technology from 3rd parties. These will always come with a contract of sorts which specify the rights and obligations associated with usage. It is a corporation's duty and responsibility to follow these obligations as well as to comply with applicable laws and/or consent decrees (e.g. Sarbanes-Oxley).

In the last few years, *software license compliance* has become a major risk for many corporations as certain software vendors have become *predatory* about adherence to the potential arcane terms of its license. Compliant systems uphold the law and comply with regulations. They adhere to the provisions of the organization's contractual obligations. They protect the intellectual property of the corporation and do not infringe the intellectual property of others.

	Compliant Systems
2.1	Protect the organization's intellectual property (IP).
2.2	Use third-party intellectual property (IP) per its license.
2.3	Store source code in a secure and managed repository.
2.4	Ensure end-user interfaces are accessible.

	Compliant Data
D1.1	Classify and manage data according to the *data classification*.
D1.2	Retain data as required by the business and by legal and regulatory requirements. Destroy thereafter.

Scalable systems (responsive solutions)

Great businesses can be built on scale. I think Amazon has built a phenomenal commerce business largely on scale. Their network effect isn't obvious to me, but boy, have they used scale effectively – Jeff Jordan, American entrepreneur

The way to really scale a venture firm is with software. – Sam Altman, President, Y Combinator

A scalable architecture is one built to adapt cost-effectively to increases (and decreases) in load. Load can come from multiple directions: from more users, from existing users increasing usage, from more data or from more data updates and transactions. Achieving scalability requires more than technology. it also needs a model, a plan, and a mindset. Think about scale every time a system is designed and built. Don't ever assume that a component will never need to scale. You do not have to have code in place on day one to achieve infinite scale, but you should at least define how it would be achieved should that day come.

Being scalable means defining, for each "scalability unit" in the system, the appropriate response to increased usage and/or content as the system grows, and the scaling unit approaches its capacity limit. Scalable systems support load increases via a proportional increase in resources in a cost-effective manner. Highly optimized systems can scale sub-linearly with load; this means that cost increases at a lower rate than capacity.

	Scalable Systems
3.1	Deliver acceptable performance under anticipated load. Degrade gracefully when load exceeds capacity.
3.2	Optimize the cost of capacity.
3.3	Set appropriate limits on auto-scaling.

Manageable systems (responsive solutions)

Bad software lives forever. Good software gets updated until it goes bad, in which form it lives forever – Casey Schaufler, Developer of the Linux Simplified Mandatory Access Control Kernel (SMACK)

Deploying manageable systems entails monitoring the health of production systems, defining procedures to modify the behavior and functionality of production systems at run-time, and tracking any problems or incidents through resolution.

Manageability includes designing systems so that resolving issues is an integral part of the design process and not an afterthought. This often requires adding instrumentation and logging. It is only when manageability is designed-in that we get the most effective use from systems and the personnel who operate and administer them. As with security and scalability, manageability is a mindset that pervades system design from day one.

It is essential for implementations to provide quantitative *and* qualitative measures of availability, responsiveness, capacity, utilization, and reliability. These qualitative and quantitative measures cover a wide range of items including: usage statistics, error events, exception events, performance metrics, availability metrics, security intrusions, capacity thresholds, and accounting events.

Even in properly designed and tested applications, failures will happen, and these are often diagnosed at run-time. It is essential that applications take special care to log all exceptional events in a manner that allows harvesting for diagnostic use. It is also vital that the volume of logged information not overwhelm either the operator interface or available disk space such that important events are not lost in a firehose of non-actionable messages.

Manageable systems have hooks to monitor, measure, and modify operational behavior (at run-time). These systems know what is happening before end users do. Issues are resolved before they become issues.

The ability to disable an account or to raise and lower the level of diagnostic reporting are two common practices in reliable run-time management systems. Where a service contract has specified Service Level Agreements (SLAs), as they always should, these should be specifically monitored.

Manageable Systems	
4.1	Respond to standard control commands dynamically.
4.2	Publish appropriate operational events and error messages.
4.3	Publish Performance and Capacity data.
4.4	Maintain a complete inventory of all operational resources

Reliable systems and data (responsive solutions)

Everything fails. All the time. – Werner Vogels, CTO Amazon

Data is a precious thing and will last longer than the systems themselves. – Tim Berners Lee

Reliable systems provide measurable service in terms of responsiveness, throughput, availability, and dependability during normal operation, as well as in a failure scenario or in case of a disaster. Each service (i.e. interface of a system asset) should have an interface contract that includes a service level agreement (SLA). Each asset that participates in the delivery of a service must exceed the minimum service levels, since it is the integration of multiple assets which are bound by the SLA and errors can either add or multiply depending on the scenario.

Reliable Systems	
5.1	Record all requests and measure adherence to your SLA.
5.2	Record all requests made to other assets and measure the dependent assets' adherence to their SLA.
5.3	Continue to meet SLA obligations in the event of a resource failure.
5.4	Continue to meet SLA obligations in the event of a site failure.
5.5	Ensure that functional testing of the solution includes at least one test case covering each of the capabilities or features supported.
5.6	Handle hard failures (unrecoverable) and soft failures (recoverable) appropriately.
5.7	Ensure all production changes are repeatable and auditable.

Reliable Data	
D2.1	Define data curation processes and follow them.
D2.2	Define data schemas and adhere to them.
D2.3	Ensure data is accurate.
D2.4	Ensure data is complete.
D2.5	Ensure data is timely.
D2.6	Define data quality control processes and follow them.

Simple systems (effective solutions)

Simplicity is the ultimate sophistication – Leonardo Da Vinci

Make solutions as simple as possible and no simpler – Albert Einstein

Decomposition into smaller pieces is a fundamental approach to mastering complexity. The trick is to decompose a system in such a way that the globally important decisions can be made at the abstract level, and the pieces can be implemented separately with confidence that they will collectively achieve the intended result. – Jim Horning, American scientist and author

There are two ways of constructing a software design: One way is to make it so simple that there are obviously no deficiencies, and the other way is to make it so complicated that there are no obvious deficiencies – C. A. R. Hoare, winner of the 1980 Turing prize

Simple systems have clear responsibilities with little or no overlap. They tessellate. They have proper placement-of-function, duplicate as little as possible and follow well-defined patterns and blueprints.

Every technology problem we seem to face today is too large to solve all at once and all in one system or by one team. It used to be the case that computer systems were bigger than computer problems. So, we ran multiple computer solutions on a single system. Now we run a single solution across grids or virtual clouds of computers. The bottom line is that the problems we are solving with computers have gotten so large that the most effective way to solve them is to first decompose them into smaller discrete problems.

This decomposition is hierarchical. We start with domains. Within domains we have assets; within assets we have modules; assets deliver services through service interfaces. Modules can be further decomposed into sub-modules as necessary. It is critical that problems be decomposed based on the problem at hand, and not on any preconceived notion of what the solution should look like.

How far do we go in this seemingly endless decomposition? There is no single, universal answer to this question. You decompose far enough so that the size of the largest problem is small enough to fit into one brain, so that it may be verified completely. You don't stand a chance of getting a large system to operate correctly if you cannot completely verify each of its smallest components.

Simple Systems	
6.1	Do not use unmaintained assets or deprecated APIs.
6.2	Do not couple an asset to an environment.
6.3	One asset, one team.
6.4	Follow placement-of-function (PoF).
6.5	Package code to facilitate independent releases.
6.6	Minimize code duplication.

Modular systems and data (effective solutions)

I intend to describe for your illumination the most common cases in which the "average" computing scientist fails to separate the various concerns. In doing so, I hope and trust that my colleagues in the profession do interpret this as an effort to help them rather than insult them. – E.W. Dijkstra, Dutch software engineer, science essayist, and early pioneer in computing science

A modular system is one that falls apart easily! – E.L. (Ted) Glaser, 1965

People who are more than casually interested in computers should have at least some idea of what the underlying hardware is like. Otherwise the programs they write will be pretty weird. – Donald Knuth

Modularity has many benefits. Modules have well-defined boundaries providing encapsulation. Crossing the boundary can only happen via pre-defined interfaces. Well-defined interfaces, that adhere to the rigors of proper versioning and strong type checking support a type of interoperability we call loose-coupling.

Loose coupling is defined as the manner of integrating two systems across an interface boundary in such a way that each can upgrade independently of the other and either can upgrade first without a dependency on the other. A loosely coupled interface cements a contractual relationship between a service provider and a service consumer. This is often called the interface contract. Loosely coupled modules can be developed and tested independently. This is called unit testing (See Chapter 8: Unit Testing). It is also called bottom-up testing because by testing the functional units independently and then re-combining them into larger units, we are proceeding from the bottom up in the structure chart of the design.

Modularity is a key enabling factor for reusability, extensibility, scalability, security, simplicity, and manageability. Component units are aggregated to provide a complete service or solution. Modularity extends beyond functionality or business logic to content. In other words, maintain proper encapsulation of content and treat content modules like you treat software modules.

Cloud-based solutions support *Infrastructure as Code* (IaC) which is the process of managing and provisioning computer data centers through machine-readable definition files, rather than physical hardware configuration. So, modularity extends to physical architecture and infrastructure as well.

Modular systems employ *separation of concerns*. They divide labor among encapsulated components that are loosely-coupled via well-defined interfaces, and data models. They do not share infrastructure. Proper modularity and encapsulation are not only about software architecture and design; they are concepts that govern the way systems are deployed as well.

	Modular Systems
7.1	Expose and consume only well-defined external interfaces.
7.2	Manage and version control external interfaces.
7.3	Do not couple external interfaces to their implementation.
7.4	Handle retries appropriately.

	Modular Data
D3.1	Databases and models are designed flexibly to support changing requirements.
D3.2	Meaning is defined separately from presentation and not inferred from presentation.
D3.3	Master data and product data can evolve independently (i.e. are not tightly coupled).[71]
D3.4	Data definition and organization supports low cost of ownership and high interoperability.

---

[71] In other words, for any data asset, you first master it in the database of record. Then you transform it into a transport format, which passes through your API, to a product database who transforms it again into a denormalized form, generally combining it with other data, and storing it in a database of access. Loose coupling requires that the two databases be allowed to evolve independently.

Maintainable systems (effective solutions)

The study of the art of motorcycle maintenance is really a miniature study of the art of rationality itself. Working on a motorcycle, working well, caring, is to become part of a process, to achieve an inner peace of mind. The motorcycle is primarily a mental phenomenon. – Robert M. Pirsig, American writer and philosopher

Maintenance is a function of every software system, once it goes into production. Therefore, a part of the real cost of developing any software or any system is the ongoing maintenance required to keep it operational.[72] This is not meant to imply that the system has bugs that escaped testing and need to be fixed. It may. In fact, it most probably will. But even disregarding that, there is always change to the surrounding infrastructure or to third-party software assets that have been incorporated. Eventually maintenance is required. In many real systems, over the course of their lifetime, the cost of maintenance can exceed the cost of initial development by quite a bit. Proper encapsulation, modularity, simplicity, adoption of standards and good, clean simple documentation all lead to maintainable systems.

Of all the methodologies for producing software more efficiently and more cost effectively, by far the best is to produce less of it! This is why reuse has achieved "holy grail" status in the software development industry. Maintainable systems are easily supported and easily modified. They can be extended into adjacent functional areas with minimal surgery.

	Maintainable Systems
8.1	Make interfaces directly callable without requiring a proprietary library.
8.2	Trace requests and failures to their source.
8.3	Appropriately comment source code and interfaces

---

[72] Studies have shown that the initial development cost of a system can be as low as 2% and as much as 15% of the total life-time cost of a system. That means between 85% and 98% of the total cost of ownership comes from maintenance and operations.

Mastered systems and data (effective solutions)

With a tad more data modeling, engineers at NASA and Lockheed Martin might have settled on either metric (used by NASA) or English (used by Lockheed) as the standard unit of measurement and not lost the $125 million Mars climate orbiter in 1999 – Joe Maguire

It is a capital offense to theorize before one has data. – Sherlock Holmes

The architecture must ensure that the data (all data) is correct and understandable to the end user. This commonly involves modeling and naming the data correctly, transforming supplied data consistently to its defined (normalized) form, preserving and protecting the data, and providing it in a context that supports its understanding. The ability to break down the data, normalize and capture the meaning, relate it to important core entities and topics are among the key practices for data which are facilitated by the master system.

Data often passes through many systems on its long and sometimes arduous path from the source to the end user. It is stored, transformed, transmitted, combined with other data, re-stored, and re-transmitted. But no matter how long and complicated a path that data has taken to reach its goal, the end user looking at the data has the right to demand, and a data provider has the obligation to affirm, the truth of that data.[73] To do that, the principles of master data management must be embraced, and every item of data must be transparently tracked through the systems it transits.

Data reuse is a powerful force for creating value. However, in an environment where data is duplicated, it is critical to data integrity to keep a record of which instance is the master (i.e. the source of truth). This is the point of control for creation, maintenance, and deactivation.

The days of making money from simply having a lot of data are gone! To play in this space in the 21st century, you must add significant value to the data, by making it easier to find initially (i.e. Search), easier to find related information (i.e. Navigation) and by managing core entities (i.e. specific items, not groups of things – like a person or an organization or a place). These more advanced capabilities are significantly enhanced by a base of high-quality data.

Data (including, but not limited to business data, content, and operational data) is handled rigorously. Data items are mastered, and their transit through systems and way-points are

---

[73] The proper architecture of data masters and master data management is a large topic and out of scope for this book. Suffice it to say, that in the PBEA definition of a data master, "the data master is right, whether it's right or wrong." Therefore, the true value of a fact, is whatever the data master says it is.

carefully managed. Values, names, mnemonics, descriptors, classifiers, and metadata are handled with the utmost rigor.

Mastered Systems	
9.1	Register the master system asset for every data asset.
9.2	Keep data quality high.
9.3	Encapsulate data.
9.4	Trace data to its source.
9.5	Do not connect end-user applications directly to data masters.
9.6	Do not lose data.

Mastered Data	
D4.1	Each data asset or each data item is mastered by one and only one system asset.
D4.2	Master data assets are modeled.
D4.3	Data enrichments are mastered.

Global systems and data (effective solutions)

If you want to make peace with your enemy, you have to work with your enemy. Then he becomes your partner – Nelson Mandela

Never before has information been so important, to governments and businesses alike. .... Globalization means that the 'butterfly effect' is everywhere at work. – Jacques Chirac

A *global* system is one capable of being localized for different languages, scripts, cultures, currencies, color conventions, rules, and regulations – without needing to rewrite and/or redesign the code. It is considered best common practice to globalize a system via resource and script files. These separate the language- and culture-dependent strings and functions from the language- and culture-agnostic business logic of the asset.

Globalizing is distinct from localizing, which is implementation for a specific locale. Examples of globalization include adoption of Unicode for string encoding and separation of strings presented to the user, from code, into resource files. Translating English strings into Japanese is an example of localizing. Localizing is more than translating. Cultural issues are also important. For example, in western cultures green normally means "up" or "positive," while red means down or negative. In some Asian cultures, these meanings are reversed. Utmost attention must be paid to iconography when creating global systems. Any hand position and many facial expressions, no matter what it means in your culture, is likely to be a curse in at least one other culture around the world. Another example is naming; a clever-sounding product name in one language may be offensive in another.

Globalizing an application can be an expensive process, so don't take it on lightly. But it is far cheaper to do during initial design than after-the-fact. So, it is generally considered to be both prudent and best-practice to develop with globalization in mind from the outset, but not localize until there is a specific business need. In other words, globalization is a core principle of the architecture, while localizing an application becomes a business decision taken on a case-by-case basis. Designing and developing global code requires a mindset, just as does security, scalability, and simplicity.

Systems and applications are global if they can support an appropriate subset of: language preference; time format preference; date format preference; time zone preference; text data in multiple languages; number formats; and text directions

Global solutions can be easily localized for use in a specific geography, including, but not limited to: language, script, culture, currency, color conventions, holidays, and sort-order.

Global Systems	
10.1	Handle data in a globalized way.
10.2	Distinguish third-party translations from company translations.
10.3	Adapt to the user's preferred locale.

Global Data	
D5.1	Number-centric data is stored in a globalized way.
D5.2	Textual data is stored in a globalized way.

PART III

System Asset Golden Rules and Measures

An Architecture Principle is like a mission statement that guides us to the achievement of our objectives. A golden rule is more specific. It is something that the architecture, design, and implementation of an asset should follow. Even though the golden rule intends to be specific, there is still a lot of ambiguity and interpretation involved in the decision as to whether a system asset truly follows the rule. As such, each golden rule has one or more golden rule measures defined.

What is a golden rule measure? It is a specific statement of what to do to adhere to the golden rule. It is intended that these statements to be simple enough that the answer is either yes or no without a complex explanation. The purpose of the *measure* is to avoid answers in the form of an essay. They form the basis of the asset checklist.

But not every measure applies to every asset, neither does every golden rule apply. As such, the PBEA allows for the definition of profiles, which relate to the behavior of an asset. If the asset exhibits the behavior, the profile is selected and all the rules and measures that are part of that profile are enabled in the checklist. An asset exhibits multiple behaviors and therefore will have multiple profiles. For now, that is enough detail about profiles. When reading this section, keep in mind that not every rule applies to every asset and there is a mechanism (through the definition of asset profiles) of form-fitting the checklist to the behavior of the asset.

This section is organized hierarchically: first by principle then by golden rule. So, there is some duplication with Part 2 of the book. But this section goes into much more detail about each golden rule. Whereas Part 2 of the book ended with the definition of the golden rules, Part 3 begins with the definition of the golden rules for system assets and elaborates each rule, providing context, golden rule measures and the body-of-evidence. The stories that make up the body-of-evidence were the actual starting point for the creation of the golden rules (as described in Chapter 9: Change Management), so they provide relevant business context as to why the rule matters (or at least should have mattered to the organization whose experience motivated the golden rule).

Each body-of-evidence story tells the tale of what happened to those unfortunate souls who, once upon a time, broke the rule and paid the price. Depending on how high that price was, an impact is assigned. Impact may be either: catastrophic, high, medium, or low. Each is also assigned a likelihood of either high, medium, or low. This is the probability that the outcome experienced in the story would happen if the rule is not followed.

The combination of impact and likelihood dictates the severity of the rule. Based on the collection of stories for each rule and the combination each event's impact / likelihood, the rule is assigned a severity of 1 (very severe) to 3 (moderately severe). Rules that would have been given a score of 4 (low impact) or 5 (low impact and low likelihood), are considered nuisance rules, not worth governing.

CHAPTER 16

Secure Systems – Golden Rules and Measures

Secure solutions are architected to balance cost and risk in accordance with company strategy. They protect valuable resources from "bad guys" who would attempt to exploit them.

	Golden Rule	Severity
1.1	Protect end-user authentication secrets.	1
1.2	Control access to important systems and data.	1
1.3	Keep web traffic private.	1
1.4	Sanitize inputs from untrusted sources before use.	1
1.5	Do not let data become code.	1
1.6	Minimize access to regulated data and protect it when used.	1
1.7	Do not place sensitive data in a URL.	2
1.8	Use third-party software safely.	1
1.9	Catch internet-facing security exposures before they are exploited.	1
1.10	Record and report on Important security related events.	1
1.11	Use standard authentication implementations.	2
1.12	Use standard encryption implementations.	3
1.13	Architect system assets to degrade gracefully when attacked.	1
1.14	Deploy system assets only into known safe environments.	1

Protect end-user authentication secrets

Data in motion is vulnerable. For example, data transiting over a network can be trivially "sniffed" by anyone with physical access to the sub-network (including desktops compromised by malware). Data on media being physically transported can be stolen or misplaced. There are simple and straightforward methods to protecting data in transport, including HTTPS, TLS (the replacement for SSL), static encryption, or physical hardening of isolated production networks.

When does this rule apply?

- When legally protected data such as un-redacted social security numbers or Driver's License numbers are transmitted across a network.
- When sensitive data crosses a security boundary (e.g. a system asset boundary, a domain boundary or across security groups within an asset.
- When sensitive data is passed between services over a network.
- When contractually protected data (such as Credit Card Primary Account Numbers (PANS)) are transmitted.
- When policy protected data (such as passwords) are stored in a browser cookie.
- When passwords are stored.

Golden rule measures

	Golden Rule Measures
1.1.1	Authenticated transactions are encrypted (e.g. Use HTTPS, not HTTP)
1.1.2	Only encrypted end-user-selected secrets are transmitted (e.g. passwords and security answers).
1.1.3	Only encrypted or hashed end-user-selected secrets are stored (e.g. passwords and security answers).
1.1.4	End-user secrets are not stored in insecure log repositories.

Body of evidence

Story	Impact	Likelihood
Company A created a feature in its product that was for "internal use only," used by the testing group. This feature was added quickly, "secretly," deeply linked into the infrastructure, and bypassed normal controls. It allowed people who knew the secret (presumably internal users) to input a special User ID and Password in a visible plaintext parameter on a URI. Almost immediately upon being released into production, the secret leaked out and the "internal-only" feature got widespread external use. Company A's security group had to spend significant time and effort finding the applications using this "internal" feature. The cost to resolve the issue was roughly 10 to 100 times the cost/time saved by hacking in the feature in the first place.	High	High

Story	Impact	Likelihood
A network sniffer sitting on an internal network during a penetration test by a third party was able to intercept several hundred valid (and indefinitely reusable) session cookies. Had this third party been malicious, they could have successfully reused the captured session cookies to completely impersonate users of the product and it would be very difficult to detect.	High	Medium
Severity		1

Control access to important systems and data

It is very easy to relax access controls to production systems and data, especially during a high-pressure release. Without adequate access control, the attack surface is needlessly magnified, and a breach becomes more likely.

Golden rule measures

	Golden Rule Measures
1.2.1	When employees separate from the organization, their access to production systems is automatically and quickly terminated.
1.2.2	There is a process in place to distinguish which users require access to production systems. Access is only granted to this sub-group, according to the principle of least privilege.[74]
1.2.3	People's access rights to production systems are regularly reviewed (e.g. annually).
1.2.4	Changes to production systems are reliably traceable to the *person* who either made each change or the person who approved it.

---

[74] Principle of least privilege – See: https://bit.ly/1NCwAPK.

Body of evidence

Story	Impact	Likelihood
Company A had an employee who needed access to sensitive resources on six different products over a multi-year period. This employee used their laptop to access these production systems as well as browse the Internet. Eventually, the laptop was compromised by undetected malware, a reverse proxy to a root account was installed, and authentication credentials were captured. That reverse proxy was then used to launch internal attacks on all six products, even though, at the time of the attack, the employee was only actively working on one of those systems. In addition to bad practices leading to the breach in the first place, the effect was 600% larger than would have happened had there been better access control to production systems.	High	High
Severity		1

Keep web traffic private

Private web traffic means that no ill-intended person can snoop in on conversations that are meant to be private. This rule is primarily related to network traffic, but many security organizations have similar policies related to voice communication as well.

Golden rule measures

	Golden Rule Measures
1.3.1	Authenticated web traffic is only transmitted on uncontrolled networks using encryption (e.g. HTTPS /TLS).[75]

---

[75] Transport Layer Security (TLS) See: https://bit.ly/2QJwApd.

Body of evidence

Story	Impact	Likelihood
An M&A lawyer was using her laptop in a Starbucks in preparation for an acquisition. She had to look up something on the Internet, so connected to the public WIFI. Sitting nearby, but out of sight, was another WIFI user, nonchalantly sipping a cup of coffee. But this person was running a sniffer on their laptop, peeking at the unencrypted traffic over the WIFI network. The lawyer had her traffic intercepted by this malicious party who deduced, from her searches, that a large merger was about to happen. She was unknowingly complicit in insider trading and securities fraud.	Catastrophic	High
Severity		1

Sanitize inputs from untrusted sources before use

Data sanitization is different from data validation. Data validation simply ensures that inputs are reasonable. For example, checking that a month is a number from 1 to 12. The goal of data validation is to get correct data, and to help a non-malicious end user correct typos and misunderstandings. Data sanitization, on the other hand, desires to strip content that may have been inserted by a hostile attacker. The goal of data sanitization is to cleanse input data of anything that could be dangerous, not to determine if the data is correct.

Following are some examples of data sanitization:

- A web application accepts a "year" field in a submit form and removes any character not between "0" – "9."

- A service that communicates with a client deployed component that accepts an XML string validates the XML against a narrowly defined schema rule, enforcing that tags contain only: (A-Z, a-z, 0-9, comma, dash, and period).

- A service that accepts what is by necessity a complex search string, removes anything not in a whitelist of approved characters. The service might then further apply a blacklist operation, removing known "bad" inputs, such as JavaScript.

- An application that takes a freeform text field URL Encodes the entire string before further processing.

- A document received from an external source may have attachments, or embedded JavaScript. These are removed before the document is stored. Inputs come via many different paths and in many forms. For example, they may be cookies, URI parameters, HTTP headers, or XML payloads. Any of these can carry malicious content.

This is not meant to imply that every interface to every system must add data sanitization. For example:

- Data that is cryptographically tunneled from a trusted source, does not necessarily have to be sanitized.

- Cookies that are properly encrypted in servers, sent without any keys to be stored by the end user's browser, and decrypted back within the safe zone of a network can be treated as coming from a trusted source.

Also note that input sanitization is not just removal of malicious changes to real input variables, it is also the protection of state that should not be changed as the result of a request. For example, if a form is not asking for a field, but somebody deliberately hacks the HTML and inserts a valid but hidden name/value pair, the injected field should not blindly update the application's state. And, if a field requires increased level of authority to be changed, that additional authentication challenge must be satisfied before the field can be changed.

Golden rule measures

	Golden Rule Measures
1.4.1	Untrusted inputs are sanitized before further use.

One useful strategy for data sanitation is to *URL Encode*[76] all inputs early in the process before using them in any way. This converts dangerous characters (such as a double quote or angle brackets) into safe sequences of characters that are displayed correctly but not interpreted as HTML code. For example, the string <"foo"> when encoded, is changed to: "<'&quot;foo&quot;'&gt;." But when displayed by the browser, it appears as <"foo">. This doesn't solve every possible problem, but it's a good start.

---

[76] URL Encode – See: https://bit.ly/2xhRXEf.

Body of evidence

Story	Impact	Likelihood
Company A ran a website that failed to sanitize inputs and failed to use parameterized stored procedures. As a result, it was breached by hostile 3rd parties via SQL injection. When discovered, the site was taken offline until a risk analysis could be performed and vulnerabilities remediated. The site remained offline for a month during investigations and cleanup. As such, the product running on the site failed to meet its revenue targets. Neither the product nor the product's VP remained with the organization.	High	High
Company B ran a community server that allowed self-registration and posting of shared content. Eventually the site began advertising pornography websites. This was inconsistent with the organization image and ethics goals. The site had to be taken down. It was never put back up, even though the site served its honest users well for many years.	High	High
There was a twitter worm going around in 2010.[77] Rumor had it that it gave lots of unsuspecting people following tweets from Robert Gibbs (the Whitehouse press secretary) their first opportunity to promote hardcore pornography. The root cause of the problem was the exploitation of a collection of half insecure features. Briefly, this is what happened: 1) Twitter recognizes URL's embedded in text and turns them into actual clickable hyperlinks. 2) Unfortunately for Twitter, they did not adhere to the security golden rule: Sanitize inputs from untrusted sources before use *(which includes browsers, Silverlight, flash, java applets, desktop applications)*. 3) Therefore, it was possible to create a carefully crafted tweet that would cause JavaScript to be executed when anyone read a tweet. The net result was that Twitter sent out a tweet that resulted in a JavaScript mouseover event if you simply let your mouse roll over the link. Because this malicious command originated from Twitter itself, the JavaScript (which is bound in the browser sandbox to only reach back to the server it came from) was free to manipulate the viewer's Twitter account. In this situation, the individual pieces were each half-secure, but when combined they could be exploited. Attacks are getting much more sophisticated as defenses get stronger, and this kind of "thread the needle" attack is now par for the course.	High	High

---

[77]: Twitter security flaw – See: https://bit.ly/2HUNq4d.

Story	Impact	Likelihood
In April 2018, Intel disclosed that a vulnerability was discovered in its processors whereby one thread running on the processor could access data in the level-one cache being used by another thread. Nobody ever considered that this was even possible until side-channel analysis discovered the problem. Intel product security head Leslie Culbertson stated: "We are not aware of reports that any of these methods have been used in real-world exploits, but this further underscores the need for everyone to adhere to security best practices. This includes keeping systems up-to-date and taking steps to prevent malware." Intel stock dropped 1% on the news.	High	High
Severity		1

Do not let data become code.

All application and service interactions with databases should use parameterized queries that prevent user input from being interpreted as commands. Parameterized procedures programmatically enforce separation between the "logic" of the operation and the "data" associated with the query. This prevents manipulations of the data from tampering with the query logic (a class of attacks that include "SQL Injection Attacks").

Any interactions with an operating system command line interface (such as interpreter or shell) should use parameterized calls to prevent user provided input from being interpreted as a command. Operating system feature invocation should programmatically enforce separation between "logic" of the operation and the data in the query. This prevents manipulations of the data from changing the query logic.

Golden rule measures

Number	Golden Rule Measures
1.5.1	All interactions with databases are via parameterized queries.
1.5.2	All interactions with the operating system are via parameterized calls.

Body of evidence

Story	Impact	Likelihood
Company A released its first Internet based product. The user interface used dynamic SQL in many of the queries that were run. A QA Engineer found that he could perform a SQL Injection attack against the login page. Luckily, it was a QA engineer working for the organization and not a "bad guy."	Medium	High
Heartland Payment Systems was a major Midwest processor of credit card payments. An internet exposed back end system failed to (a) sanitize inputs and (b) use parameterized procedures to execute SQL commands. An attack on this interface used SQL injection to introduce network sniffing software deep into Heartland's infrastructure. As a result, it is estimated that 130,000,000 (!) credit card numbers were compromised. Excluding the impact of the actual fraud, simply re-issuing a credit card with a new number, costs between $5 and $30 per card. Heartland's stock price, which was trading as high as $30 per share, dropped to as low as $4 per share after the breach was made public.	Catastrophic	High
Severity		1

Minimize access to regulated data and protect it when used

The invasive and ever-changing PCI[78] regulations can incur high costs for those systems that abide by them. As such, access to PCI data should be constrained, and if possible, eliminated altogether. This translates to all other highly regulated data as well.

When does this rule apply?

- When a User ID is logged to facilitate security and problem resolution.

- If a system processes or stores: user passwords, social security numbers, driver's license numbers, medical information, credit card numbers, et al.

---

[78] Payment Card Industry (PCI) See: https://bit.ly/2BNOMdg.

- When an application logs any data classified as Sensitive Personally Identifiable Information (SPII) to a non-secure repository. For example, when a 'masked' credit card number is logged, the first 12 digits of the credit card number should be replaced with an "*" character, and the last four digits should be stored intact. The repository should also be registered.

Golden rule measures

	Golden Rule Measures
1.6.1	PANs (i.e. Credit Card Primary Account Numbers) are not stored, transmitted, or processed unless the system asset is approved for such use, tracked, and regularly audited for PCI compliance.
1.6.2	Highly-regulated (SPII) data is not stored, transmitted, or processed unless the system asset is approved for such use, tracked, and regularly audited for compliance to appropriate regulations. For example: HIPAA for medical records, DPPA for drivers' licenses.
1.6.3	If highly-regulated (SPII) data must be used, then it is masked wherever possible.
1.6.4	If highly regulated (SPII) data must be used, then it is encrypted when transmitted or stored (including in log files).

Body of evidence

Story	Impact	Likelihood
Company A had several applications that were capturing search strings in poorly controlled logging repositories. Unfortunately, the Company's privacy statement for its products indicated that search strings entered by end users into its products were considered private. The project to remediate these repositories cost 10-100x the original cost of the project.	Medium	High
Company B was not compliant with PCI rules (which apply to any system asset that touches a credit card number). They were breached and taken to court. As a result, they were held responsible for all expenses relating to the breach, including unauthorized charges, and costs to reissue consumer cards. For example, Target agreed to a $39M settlement with the credit card companies because they could not prove they were fully PCI compliant at the time of the 2013 breach (even though before the breach, they thought they were compliant).	Catastrophic	Medium

Credit card companies created and issued a new set of rules for anyone accepting credit card payments. One of these rules precluded any plain-text storage, display, or transmission of Credit Card numbers. Company C was compliant with the previous set of requirements, but once the new requirements were issued, multiple systems became non-compliant. Company C was now presented with a choice: (1) Spend $1 Million to remediate the non-compliant systems. (2) Risk being assessed fines of up to $40,000 per day for non-compliance. (3) Walk away from $100 Million per year in automated payments.	High	High
Between 2016 and 2018, nearly $370 million was paid to settle data breach lawsuits in the US. Among them, two settlements totaling nearly $45 million by Home Depot, and a $28 million settlement by the poster-child of data breaches, Target.	Catastrophic	High
In September 2017, Equifax announced that it had been breached sometime between May and July of that year and that credit card numbers and other personally identifiable information, such as social security numbers for over 190,000 Americans were compromised. Equifax traced the breach to a small number of servers running an old version of the open source Apache Struts library, which was not patched. Before the end of the month, Equifax's CEO, Richard Smith stepped down amidst the scandal that followed. Months later, victims of the breach were still struggling to recover. On 10 January 2018, Sens. Elizabeth Warren (D-Mass.), and Mark Warner (D-Va.), introduced the Data Breach Prevention and Compensation Act, which would raise the security requirements for data stored at credit agencies and give the organizations more to lose when that information gets stolen. It's the third piece of legislation aimed at tightening the leash on credit reporting agencies after the 2017 Equifax data breach.	High	High
For the data breach du jour, see SC Magazine[79] or The RISKS Digest.[80]		
Severity		1

---

[79] SC Magazine – See: https://bit.ly/2DfVC9X.

[80] The RISKS Digest – See: https://bit.ly/2GskDBK.

Do not place sensitive data in a URL

If a referrer field, bookmark, or analytics element contains sensitive data, it could inadvertently leak all information necessary to impersonate an end user or leak the end user's private information.

Golden rule measures

	Golden Rule Measures
1.7.1	Sensitive data is not placed into a URL (e.g. as a parameter).
1.7.2	HTTP(S) links to third party sites do not disclose sensitive information (e.g. session or authentication information in a "referrer" field).

Body of evidence

Story	Impact	Likelihood
Company A had a web application which used an HTTP GET operation to log into its application. Since they were using HTTPS, and the parameters were encrypted over the Internet, they thought they were safe. However, all HTTPS transactions were decrypted once inside the organization's firewall and the front-end web server logged all incoming URLs which included the Log on transaction. As such, the unencrypted User ID and Password combinations were stored in the log file as was other sensitive data. In addition, the log repositories were accessible by anybody with the operational credentials (which was pretty much everybody).	Medium	High
Severity		2

Use third-party software safely

Many software companies have specific divisions solely devoted to auditing companies' use of their software and deriving revenue from fees and fines associated with non-compliance. License compliance can be a significant financial exposure.

Understanding trusted code repositories

Third-party code should be reviewed and controlled, and its access and usage should be managed. This includes code that might be dynamically loaded into the end user's browser from a third-party repository (e.g. JavaScript routines) as well as open source code that might be downloaded by a developer and compiled into an application.

Using code from a third party opens privacy and security risks, so appropriate controls should be put in place to counterbalance these risks. At a minimum it means understanding which third-party code repositories are being used and by which system assets. Uncontrolled source code, even if okay today, could change in the future to include a variety of straightforward attacks (for example causing the user to be prompted to download and install malware) or inadvertently incorporate licensable intellectual property. An example of a control that could be put in place when a third-party JavaScript library is incorporated into an application would be to host that library on an organization server and only update the library after an independent review has taken place.

Does loading a JavaScript library such as jQuery from Google's CDN break the rule?

Maybe. If the Google CDN has been placed on the list of trusted repositories, then there is no problem. If not, the rule has been broken. This is because Google and sites like it can be considered an abstract risk. Depending on how much control Google places over the repository (which could change at any time), the repository could be considered *trusted* or not. As such, some additional due diligence is recommended where code is concerned, allowing the organization to match the criteria for trust to their risk profile.

Understanding licensing risk

Software Asset Management (SAM) is a process implemented by many organizations to limit the risk of being assessed fines due to improper use of licensed software. (See Software Asset Governance in Chapter 6). Many software vendors are exercising with greater frequency their right to audit the use of their software to ensure adequate licenses are in place and paid for by enterprises. Accordingly, companies should regularly check what software is installed on its equipment, including its servers, PCs, laptops, and mobile devices – to confirm that it has the required amount and type of licenses and thus avoid liability for infringement or breach of contract.

It is an unfortunate truth in the industry, that some companies have become predatory regarding software license compliance such that there is no such thing as an innocent mistake. Fines are often assessed in the $millions, so the risk is quite real. Each enterprise should decide for itself how to balance the investment in a software asset management process with the business risk of being *out-of-compliance*. There is no right or wrong answer, but there are industry consortia[81] and industry research groups[82] that provide guidance.

Golden rule measures

	Golden Rule Measures
1.8.1	All third-party software is registered (in the Software Registry).
1.8.2	Third-party software classified as *prohibited* is not being used.
1.8.3	License ownership vs. usage for all third-party software is tracked according to the rules laid out in the license agreement for that software.
1.8.4	A mechanism exists for each compute instance hosting the system asset to automatically report the software installed on it (and any usage related to licensing).
1.8.5	Code is only downloaded from trusted repositories. This applies to open source as well as dynamically loaded code.

Body of evidence

Story	**Impact**	**Likelihood**
Company A decided to build its brand-new web application with a brand-new group of software developers who could "code like the wind" and release features very quickly. These developers were used to searching GitHub for any "new and cool" code. In fact, this approach was how they achieved their results. Unfortunately, for Company A, it was a target for *bad-guys* who constantly probed their networks for weaknesses. This new team incorporated a third-party JavaScript library from an uncontrolled source into their application, which was compromised. Malware was installed on all the servers, which reached across every device accessible to the compromised hosts, installing Cryptolocker on each. Company A received a ransom demand far more than the value of the new product. Luckily for Company A, their network was well segmented, so the only devices compromised were the servers of the new product and all the developers' laptops. Rather than pay the ransom, the organization decided to shut down the product, disband the group, and wipe all the infected laptops.	High	High

---

81 Software Asset Management – See: https://bit.ly/2MPC8Nu.

82 Gartner Peer Insights – See: https://gtnr.it/2F0maMD.

Story	Impact	Likelihood
Company B launched a product which incorporated a "free" third-party web analytics package. Unknown to Company B, this third party was hosted somewhere out of reach of U.S. laws and it installed private cookies that tracked the end user's page views, as well as stole private information. The third party then resold the information to other parties on the dark web. Suddenly, there was a massive increase in the incidents of Identity theft associated with end users of Company B's product.	Catastrophic	High
Company C inadvertently integrated a piece of software that was free for non-commercial use into one of its for-sale products, because the developers of the product were unaware of the license terms-of-use. This piece of software had a Copyleft clause which implied that all derivative works (which included all the proprietary application code deployed with the open source) had to carry the same "free to distribute" license. The organization was forced to pay a substantial penalty as well as a recurring license fee, to continue selling its product. "Free" turned out to be very expensive, indeed.	High	High
Company D standardized on the Oracle database for all its products. They had a software license management group who diligently counted all license usage to ensure they remained compliant. At some point, an optimization exercise was done hoping to save some money by reducing the number of computers in the data center by increasing virtualization. The Data Center optimization team performed a detailed evaluation and chose VMWare for their virtualization layer. Unknown to the optimization team, Oracle's licensing terms for running in virtual machines, did not recognize "soft virtualization," such as that provided by VMWare as *valid*. In these situations, a license was required for every physical core of any computer running a database, even if the database was only running in one VM, associated with one core on a 128-core machine. To make matters worse, when VMWare implemented the ability to move virtual machines across physical machines in a cluster, Oracle now required a database license be assigned to every core of every CPU of every host in the entire cluster if just one core on one host was running an Oracle database. When Oracle came in and performed an audit, Company D found itself thousands of licenses short (even though it thought it was compliant, by the licensing rules it understood). The initial assessed fine was considered "outrageous." In the end, Company D spent three years negotiating the settlement and thousands of person-hours of effort managing the process.	High	High
Severity		1

Catch internet-facing security exposures before they are exploited

If an application security defect lingers in an internet-facing product, it could be exploited and result in a security breach.

Golden rule measures

	Golden Rule Measures
1.9.1	Penetration testing is regularly[83] performed on all internet-facing products, and any system asset directly or indirectly exposed to the Internet).
1.9.2	Network vulnerability scans are performed regularly.

Body of evidence

Story	Impact	Likelihood
In Company A, a JBoss console was unknowingly installed by a DevOps system administrator when installing other requested software. At some point, a different application had needed the JBoss console so it was added into the default Operating System package that was used to make images. Neither the developers nor the administrator knew the JBoss console was there, so nobody changed the default password. Eventually, an attacker discovered it, and installed malicious software which gave him access to Company A's production network.	High	High
Company B put lots of protection in front of its internet-facing applications, including umpteen firewalls, intrusion-prevention software, intrusion-detection software, et al. But there was very little protection (other than a single firewall) between its content systems and the Internet. The content systems would regularly access websites over the Internet to "scrape" new data. Eventually those systems were compromised with spambot software. Company B was written up in the Industry press as a one of the largest originators of spam on the Internet over a 3-month period. This was very embarrassing to the executive team who took immediate action to initiate a "witch hunt" and find those responsible.	High	High
Severity		1

---

[83] How often should penetration testing be done? Some would say "constantly", if it was affordable. Others would say annually is enough. Each organization needs to decide for itself how often "regular" testing is performed depending on how likely they are to be a target of an attack and their risk profile.

Record and report important security related events

Creating a full list of security related events would take a volume of its own and several have already been written. PBEA expects that any organization adopting the model will revise the list of security events. At a minimum, PBEA recommends capturing all authentication related events and that every event captured be traceable to specific requests and transactions and to user identity where possible.

Golden rule measures

	Golden Rule Measures
1.10.1	Both successful and failed authentication events are captured.
1.10.2	Both successful and failed credential management events are captured.
1.10.3	Auditable records for sensitive transactions (e.g. privacy related, regulated data related, cost related, et al) are captured and retained.
1.10.4	Recorded events include: a reliable timestamp, originating IP address, user identity, and specific information about the activity, wherever possible.
1.10.5	Event records are retained for at least 90 days[84] online and off-line for at least one year.

Body of evidence

Story	Impact	Likelihood
Company A discovered that an ID for the end user of one of its on-line products was compromised. Unfortunately, its logs were insufficient in both the amount of data captured and the time the logs were retained. As such, the organization was unable to detect whether other user IDs were similarly compromised or how long ago the known ID was compromised. To mitigate the risk, they were forced to immediately require that all existing users change their online IDs and passwords, which was extremely disruptive to both the user population and the business.	High	High

---

[84] 90-day on-line retention is common, but industry or country regulations and/or company policy may dictate otherwise.

Story	Impact	Likelihood
Company B discovered that one of its online products had been breached. Thorough analysis revealed that the breach had begun months prior to the discovery. The hackers had been regularly introducing more and more malware to branch out and infect more systems. Measuring the extent of the attack was extremely difficult because the systems were insufficiently instrumented to detect the aberrant usage.	High	High
Company C produced a product that included sensitive information. Both the Federal Trade Commission and certain customers required that Company C submit to annual independent security audits. The first audit revealed that the company could not prove that it was logging security-related events. Even though the organization claimed that it captured the required information, the fact that it could not produce the logs as evidence during the audit resulted in a negative finding. This resulted in additional cost and negatively impacted the organization's reputation.	Catastrophic	High
During a high-profile breach involving an acquired company, an investigation was launched to identify potentially fraudulent use. Tens of thousands of potentially fraudulent transactions were initially identified. Detailed logging on the systems allowed all but 0.002% of these actions to be classified as "low risk" rather than "high risk." While the fact the breach occurred at all was still a serious issue, the organization's logging and auditing infrastructure significantly reduced both its litigation risk and remediation cost. (A high-risk remediation average $60 per instance, while a low risk remediation was less than half that).	High	High

Story	Impact	Likelihood
Company D's flagship web application suddenly started experiencing slow performance and intermittent total outages. Detailed log records allowed investigators to quickly realize that the system was undergoing a distributed dictionary attack (a collection of compromised hosts at many different IP addresses were making wild guesses at valid ID's and passwords for system accounts, submitting millions of requests hoping to find a random correct guess). The sheer volume of these requests (coupled with the fact that authentication and authorization were not separated, and that a failed authentication request consumed significant database resources (attempting to retrieve authorization information) turned the dictionary attack into an all-out denial-of-service attack. Analysis of the log file entries allowed the organization's Information Security group to reactively start blocking the IP addresses that were part of the attack. Quickly, the denial-of-service aspect of the attack was resolved (as the worst offending IP's were quickly blocked). Eventually, the dictionary attack aspect of the problem was resolved as well. It is likely the attackers just grew tired of recruiting new botnet systems to find an unblocked IP address.	High	High
Severity	1	

Use standard authentication implementations

Authentication solutions will change over time, both for end-user applications as well as for employee access to systems. The solution(s) that are standard at any one time should be identified. By "standard" authentication implementation, we mean the "standard" solution to the "authentication" problem as described by: *technology standards registry* in Chapter 8. In general, there will be different standard solutions for authenticating end users and employees. This is accomplished by defining end-user authentication and employee authentication as two distinct *technology problems.*

Golden rule measures

	Golden Rule Measures
1.11.1	Standard authentication systems are used for end-user applications and services. (NOTE: an end-user application may not require authentication, if all its exposed content and services are free.)

Body of evidence

Story	Impact	Likelihood
An asset built its own authentication system for access to operator and administrator interfaces. Every member of the development and DevOps teams, including contractors, were given an ID. Over time, as people joined the team and left, it became customary to just hand the credentials for an employee or contractor who had just left to a new person joining the team as opposed to going through the administrative effort of removing old credentials and adding new ones. After a time, a disgruntled ex-employee whose access credentials were not revoked took malicious action and caused a product outage during peak usage.	High	Medium
A new asset built a new authentication system correctly, but for use only by that asset. Since company policy required regular code reviews on all authentication systems, it quickly became costlier to have the extra authentication system than it would have been to just interface to the proper one. In addition, the number of opportunities for coding defects and security vulnerabilities was needlessly increased.	Medium	High
Company A had a collection of one million identities in one master repository and another two million identities in a second master repository. About 500,000 of these identities were for the same people. The rest were unique to one product or the other. End users who subscribed to both the products had to maintain multiple user IDs and passwords and sign on individually to each product. The organization lost 6% market share over the course of one year. Surveys indicated that a key reason was because a competitor had an equivalent product offering, at a similar price, but with a much less painful sign-on experience. The competitor used a single, seamless log on process which covered all their products.	High	Medium

Story	Impact	Likelihood
Company B adopted Google Analytics for its website analytics solution. Google Analytics is a SaaS solution with its own identity & access management (IAM) solution. Company B used Active Directory to manage internal network access, but as Google's IAM did not federate with the organization's Active Directory, they manually provisioned accounts for all the employees who needed access to the analytics. As there was neither an automated nor manual process to keep credentials synchronized between the two IAM solutions, they fell out of sync. Employees who were terminated had their company credentials revoked, but their Google Analytics access remained. The terminated employee had full access to all the proprietary company data that he held in his former role.	Medium	Medium
Severity		2

Use standard encryption implementations

Encryption implementations are notoriously difficult to get right and very expensive to build. It is therefore best to do them once and do them right. By "standard" encryption implementation, we mean the "standard" solution to the "encryption" problem as described in Chapter 8: Technology standards .

Golden rule measures

	Golden Rule Measures
1.12.1	Only standard Encryption implementations are in use.

Encryption is only obfuscation until it includes all of the following:

- Strong keys (i.e. random with sufficient entropy).
- Rotating keys.
- Securely managed keys.
- Revocable keys.
- Tamper-resistant keys (i.e. that carry checksums validated off box).
- Auditable key lifecycles (generation, distribution, access, revocation).
- Secured key storage and access.

Body of evidence

Story	Impact	Likelihood
A product initially used a locally-written encryption algorithm. When that developer left the organization, the resulting intellectual property confusion delayed a product release until the encryption solution could be replaced with a licensed package (at a cost of several weeks and $70K).	Medium	Medium
Severity		3

Architect system assets to degrade gracefully when attacked

Any system asset which is either directly or indirectly exposed to the Internet is a potential victim for a denial-of-service attack. By taking appropriate steps while architecting the system asset, the impact of a potential attack can be greatly diminished.

Golden rule measures

	Golden Rule Measures
1.13.1	Systems are designed to smooth out activity spikes over time (e.g. by making the site highly and rapidly scalable, or by queuing requests and ensuring that a single requestor doesn't swamp the system at the expense of all other users).
1.13.2	Systems are designed to use the minimum amount of resources to determine that a request is invalid.
1.13.3	Systems do not crash when they receive requests at a rate far above what is anticipated.
1.13.4	Systems only accept requests from expected sources that have been authenticated.

Body of evidence

Story	Impact	Likelihood
Company A's authorization system, to validate an end user's credentials, retrieved all data about the end user, in addition to the password check. Given the computationally intensive and I/O expensive operation, used for authorization, a minor dictionary attack caused the authentication system to crash resulting in a complete product outage.	High	High

Story	Impact	Likelihood
Company B was very diligent about the building redundancy into its products but implemented a single server for domain name resolution. Because of a minor denial-of-service attack against the product URL, the DNS server overloaded and went down. The entire product became unavailable as a result, not because it wasn't working, but because it suddenly became impossible for end users to reach it via the product URL.	High	High
Severity		1

Deploy system assets only into known safe environments

While the concept of an environment is associated with groups of assets and falls under the authority of a Technology Owner (see Part 5: Technology Ownership), each asset owns its own deployment and should know whether it is being deployed into a known environment that has been reviewed and classified as *safe*.

Golden rule measures

	Golden Rule Measures
1.14.1	Every environment an asset is deployed into is known to have been vetted and deemed *safe*. The Security Assessment should be published and available on request.

Body of evidence

Story	Impact	Likelihood
A product manager grew frustrated with the time and process overhead for getting infrastructure resources deployed in the data center. Since their plan was falling behind schedule, this manager used their corporate credit card to secure their own hosting. Two years later, because of poor physical security practices or a failure of the development team to do patching, the environment and all its data was completely compromised by the exploitation of a known and common vulnerability.	Catastrophic	High
Severity		1

CHAPTER **17**

Compliant Systems – Golden Rules and Measures

Compliant solutions uphold the law and comply with regulations. They adhere to contractual obligations. They protect the intellectual property of the corporation and do not infringe the intellectual property of others.

	Golden Rule	Severity
2.1	Protect the organization's intellectual property (IP).	3
2.2	Use third-party intellectual property (IP) in accordance with its license.	1
2.3	Store source code in a secure and managed repository.	2
2.4	Ensure end-user interfaces are accessible.	1

Protect the organization's intellectual property

Intellectual property that is not marked can be copied and claimed by anyone. This pertains to content, source code, and JavaScript files as all of these are protected by patents, copyrights, and trademarks.

Golden rule measures

	Golden Rule Measures
2.1.3	A copyright notice is included in each source code module.
2.1.4	A copyright notice is included in source code delivered as part of an HTML page, such as a JavaScript routine.
2.1.5	A copyright notice is included in public documentation (e.g. for a public API).

Body of evidence

Story	Impact	Likelihood
In 2012, Oracle sued Google stating that Google had copied their Java APIs, and even though Google wrote their own implementation of those APIs, that merely copying the interface specification was copyright infringement. The court agreed that Google had copied portions of Java but that these copied portions were mere APIs; as such, they could be repurposed by developers without a license under the "fair use" doctrine and was not protected by copyright law. "So long as the specific code used to implement a method is different, anyone is free under the Copyright Act to write his or her own code to carry out the same function or specification of any methods used in the Java API," wrote district judge William Alsup. Upon appeal, the Federal Circuit reversed this decision in 2014, holding that the "structure, sequence, and organization" of an API was in fact protectable by copyright.	Medium	Medium
Severity		3

Use third-party Intellectual Property (IP) in accordance with its license

This includes, but is not limited to, aspects such as time-based or market-based embargoes, royalty payments, contractually obligated presentation format, copyright rules, and time limitations on retention of copies.

When might this rule apply:

- A system asset that processes news, receives a copy of a certain publishers' story (e.g. an earnings announcement) before the publisher releases that story to the general public. The license might require that the story may not be distributed before a specific *embargo* time (e.g. 9:00AM EST).

- The license for a specific publication might allow its resale into certain markets, but not other markets (e.g. Academic markets).

- Resale of certain publications might require payment that is a percentage of revenue received or based on end-user usage.

Golden rule measures

	Golden Rule Measures
2.2.1	Embargos, restrictions, and contractual obligations are honored when using third-party materials, including (but not limited to) third-party software and data.
2.2.2	When using third-party data with a royalty component, records are generated allowing calculation of the royalty payment.
2.2.3	If a derived document contains materials from more than one copyrighted source, then the copyright from each Intellectual Property (IP) owner is included in the derived document
2.2.4	If a document contains an attachment (e.g. a table, picture, or multimedia file) with a different intellectual property owner than the document itself, then the intellectual property owner of the attachment is also identified.
2.2.5	Data with contractual restrictions is only distributed to products and customer segments allowed by the contract.

Body of evidence

Story	Impact	Likelihood
Company A was an aggregator and redistributor of news and research. The payment for third-party news was per source, and per publication and was independent of how many end users read the stories. But the payment for third-party research depended both on how many end users accessed the research and when. If an end user accessed the research document within a week of being published, it was one fee; after that it was another fee. During an audit, it was discovered that Company A's algorithm for calculating the two royalty amounts for research content was different than what was stated in the latest contract. A *large* fine was assessed.	High	High
Company B was in the business of redistributing company earnings reports. In order not to give anybody unfair (or insider) knowledge, each redistributor of the report was given an advanced copy before market open, with a distribution embargo of 9:00AM EST. Unfortunately for company B, their distribution system had the wrong internal clock setting, so even though it did not send the report before the 9:00AM embargo time, the timestamp it sent out with the earnings report said 8:59AM. An investigation ensued involving the organization who issued the earnings report as well as the SEC. Even though company B was found innocent, the distraction consumed a large amount of the organization's resource as well as legal fees.	High	High

Story	Impact	Likelihood
Company C licensed content from company D that was only allowed to be incorporated into certain products and only allowed to be sold within certain customer segments (where company C and company D did not compete). The content systems group in company C did not implement internal restrictions, because *entitlements* was the job of the end-user-facing application not the content systems. A few reorgs and a spin-off later, a new product that sold into one of the restricted segments incorporated the restricted data. The organization had recently been spun-off from a larger company and all the individuals who understood the contractual restrictions either stayed with the old company, resigned, or were fired. So, nobody remaining knew the detailed terms of the agreement (and if they did, they ignored them). When company D discovered the violation, company C was served with a cease-and-desist notice. They had 90 days to either remove the restricted data from their product or stop selling the product. When the data contract came up for renewal, company D declined to renew it.	High	High
Severity		1

Store Source code in a secure and managed repository

Improper control over source and deployment undermines the integrity of many other controls.

Golden rule measures

	Golden Rule Measures
2.3.1	All source code is stored in a standard[85] Source Code Management system and follows approved maintenance processes (e.g. off-site backups).

---

[85] By standard, we mean the standard solution to the *source code control* problem as defined in the Technology Standards registry.

Body of evidence

Story	Impact	Likelihood
Company A stored its source code in an unmanaged repository that was backed up *now and then*. When the Database in the repository had a critical failure, the organization lost over a week's worth of source code and all the configuration data (which was not backed up at all). As a result, the organization was unable to rebuild the software and had to recreate both the latest weeks' worth of code as well as all the build processes from scratch.	Medium	High
Company B had two data centers and religiously backed up its code, which was mastered in one data center and copied to the other each night. Unfortunately for company B, both of its data centers were in the World Trade Center, so other than an old backup that somebody had taken home, everything was lost on 11 September 2001 (9/11).	High	Medium
Severity		2

Ensure end-user interfaces are accessible

The United States government (and the governments of many other nations) has defined a set of techniques for compliance with accessibility mandates when using various presentation technologies.

Golden rule measures

	Golden Rule Measures
2.4.1	Test applications for accessibility according to company guidelines.

Body of evidence

Story	Impact	Likelihood
Company A wanted to expand the sale of its products to the U.S. Federal Government. However, the user interfaces of its products did not comply with Section-508[86] accessibility guidelines. As such, they were not able to sell into US Government markets.	High	High
Severity		1

---

[86] https://bit.ly/2dfvXRA. Note: Section 508 guidelines will eventually be updated to adhere to WCAG v2.0 (ISO 40500). https://bit.ly/2JVgC8U.

CHAPTER 18

Scalable Systems – Golden Rules and Measures

Scalable solutions support load increases (and decreases) via a proportional increase in resources in a cost-effective manner.

	Golden Rule	Severity
3.1	Deliver acceptable performance under anticipated load. Degrade gracefully when load exceeds capacity.	2
3.2	Optimize the cost of capacity.	2
3.3	Set appropriate limits on auto-scaling.	1

A scaling group is a set of resources that scale as a unit. For example, after a certain number of web servers are configured, the size of a load balancer must increase as well. The web servers and the load balancer constitute a single scaling group:

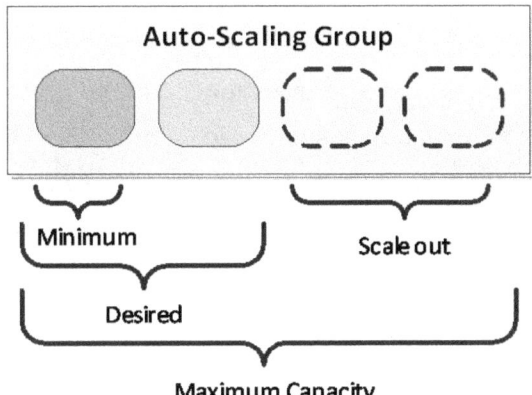

Most cloud providers allow the definition of auto-scaling groups to dynamically provision the correct number of instances to handle the load for an application. The autoscaling groups allows the specification of the minimum number of instances in each auto-scaling group, ensuring that the number of instances never goes below this size. It also allows specification of the maximum number of instances. By specifying scaling policies, auto-scaling can launch or terminate instances as demand on the application increases or decreases.

For example, the above Auto Scaling group (from Amazon EC2) [87] has a minimum size of 1 instance, a desired capacity of 2 instances, and a maximum size of 4 instances.

Deliver acceptable performance under anticipated load

Not only should assets deliver acceptable performance under anticipated load, but they should also degrade gracefully when load exceeds available capacity. Graceful degradation is the ability of an asset to support limited functionality even when it cannot fully meet its SLA. An asset should never crash when anticipated load is exceeded. In graceful degradation, the operating efficiency or speed declines in proportion to the overload. For example, if a system's average response time is one second and its SLA guarantees 95% of responses within two seconds, then under excessive load, it might take three seconds to respond. As load becomes even more excessive, response time may go to 5 seconds or 10 seconds. Eventually the system might return an error message indicating it is in an overload condition. One common approach to achieving this kind of behavior is to enqueue all requests received and to dequeue requests in a FIFO manner when the asset can process the next request.

Graceful degradation is not only important for smooth operation, but it is also a strong defense against a *denial-of-service attack* (See golden rule 1.13 – Architect Systems to degrade gracefully when attacked)

Performance should be tested in an environment which simulates the actual production environment, including all other system assets which could reasonably affect performance. The performance measures that are collected should allow direct testing of all SLAs provided to end users. Performance requirements should be treated as business requirements, not technical requirements.

Golden rule measures

	Golden Rule Measures
3.1.1	Responsiveness is validated vs. SLA under anticipated load.
3.1.2	How high the load can go before the response time SLA fails is measured.
3.1.3	How high the load can go before the service becomes unavailable is measured.

---

[87] Amazon EC2 auto-scaling – See: https://amzn.to/2yQNQl9.

Body of evidence

Story	Impact	Likelihood
Company A had an annual budgeting process which was rigorously adhered to. If it wasn't in the budget, it waited until next year, or required escalation all the way to the CFO. One product failed to properly anticipate how high its load would go during the peak and had significantly degraded performance when end users needed it most. As a result, end users began moving to competitor's products adversely impacting revenue, and company reputation.	High	Medium
Severity		2

Optimize the cost of capacity

PBEA adopts a DevOps philosophy which aligns development and operations under common ownership. Architecture decisions affect not only how software is developed, but how it operates, how it performs, and how much capacity is required to meet performance SLAs. It is only sensible that the cost of capacity factor into architecture decisions especially since development costs are one-time, but Operational Expense (OpEx) is ongoing.

Golden rule measures

	Golden Rule Measures
3.2.1	Load is efficiently balanced across available resources.
3.2.2	Capacity is added (and removed) with minimal engineering costs and delays.
3.2.3	The size of each incremental increase or decrease in capacity is minimized.
3.2.4	The purchase of new capacity over the period is optimized. • Assets with predictable fixed workloads should use low cost options based on volume discounts and/or long-term commitments. • Assets with unpredictable workloads should purchase capacity to minimize long term commitments.
3.2.5	Components scale either horizontally [88] (preferred) and/or vertically [89] while minimizing disruption to service.

---

[88] Horizontal scaling - scale by adding more machines into your pool of resources.

[89] Vertical scaling - scale by adding more power (CPU, RAM) to an existing machine.

Body of evidence

Story	Impact	Likelihood
Company A had a traditional annual budgeting process and ran its own data centers. Additional capacity needs had to be anticipated over a year in advance, with little to no knowledge of revenue targets and customer growth projections, so were almost entirely guesswork, especially for new products. In addition, it could take anywhere from six weeks to six months for new capacity to be added to the data center floor. Purchase orders had to be produced and approved. The data center group liked to aggregate the capacity needs for many products into a single large purchase order to receive a volume discount from the vendor. Larger purchase orders required more senior approval, so took longer to be approved. Once the purchase order was approved, systems had to be ordered, shipped, and arrive on the loading dock. Once the systems arrived, space had to be found in the data center. Sometimes this required new racks to be installed. Sometimes it required old systems to be removed from existing racks. Then the systems had to be installed in a rack and get wired up. The group that installed the systems in the rack and the group that wired the systems into power and the network were unionized, and each group was a different union. Negotiating with the unions took additional time and only the respective unions could perform the tasks they were assigned. Once installed, systems had to be tested, and finally get configured into the scaling group for the asset that needed the additional capacity. Then the operating system image had to be installed and configured. Then the foundation software and application software were installed. Finally, the fully installed and configured system was tested once again and configured into the scaling group for the system asset that needed the additional capacity. Due to the length of time required to add new capacity and the ambiguity associated with predicting capacity needs, most people played it safe and overestimated. But not everybody. Some of company A's products used less than 0.1% of their available capacity on average, while other products did not have enough capacity to meet customer needs, resulting in performance problems and service brownouts. The result was customer dissatisfaction and frustration in both the product management and product development groups.	High	Medium

Story	Impact	Likelihood
Company B implemented an agile budgeting process. Capacity needs were modeled based on user growth and data growth as a whole (not by individual group). End user growth was modeled off revenue projections. As revenue projections changed during the year, so did capacity projections and budget. In addition, company B's products were completely deployed in the cloud, so all capacity was treated as an operational expense (OpEx) and required no up-front capital outlay. The OpEx growth was proportional to user growth, which was proportional to revenue growth, so the model worked. Each product was architected to have just enough capacity (plus a 10% buffer) to meet its SLAs at peak usage, and to add capacity as more customers subscribed to the service. Hence revenue growth offset any OpEx growth. Company B typically spent less than half as much as Company A to run its products.	High	Medium
Company C implemented the same budgeting process as company B, except they architected their products to not only add capacity when needed (just-in-time), but also to remove it when not needed. Company C sold primarily to a U.S. audience and when they modeled the traffic on their systems, they saw a very predictable pattern. System load was about 40% on average, but between 6:00 PM EST and 8:00 AM EST, utilization averaged less than 10%. Between 8:00AM EST and 6:00 PM EST, utilization averaged around 60%, and between 9:00AM and 10:00AM, utilization peaked at 95% load for 10 minutes. This model had some seasonal variation but was otherwise predictable. They re-architected their systems to allow capacity to be both added and removed. Systems such as databases, which maintained state only scaled up, never down. As a result, they were able to meet SLAs running just two web servers at night, six during the day (on average) and ten during the peak(s). Company C was able to reduce their operational expense an additional 20% using this approach to capacity modeling.	High	Medium
Severity		1

Set appropriate limits on auto-scaling

Auto-scaling is the process of adding (or removing) resources automatically, based on algorithms without human intervention. Auto-scaling may be triggered based on different factors (or combinations of factors. The scaling plan for a scaling group should be based on the operational characteristics of the asset and appropriate testing.

Common metrics used to drive auto-scaling include:

- CPU utilization
- Memory utilization
- Request rates
- Queue length
- Load Balancer utilization

Golden rule measures

	Golden Rule Measures
3.3.1	Define scaling groups and scaling plans for all resources.
3.3.2	Set appropriate limit(s), including an absolute maximum and how quickly resources may be added.
3.3.3	Generate alarm(s) when the limit(s) are reached.

Body of evidence

Story	Impact	Likelihood
Company A engaged in a year-long project to migrate its product technology from a traditional data center to the cloud. At the same time, they went through a transformation to agile development methodology and to DevOps. For the most part things got better. Software was released more often and bugs that had been missed during the testing phase were quickly found and fixed. Usage of the product began to grow steadily, which made everybody happy. But because of the increased usage, the product started to have brown-outs during periods of high load (usually at the start of each day). To get to the cloud quicker, only the technology was adapted to the cloud (without re-architecture). Many of the old operational processes were migrated to the DevOps organization but not adapted to the cloud model. This included the process of adding capacity, which was still done manually with a long approval process. A project was initiated in the DevOps group to implement auto-scaling, so that the system would automatically detect that it was underperforming and add capacity during peak periods. As the DevOps function was relatively new, it was not integrated with either the architecture or software development methodology. So, while the auto-scaling implementation went seemingly flawlessly, the group failed to implement absolute maximums on auto-scaling, defaulting instead to firing alarms that sent emails to human operators. Eventually a software release went live that had a memory leak, which under certain circumstances caused the system to completely bog down within seconds. Even though the auto-scaling system fired off multiple alarms indicating that capacity was being added, the human process took time to react and stop the system from adding capacity non-stop. It took additional time to fix the problem, remove the extra capacity and reboot the remaining instances. As such, that month's bill was 'a whopper.'	High	High
Severity		1

CHAPTER 19

Manageable Systems – Golden Rules and Measures

Manageable solutions have hooks to measure operational behavior and adapt dynamically. These systems know whether problems are about to occur before they happen and long before any end user experiences a problem. Issues are resolved before they become issues. A manageable system doesn't just publish operational events and error messages. It also provides the tools to interpret and correlate them, so that incident response and problem resolution can follow quickly.

While manageable systems are almost always fully automated, requiring no human intervention for most scenarios, a fully manageable environment should also include the ability for a suitably authorized operator to "break the glass"[90] and invoke manual override. This provides a quick means for a person who does not usually have privilege to access certain information or functions to gain that access when urgently necessary.

Systems must develop, document, implement, and test break-the-glass procedures that could be used in the event of an emergency. These systems must have clearly-stated and widely understood procedures for allowing access via alternate or conventional methods.

Any actual emergency access must be logged for later review and audit. Typically, a special audit trail is created to monitor such access. Standard access controls should be established, with rules that minimize the number of times this "break-the-glass" access actually occurs.

Break-the-glass access should be based upon pre-staged "emergency" user accounts, managed in a way that can make them available with reasonable administrative overhead. This solution can require operators to log into one of these elevated privilege accounts before access is granted. The break–glass mode is intended to specifically cover emergency cases and should not be used as a replacement for implementing proper automated procedures.

---

[90] "Break the glass" draws its name from breaking the glass to pull a fire alarm, access a fire extinguisher, or access a fire axe. See also: https://bit.ly/2Sc45oK.

	Golden Rule	Severity
4.1	Respond to standard control commands dynamically.	1
4.2	Publish appropriate operational events and error messages.	2
4.3	Publish performance and capacity data.	1
4.4	Maintain a complete inventory of all operational resources.	1

Respond to standard control commands

Any system running in production, no matter how well architected and tested, may have problems that were unanticipated, especially during events that were unexpected. As such, all systems should be built with hooks that would allow a human operator to direct certain actions including the minimal set enumerated below.

Standard control commands include:

- The ability to disable an account.
- The ability to raise or lower the level of diagnostic reporting.
- The ability to gracefully start and stop the service.
- The ability for a properly authorized operator to take manual control of a system.

If all goes well, the system may run for years unattended with all operational issues automatically corrected. But systems are complex and it's hard to anticipate every scenario. The first time you run into one that you never thought could ever happen, you will be glad these hooks are already there.

Golden rule measures

	Golden Rule Measures
4.1.1	System responds to start and stop commands for the entire service or to a single resource.
4.1.2	If an account is disabled, system disables access in an appropriate amount of time.
4.1.3	System allows diagnostic level to be raised or lowered without disconnecting users.

Body of evidence

Story	Impact	Likelihood
Company A released a new product which had a memory leak that was not caught during testing. The bug caused the application server to eventually run out of memory and crash. The applications servers were configured in a scaling group, but when one crashed, it caused a cascade failure that took the entire scaling group off-line resulting in a service outage. If the resource that was running out of memory was rebooted before it failed, the rest of the servers in the scaling group would handle the load until the rebooted server came back on-line, but unfortunately the system did not handle standard control commands, so the DevOps group was unable to reboot the failing server and was unable to add new servers into the scaling group without changing a configuration file and restarting the entire group. This caused a 10-minute service disruption about once per hour until the bug could be found, fixed, and the fix deployed.	High	High
Company B released a mobile application for both iPhone and Android. About a week after deploying the app into the Apple App Store and Google Play, a security issue was discovered. Internet requests were being made over HTTP (rather than HTTPS) potentially exposing sensitive data. The app was updated and re-released. But neither Apple nor Google provide a mechanism to force users to upgrade apps once they were downloaded. Had the app implemented the ability to turn off access until a new version was downloaded, the risk associated with the security issue could have been significantly reduced.	High	High
Severity		1

Publish appropriate operational events and error messages

Security incident response, financial management, and application performance analysis depend on operational events containing the association between the Infrastructure and the asset. If operational events don't contain standard tags these functions will be impaired or cannot be performed. Without operational events, there is a risk of an outage occurring wherein the Incident Response teams cannot track back to a root cause. This situation can lead to longer times to recover, meaning that availability and reliability SLAs are not met. In certain circumstances these can translate into both financial damages and reputational risk as well as unsatisfied customers.

Every system is expected to publish logs that describe events that are occurring within the application flow as well as metrics that can be used to determine if the software is operating within expected levels. Each event is time-stamped and classified as either *informational*, a *warning* or an *error*. It is also best practice that application logs trace events to a transaction ID that can be used to collect the tree of events that were triggered by a single end-user operation of business event (like a data update). By adopting a standard pattern to all metrics and events, logs and metrics may be aggregated together across multiple assets to determine the root cause of a problem.

Golden rule measures

	Golden Rule Measures
4.2.1	Operational events are published that support troubleshooting during both testing and live operation.
4.2.2	Operational events and error messages can be easily traced to the individual who owns correcting the problem.

Body of evidence

Story	Impact	Likelihood
Company A did not define standards for error messages or operational events, allowing each group to do what it thought best. As such, some assets streamed information messages for every little thing it did, and others barely logged anything at all. When an error occurred, sometimes it referred to the asset, sometimes it only referred to the name of the original source code module, which had changed names several times over the years. Initially, things worked okay. The organization was small, and individuals created little 'cheat sheets' that let the people who were monitoring live operations, know that when the error message said 'this,' alert that group. But as the organization grew, and people left or changed jobs, the tribal knowledge was lost, and troubleshooting became harder and harder. Eventually, standards were set, and a complete redesign of the way errors were handled had to be done, at significant cost and time. Everybody agreed that in retrospect, a few hours of design up front would have saved months or years of redesign and rework in the end.	Medium	High
Severity		2

> Events initiated by an end user are assigned a Transaction ID that is carried in every call to a system service resulting from the initiating event. Application logs should include the Transaction ID, allowing the call-tree to be linked back to the original event. The same approach should be taken if the initiating event is a data update.

> *Tribal Knowledge*[91] should never be part of a diagnostic procedure. Everybody should consider it their responsibility to properly document any discovery of tribal knowledge.

Publish performance and capacity data

Performance is generally defined as response-time and latency (see Chapter 8: Architecting Responsive Solutions). Performance data is a metric indicating how well an asset is meeting its performance SLA.

Capacity, on the other hand, has to do with the amount of resource that is allocated to a service. By resources, we do not mean just the number of servers and how much network bandwidth. We also include resources inside the server such as CPU and memory utilization as well as storage utilization. Capacity maps one-to-one with cost.

Without publishing performance and capacity data there is the risk of a performance issue occurring that cannot track back to a root cause. This can lead to SLAs not being met. In certain circumstances these can translate into both financial damages and reputational risk as well as unsatisfied customers.

Golden rule measures

	Golden Rule Measures
4.3.1	Performance and capacity data needed to support SLA measurement is published.
4.3.2	Performance and capacity data needed for troubleshooting performance issues is published.
4.3.3	Performance and capacity data needed to support capacity planning and auto-scaling is published.

---

[91] Tribal knowledge is any unwritten information that is not commonly known by others within a company and not written down in an accessible location. This term is used most when referencing information that may need to be known by others to produce quality product or service. (See: https://bit.ly/2SaLY2x)

Body of evidence

Story		Impact	Likelihood
Company A was a small company that was acquired by Company B, a much larger company. While company B had standards for publishing performance and capacity data, the much smaller Company A did not. During the *technical due diligence* process, the defect was noted, and money was added into the acquisition business case to correct the deficiency. But meeting financial goals were prioritized way ahead of aligning operational processes, so products were integrated and migrated into strategic data centers, while duplicative roles were eliminated first. At the end of the first milestone, the organization's traditional operations group became responsible for the live operations of the acquired product, but since that product did not produce performance or capacity metrics, the first ones to realize that it was performing poorly were the end users.		High	High
Severity			1

Maintain a complete inventory of all operational resources

A Resource Inventory lists all compute, network, storage, and software as a service (SAAS) resources supporting each asset. In the cloud, this is essentially what gets billed; if resources are tagged with an AssetID, this inventory should be relatively easy to maintain.

Golden rule measures

	Golden Rule Measures
4.4.1	An inventory of all operational resources is maintained.
4.4.2	Each resource is traceable back to the individual and team immediately responsible for the resource and to the asset and asset owner.

Body of evidence

Story	Impact	Likelihood
Company A commonly used open source software, including the Apache Struts library. Company A's CMDB had a complete list of all the computing systems on its network, but over the years lost track of who was responsible for the system or even which product is supported. It was estimated that 10% - 15% of the servers running in the data center were running products that had zero users. But nobody could be sure, so they were left running. A handful of systems had an old version of the Apache Struts library installed, which had a known vulnerability. Since nobody owned the systems, nobody patched them either. Bad guys found the vulnerability before the organization and installed malware on the vulnerable servers, which were then used to reach out and attack other servers on the network. All it takes is one neglected server among thousands (or even millions) to provide an attack vector that can lead to every data center being infected, resulting in massive financial loss and/or penalty.	High	High
Company B maintained a CMDB that was thought to be about 80% accurate. Everybody knew it was not fully dependable, but there was never enough time and money to correct it. In addition, new products and services were being released at an ever-increasing rate and to support the new agile delivery method, many of the data center processes were being bypassed because they were too manual and too slow. As the CMDB became less and less dependable, it became increasingly difficult to trace server slow-downs and failures back to the individual who cared enough and had the budget authority to get the problem fixed. Company B's service steadily degraded until it made the decision to completely reorganize and transition away from shared central ownership, to full service ownership and DevOps. The transition took almost 24 months to complete and during this time, customer satisfaction hit an all-time low.	High	High

Story	Impact	Likelihood
Company C was organized with independent product groups, but a central shared resource that ran the data centers. The product groups were responsible for the initial purchase of all hardware and software for deploying the product into the data center, but once it was deployed, the data center group owned the budget for hardware maintenance, software maintenance, and for capacity upgrades. The servers they bought were depreciated over three years, and after the three-year depreciation cycle, the servers were replaced with brand new servers. Part of the justification for refreshing the servers every three years, was that the server vendor increased the cost they charged for maintenance, so it was "cheaper" to just refresh (or so the vendor's sales executive claimed). Over the years, the data center group, to manage an ever-tighter budget, came to depend on the server refresh to manage the cost of capacity increases, because due to Moore's Law,[92] in the next refresh, they could buy bigger servers, with more CPUs for the same amount of money. Unbeknownst to the data center group, many of the servers they were refreshing ran databases that were licensed based on the total number of physical cores of the underlying hardware regardless of virtualization and how many virtual cores were actually allocated to running the database software. The issue was known to the asset owner, but as the asset owner did not own the underlying hardware provided by the data center shared service, the asset owner was unaware that this was happening. During an internal license verification project, it was discovered that Microsoft SQL Server had been inadvertently over deployed (by hundreds of licenses). Had the issue been caught during a formal audit rather than an internal license review, the cost would have run into the $millions.	High	High
Severity		1

---

[92] Moore's Law – See: https://bit.ly/1Nx7yBk.

CHAPTER 20

Reliable Systems – Golden Rules and Measures

Reliable solutions do what is expected when expected. They provide measurable service in terms of responsiveness, performance, availability, and dependability [93] during normal operation, as well as in a failure scenario or in the event of a disaster. Each service should have a Service Level Agreement (SLA). System level reliability generally implies no single points of failure for that system asset. Under extreme circumstances, where there may be multiple independent system failures, a service may remain reliable by treating the case as a site failure. You cannot test away all problems, so a reliable architecture makes problems easy to find and fix when they occur. Architecture issues affecting reliability are the most insidious, so find them as early in the process as possible and:

1. Design and build systems with failure in mind. Nothing is 100% reliable.
2. Always think about scaling and graceful degradation of service as utilization approaches capacity.
3. Monitor SLAs (your own and those of all services upon which you depend). Alarm when SLAs are out-of-bounds.

	Golden Rule	Severity
5.1	Record all requests and measure adherence to your SLA.	1
5.2	Record all requests made to other assets and measure the dependent assets adherence to its SLA.	2
5.3	Continue to meet SLA obligations in the event of a single failure.	1
5.4	Continue to meet SLA obligations in the event of a site failure.	2
5.5	Ensure that functional testing of the solution, includes at least one test case covering each of the capabilities or features supported.	2
5.6	Handle hard failures (unrecoverable) and soft failures (recoverable) appropriately.	2
5.7	Ensure all production changes are repeatable and auditable.	1

---

[93] By dependability, we mean: low error rates and predictable behavior.

Record all requests and measure adherence to your SLA

Each system asset should have a service levels agreement which clearly defines the individual metrics. Each system asset should measure its adherence to its own SLA and generate alarms if it is not being met. Not every asset need be treated the same, even when they are integrated into the same business capability. Testing should determine whether the system asset can meet its SLA; operational monitoring should verify that it actually does.

Golden rule measures

	Golden Rule Measures
5.1.1	A response time and dependability metric are defined for each public API as part of the SLA.
5.1.2	An Availability metric is defined for the asset as a whole.
5.1.3	A Recovery Time Objective (RTO) and a Recovery Point Objective (RPO) are defined for the asset as a whole.
5.1.4	Appropriate limits based on reasonable use cases are defined. Limits might include the total number of records that may be returned in a single request, or the total amount of time a query may run.
5.1.5	Regular data backups are performed as necessary to achieve the SLA.
5.1.6	The asset is tested to ensure it can meet its SLA, within financial constraints.[94]
5.1.7	The asset is monitored during live operations to ensure that it continues to meet its SLA. Alarms are generated if service levels are not being met.

Body of evidence

Story	Impact	Likelihood
Company A fully documented its Recovery Time Objective (RTO) and Recovery Point Objective (RPO) but did not test for them. As a result, they did not actually meet the documented RPO when the service went live.	Medium	High
Company B tested its SLA before releasing the new version, but its test environment did not mirror the production environment. The tests passed, but during live operations, the service failed.	High	High

---

[94] In this context, financial constraints are assumed to cover all environments, but the main point is that you should not let any system continue to add capacity beyond a reasonable limit and that reasonable limit should be enough to meet your SLA.

Story	Impact	Likelihood
Company C's *CustomerAccount* service was having performance problems. The service started slowing down until it eventually became unusable. It was determined that some other user of the service requested a list of 100,000 accounts with full details. The *CustomerAccount* service could handle no more than 5,000 accounts in a single request and still meet its response-time SLA. In addition, there was no legitimate business use case that required more than 2,000 accounts to be requested at a time. However, the CustomerAccount asset did not set any request limit in its SLA nor did it implement request throttling. When it received the request for 100,000 accounts it attempted to retrieve all 100,000. Eventually, the request consumed all resources, causing the server to fail without returning any data. The calling service hit its time-out and retried the request, which took down the next server in the scaling group. And so on until all servers had failed taking down the service and causing an outage. Had the account service set a limit (like 2000 accounts per request) and returned an error for the out-of-bounds request, the issue would have been averted. Had the requester implemented an exponential back-off algorithm, the service failure would have been avoided.	High	High
Severity		1

Record all calls made to other assets and measure the dependent assets' adherence to their SLA

Failure to analyze the upstream and downstream effects of an asset may result in the unexpected inability to meet other performance, availability, and recoverability service levels.

Golden rule measures

	Golden Rule Measures
5.2.1	The SLAs of all dependent systems are measured and tracked.
5.2.2	If a dependent system fails to meet its SLA, an alarm is generated.
5.2.3	If the failure of a dependent system to meet its SLA causes this system to not meet its SLA, a different alarm is generated.

Body of evidence

Story	Impact	Likelihood
Company A had just finished the migration of its core search engine from a mainframe to a modern scalable architecture, which was deployed across two of its data centers. Testing had gone well, and initial customer reaction was positive. As more customers came onto the system, an intermittent slow-down in search response-time began to be noticed. There were no operational alarms but there were customer complaints. Problem resolution calls were scheduled with at least one senior individual from every system represented. But each call ended without identifying the root cause of the problem. Each system owner looked through their own logs and metrics claiming that "their" system was operating properly. After a few days of this, technology and product management got together and decided that the normal problem resolution process was not working. So, they called for a "war room." This meant that one or more senior representatives from each system in the search pipeline had to sit in the same room until the problem was solved. The first thing that was recognized was that each system owner only had statistics for their own system. There were no formal SLAs defined, so the interpretation of the logs as to whether they represented correct behavior was up to everyone to decide for themselves. In addition, the organizational mentality was such that people feared for their jobs and nobody wanted to be at fault, even if it meant the customer problem was not found and fixed. Since the network layer and the storage subsystem were "part of" the search pipeline, but were accessed through operating system calls, a very expensive consultant from the Operating System (OS) vendor was also brought in, to sit in the war room and interpret the OS logs. Each time one of the system representatives noticed a "blip" in their log file, they would call it out and everybody else in the room would scan back through their own log files to see if they noticed anything "odd" around the same time. After about a week of this process as the individuals began to understand how their systems behaved in the context of the others, a slow-down event occurred that each group was able to trace to a log file entry. In the end, the problem turned out to be an intermittent overload between the network and disk subsystems that was finally discovered because an Operating system call underneath the database subsystem timed-out. Had there been clearly defined SLAs as to the expectation of disk retrieval performance under specified load conditions, the problem could have been found in 7 minutes, rather than 7 days.	High	Medium
Severity		2

Continue to meet SLA obligations in the event of a single failure

A single resource failure means that one thing failed, usually a server (or a disk or a network device). In general, platforms and assets should be architected with no single points of failure, meaning that there should never be a service outage in the event of a single resource failure. This is only practical given the sheer magnitude of resources that make up any modern product. Components such as disk drives have moveable parts that eventually wear down and eventually fail. Component failure is pretty much guaranteed to happen in any modern system. (See Chapter 8: Failure Scenarios).

Golden rule measures

	Golden Rule Measure
5.3.1	If there is a single resource failure (e.g. a database), the system continues to meet all SLA obligations.

Body of evidence

Story	Impact	Likelihood
Company A built its systems with failure in mind, or so they thought. They spent a lot of money to build at least two data centers in each region and a lot more money creating complete duplicate infrastructure in each data center as well as between data centers. There was four of everything. What could go wrong? The answer, of course, is "Murphy's Law." Each server group was configured so that it connected to two core network switches, but to save money, each computer system only had one network card. So, the server group was split into the "A" servers, which connected to the "A" switch and the "B" servers which connected to the "B" switch. Availability testing was done to ensure that if a server failed there was sufficient capacity to handle peak load. As luck would have it, the network switch was the component that failed, which "took out" half the servers at once. Even with half capacity, the system kept working, except when there was a momentary peak, at which point the other switch overloaded and the rest of the servers failed causing a service outage. During this time, operations staff was "working on the problem," but had not forced the service to switch to the other data center, because switching data centers required that every product switch at once, so people felt there was just too much risk involved. Nobody really trusted the *disaster recovery* processes. Had fail-over been automatic the outage could have been averted. Had switch failure been part of the high-availability testing, the operations staff would have been better prepared.	High	High

Story	Impact	Likelihood
In October 2018, Lion Air flight JT610 plunged into the Java Sea thirteen minutes after takeoff, killing all 189 people on board. The cause of the failure was isolated to a new system on the new Boeing 737 Max that was unknown to the pilots and was designed to automatically correct the planes angle-of-attack to prevent a stall. The prevailing theory on the cause of the crash was that faulty signals from a sensor caused the plane to relentlessly push the nose of the plane down even as the pilot fought to pull back on the stick and bring the nose back up. Following is an extract of an article from the Seattle Times[95]. There is another follow-up in the New York Times.[96] The fact that the plane's nose could be automatically and repeatedly pushed down due to one false signal shocked Peter Lemme, a former Boeing flight controls engineer, who said it looks like a design flaw. "To contemplate commanding the (horizontal tail to pitch the jet's) nose down clearly is a major concern. For it to have been triggered by something as small as a sensor error is staggering," Lemme said. "It means somebody didn't do their job. There's going to be hell to pay for that." Likewise, Dwight Schaeffer, a former Boeing electronics engineer and senior manager who oversaw development of systems, including the 737's stall management computer, said the brief description in the FAA's airworthiness directive "blows me away." "Usually you never have a **single fault** that can put you in danger," said Schaeffer. "I've never seen any such system." A former Boeing vice president — who asked for anonymity, — said he is also surprised at the suggestion in the FAA wording of "a **single point of failure**" that could bring down an aircraft.	High	High
Severity		1

---

[95] The Seattle Times – See: https://bit.ly/2Txn75y.

[96] The New York Times – See: https://nyti.ms/2MNcPM1.

Continue to meet SLA obligations in the event of a site failure

A site failure is defined as all the asset instances located in a single site (i.e. data center or availability zone) failing at the same time. As with a single asset instance failure, a physical implementation that spans sites should be at least partially resilient to a site failure. (See Chapter 8: Failure Scenarios).

Golden rule measures

	Golden Rule Measure
5.4.1	If an entire site fails (for example one AWS availability zone), the system continues to meet all SLA obligations.

Body of evidence

Story	Impact	Likelihood
On February 28, 2017, many websites went down at the same time. A simple human error at Amazon S3, caused an outage.[97] The S3 billing system was behaving sluggishly and was being debugged. During the process, someone entered a command to remove a few servers from one of the subsystems, but typed the command in wrong, taking down many more servers than expected. Many websites depended on the S3 service and when it failed, they failed as well. But while some Amazon S3 customers fell victim to the outage, others did not. Netflix was one of the companies that survived with no loss of service. Back in 2012, a power outage at Amazon caused Netflix to suffer three hours of downtime. So, Netflix engineers began to systematically eliminate *single points of failure* in their architecture. A 2014 report showed that the cost of one hour of downtime for Netflix was about $200,000. The organization lost revenue from an outage whether it was their own fault or the fault of their cloud provider. Service outages were bad for business and tarnished the brand, regardless of fault. The updated Netflix cloud architecture was spread across 12 regions globally, each of which has multiple *availability zones*. Each zone had at least one data center along with associated power, networking, and connectivity. Because these zones are connected to each other, Netflix had been able to design their cloud infrastructure in such a way that their applications switched between zones automatically when failures occurred, avoiding service disruptions.	High	Medium

---

[97] 2017 Amazon S3 outage – See: https://bit.ly/2taqF22.

Story	Impact	Likelihood
Company A ran two data centers with a high bandwidth link between them. One of the data centers was considered the "live" data center and the other was considered the backup or "D/R" data center. Twice per year, as per company policy, the operations group ran a D/R test. They would have run the test quarterly, but each test took almost half a year to plan, so twice a year was about the best they could do. The process for running the test was to first kill the link between the two data centers, then product by product, switch to the D/R site and test that the product was still running. Since almost every product required the switch to be done manually by following a run book, this took quite a while. Invariably, one product would not survive the test, and a long, detailed report would be written. The report would be distributed, but very little would be done, since the problematic products were generally the ones "on life support" (i.e. there was no new investment in the product and no assigned development team). A few months after the organization released its new flagship product, a D/R test was done. Because the product was brand new and had very few customers comparatively, it was near the bottom of the list of products to be manually switched over to the new data center after the inter-data-center link was cut. The new product was architected to be live/stand-by. Each system that took in new data, streamed updates to the backup site, where duplicate systems would process in parallel with the live site. Periodically the live and stand-by systems would verify that the databases remained synchronized. During this test, which was the first one for the new product, when the inter-data-center link was cut, the synchronization queue backed up and the live product failed. Since nobody had done the manual switch to the backup site, this caused a complete service outage to the organization's brand-spanking-new flagship product.	High	Medium
Severity		2

Ensure that functional testing includes at least one test case covering each of the capabilities and features supported

Functional Testing is the process of ensuring that an asset delivers all agreed-upon business functionality. Other types of testing include: non-functional testing (e.g. performance testing or resilience testing), and security testing (e.g. penetration testing). See Chapter 8: Architecting testable solutions.

Golden rule measures

	Golden Rule Measures
5.5.1	New functionality and/or changed functionality is covered by at least one test case verified before deployment to production, and the results retained for independent review.
5.5.2	All required functional tests pass before the asset is deployed to production.
5.5.3	All test results are maintained for independent review.

Body of evidence

Story	Impact	Likelihood
Company A had no formal standards for functional testing and no real way of measuring whether every feature that was exposed to customers functioned as defined. The organization's premiere product was built from over 50 independent services that were individually developed and released by over 20 different teams. Each team tested its service thoroughly and when it was satisfied, released into production. The end-user experience was fully tested only when an upgrade to the user-facing application was released, but when an internal system was released, impact on the end user may or may not have been tested, depending on whether the development group believed what they changed should or should not have had an impact. Formal placement-of-function was considered a nice-to-have, not required, and as such, there was no end-to-end view of whether a change to one asset impacted another or the end user. As such, it was common for end users to find bugs and issues appearing and disappearing with little or no communication from their sales representative.	Medium	High
Severity		2

Handle unrecoverable failures and recoverable failures appropriately

An error implies either that something unexpected occurred, or something expected, but known to be improper occurred (e.g. making a request to a database that doesn't respond). Some errors are recoverable, some are unrecoverable. A recoverable error is one that should be investigated but does not indicate a complete failure. An unrecoverable error generally indicates that the system should be stopped, and replaced, because it will likely continue to fail. A server crash is an example of an unrecoverable error. Hardware failures and running out of memory are also generally unrecoverable.

Golden rule measures

	Golden Rule Measures
5.6.1	Recoverable failures are differentiated from unrecoverable failures.
5.6.2	Recoverable failures are handled appropriately.
5.6.3	Unrecoverable failures are handled appropriately.

Body of evidence

Story	Impact	Likelihood
Company A built an application which used a service provided by Company B to retrieve a logo for the end user's company. This logo was displayed on the application's logon page. Logo display was a non-critical function so testing of the functionality was light. One day, Company B's logo service failed. Company B's SLA guaranteed 98% availability and 3 – 10 hours to restore the service after being notified of an issue. So, even though the service failed, they were well within their SLA, and did not treat the problem as urgent. Unfortunately for Company A, this dependency failure was not tested, and their logon service failed, making their application unusable, which was a critical failure for Company A.	Medium	High
Severity		2

Ensure all production changes are repeatable and auditable

A manual change is one that is executed by a person either using a script or ad-hoc. While a human operator following a script (or a run-book) is usually repeatable, an automated process is guaranteed to be repeatable. There are tradeoffs. As processes become better defined and predictable, they should be automated. But whether executed by a human operator following a run-book, or an automated script, it is imperative that any change to a production environment be repeatable and auditable.

Golden rule measures

	Golden Rule Measures
5.7.1	Production changes can be repeated with little or no opportunity for human error.
5.7.2	Production changes are reviewed before being applied or afterwards.

Body of evidence

Story	Impact	Likelihood
Company A architected its systems to be highly reliable and scalable. Shortly after a new release, one of the servers in a scaling group failed, but the service did not go down since there were sufficient additional servers in the group to carry the load; especially since it was the evening and usage was low. The operator on-call analyzed the log files and determined that the root cause of the problem was that the server ran out of file handles. So, the operator went into the system and tweaked an operating system variable to increase the number of file handles. The server came back up and the system ran fine (or so the operator thought). He filed the issue, but as it was 'fixed' and there was no *incident* it was treated with no urgency. In the morning, the night shift operator handed off to his colleagues and went home thinking he had 'saved the day.' Unfortunately for Company A, the root cause of the problem was a bug in the software that did not properly close files. The next day, as people got into work and traffic increased, all the other servers in the group failed almost simultaneously and the service went down, causing an outage. Had the operator applied the change in an automated fashion and properly assessed the root cause of the problem, the outage could have been averted.	High	High

Story	Impact	Likelihood
Company B implemented high availability for one of its core databases by deploying a redundant database in a second availability zone. The two databases were configured in a live / stand-by configuration where one database handled all requests, but the data in the backup database was constantly synchronized with the live database. The DevOps group wanted to check configuration changes on the database, so they experimented on the backup database. Their reasoning was: It wasn't being used for anything, right? Except that it was. It was the backup in the event of a failure. One day, the inevitable happened and the live database failed. Request traffic was switched to the backup, which initially handled the incoming load. Unfortunately, over the course of multiple experimental configuration changes the backup database configuration had meandered so far from the original configuration that it too failed and the service went down.	High	High
Severity		1

CHAPTER 21

Simple Systems – Golden Rules and Measures

Simple solutions have clear responsibilities with no gaps and no overlap. They tessellate. They have proper placement-of-function and duplicate as little functionality as possible based on organizational reality. They follow well-defined patterns and blueprints.

	Golden Rule	Severity
6.1	Do not use unmaintained assets or deprecated APIs.	1
6.2	Do not couple an asset to an environment.	2
6.3	One asset, one team.	1
6.4	Follow placement-of-function (PoF).	2
6.5	Package code to facilitate independent releases.	2
6.6	Minimize code duplication.	2

Do not use unmaintained assets or deprecated APIs

There will always be assets and APIs that have more debt than is worth paying off and should be replaced rather than repaired. As platforms and organizations grow, the number of systems that are unmaintained or under-maintained grows as well. If an asset has zero investment budget and has had its maintenance budget consistently cut over the years, it likely falls into this category. There may be no alternative asset, but at a minimum, building a new asset that depends on one which is not being adequately maintained needs to be captured as technical debt. The same goes for using deprecated APIs. PBEA defines a deprecated API as one that has been replaced by a new API with equivalent or greater functionality.

Golden rule measures

Number	Golden Rule Measures
6.1.1	Assets with new investment do not use functionality or APIs offered by assets that are unmaintained.
6.1.2	Assets with new investment do not use deprecated APIs.
6.1.3	If an unmaintained asset or a deprecated API is used, it is identified on architecture diagrams and architecture debt is assessed.

Body of evidence

Story	Impact	Likelihood
Company A has been a technology company for 50+ years. Their first product was built on a mainframe and predated the Internet. They built and deployed their own hardware and managed their own telecommunications lines to their customers. When the Internet started becoming popular, they built a new Internet-based application that ran on a PC, replacing their need for proprietary hardware or telecommunications management. To get to market quickly, the new application was built using all the old mainframe infrastructure. The organization incrementally replaced the mainframe infrastructure over the next few years but was still unable to retire the expensive mainframe because internal editors and salespeople were still using the legacy product and had no alternatives. The organization had carefully tracked all the interfaces used by its customer-facing products but forgot to track all the internal applications and tools that depended on the legacy mainframe.	High	High
Company B built a new strategic system. To meet aggressive timeframes, it was decided to pull data from an existing legacy system rather than go directly to the strategic source. This resulted in a prolonged and complex project to retire the legacy system, given the complex spider-web of dependencies. Additionally, as there was no investment in the legacy systems, it became the source of performance and reliability problems for the assets that depended on them.	High	High

Story	Impact	Likelihood
An article published in TechNewsWorld[98] describes how legacy systems intertwined in the infrastructure of companies' operation become the root causes of regulation issues, security issues, performance issues, and lack of agility.	High	High
Severity	1	

Do not couple an asset to an environment

Assets need to be able to run in any environment (Development, Testing, Production) with minimal changes to configuration definitions. For example, an asset that hardcodes the absolute addresses of its API providers would be tightly coupled to a specific environment (which is bad).

Golden rule measures

	Golden Rule Measures
6.2.1	Any parameter that might be tied to a specific environment (which could include the URL of APIs it calls) is configurable so it can easily change during a staged deployment.
6.2.2	External interfaces, including user interfaces, are exposed via an infrastructure-agnostic addresses, such as DNS aliases, not IP addresses or host names.

Body of evidence

Story	Impact	Likelihood
Asset A's interface was explicitly tied to a specific IP address. When the hardware failed, resolution required the machine to be rebuilt and reconfigured manually. With the external interface address coupled to the hardware the effect was compounded as all the API consumers requiring revectoring the API call to the IP address of the replacement machine. The result was an availability impact (possibly customer visible) and increased operational expense to resolve.	High	Medium

---

[98] TechNewsWorld – See: https://bit.ly/2SgzExR.

Story	Impact	Likelihood
Asset B's code contained hardwired host names (for multiple internal and external system dependencies). To migrate the system from the *development* environment to the *testing* environment and from test to *production*, all these settings had to be changed and the code recompiled. During this process, a setting was missed and was left pointing to the development environment rather than to production. A second setting was not changed to reflect the new host name that asset B was deployed on. The end-result was several failed rollouts, incorrect functionality, and incorrect data.	High	Medium
Asset C's code contained hardwired host names. When recompiling the code to change from the testing environment to the production environment, either the wrong version of the code was retrieved, and/or the compilation activity was not 100% successful. Things that worked in the testing environment no longer worked in production. This resulted in increased operational costs and missing the release window, which delayed the launch of new revenue-generating features.	High	Medium
Severity		2

One asset, one team

In any large organization there will be dependencies that have to be managed. There will also be the temptation to align organizations by skillsets (e.g. the database team). Don't succumb to these temptations. **The bigger an organization gets, the more important it is to clearly define ownership.** Yes, most enterprises will have an organizational matrix that blurs responsibility and accountability across groups– but that does not necessarily imply a problem as long as, for assets, we adopt the *one asset, one team* model. For each asset, we define exactly what is owned and by whom, with no overlapping responsibilities or accountabilities. PBEA defines the role of *asset owner* to be this single owner of an asset end-to-end. The asset owner is responsible and accountable for all aspects of the asset lifecycle from ideation to operations. They may depend on others for services, but if the asset fails to meet its SLA, it's the asset owner's responsibility to fix it. If the asset goes down at 3 AM, it's the asset owner's responsibility, even if it was the disk array that failed, and the disk array has to be fixed by an operations group that does not directly report to the asset owner.

Golden rule measures

	Golden Rule Measures
6.3.1	One team is responsible for all aspects of development including: system architecture, system design, API design, security design, software development, testing, release, and maintenance.
6.3.2	One team is responsible for all aspects of operation including: deployment, operational monitoring, operational security, SLA adherence, incident response, problem resolution, administration, and reporting.
6.3.3	The development team and operations team are responsible to the asset owner.
6.3.4	Compute resources are not shared by more than one asset (i.e. assets adopt a shared-nothing[99] architecture).

Body of evidence

Story	Impact	Likelihood
Company A was organized with individual product development teams, but with a central, shared data center organization that was responsible for managing all the hardware in the data center as well as deployment and operations of all products running in the data center. To avoid the cost of buying new hardware, the data center group deployed a new asset onto the same hardware as an existing asset (without virtualization), because the hardware seemed to have spare capacity. Instead of abstracting away the hardware through virtualization, it was felt to be quicker to just share the box. Over time, the two systems outgrew the capacity of the box, but as they were not logically separated, upscaling became politically complicated. Neither of the product teams felt that they were responsible for the cost of the upgrade. In addition, the physical coupling between the assets hindered agility by forcing monolithic release of changes. Scaling flexibility was compromised because upgrading the shared infrastructure had to be negotiated across multiple teams. Updating the version of the operating system was also complicated by the fact that one team wanted the newest version of the operating system in their next release and the other did not have the resources to perform the necessary testing by the deadline.	High	High
Severity		1

---

[99] Shared-nothing architecture – See: https://bit.ly/2SpfWPN.

Follow Placement of Function (PoF)

Placement-of-function is the process for clearly mapping business requirements to the integrated set of assets that deliver those requirements (See: Chapter 1: Placement of Function).

Golden rule measures

	Golden Rule Measure
6.4.1	A PoF artifact exists that defines the business requirements and user stories this asset is responsible for delivering (in association with other assets).
6.4.2	The architecture and implementation follow placement-of-function.

Body of evidence

Story	Impact	Likelihood
Asset A wished to use functionality already implemented in asset B. Asset B did not expose a clean and simple interface to consume the desired functionality. Asset A ended up duplicating the functionality in asset B, since they couldn't wait for asset B to expose it, even though building a new interface in asset B was 1/10th the cost of duplicating the functionality. This resulted in additional initial cost to upgrade asset A and every time the duplicated functionality had to be updated, it had to be updated in two places. Initial cost was higher, OpEx was higher, ongoing support cost was higher, but time-to-market drove behavior, so the duplication was done (and it was not an isolated case). Over time the two implementations diverged, resulting in inconsistent behavior depending upon which route was taken.	High	Medium
Severity		2

Package code to facilitate independent releases

Physical packaging and deployment boundaries enable loose coupling that simplify lifecycle and release management. Use of dynamic libraries and services enable clients and providers to evolve independently of one another, so long as compatibility is maintained. This, in turn, avoids the need to perform costly lockstep deployment of multiple interdependent components at the same time.

Poor physical separation of concerns increases overall system coupling and often results in monolithic solutions that are costly to adapt to varying degrees of change.

Golden rule measures

	Golden Rule Measure
6.5.1	Code is packaged so that independent assets and modules may be released and promoted to production independently.

Body of evidence

Story	Impact	Likelihood
Company A had a small software development group with very few formal processes. This worked very well while they were small. The whole system was deployed across a very small number of servers and the code that was deployed to each server group was built as a unit with little or no logical separation between the components other than how they were deployed physically. As the organization grew, portions of the system were split off so that they could be owned by different development groups who could operate somewhat independently, but since the code was not packaged logically, the various groups still had to stay closely coordinated when it was release time. This slowed down the whole process. As the group grew, the process slowed down even more until they were finally forced to stop all new feature development and rearchitect the underlying organization of the system, as well as how it was packaged and released. During the feature hiatus, tensions between product management and product development grew, even though in the beginning they were one happy team.	Medium	High
Severity		2

Minimize code duplication and complexity

Code duplication is not inherently bad, but left unchecked and unmeasured, it almost always leads to increased code complexity. Code complexity **is** inherently bad, but it is often hard to measure. There are several industry standard metrics for code complexity. Each has its promoters and its detractors. Like with overall technical debt, code duplication should be balanced with the needs of the business.

Golden rule measures

	Golden Rule Measures
6.6.1	A method has been defined to measure code complexity and duplication. What is considered 'acceptable' has been defined.
6.6.2	Code complexity has been measured for this system and regularly updated.
6.6.3	The system meets minimally acceptable standards for complexity.

Body of evidence

Story	Impact	Likelihood
In one development group of Company A, a software engineer implemented a new feature by taking a file containing the implementation of a similar feature, copying it, renaming the global declarations, and slightly modifying the implementation. Now the product had two large files that were almost identical apart from some naming. During a code review, the duplication was identified, but the developer said he did not have time to do it any other way and by the way "it worked, so what's the problem?" A few bugs were found in one version of the code and they had to be fixed in two places decreasing maintainability and increasing cost. Still it was considered "no big deal." But as the product aged and grew, new software engineers were added to the group and others left. The group's onboarding process was "go read the code," which they did. Following what was done before, new software developers duplicated code modules when it was quicker, resulting in a very large code base, a large fraction of which was duplicative. The effort required to maintain the code grew quickly, so quickly in fact that to stay within budget, code maintenance was outsourced. Things got worse, not better. Budget cuts led to a large amount of	High	Medium

Story	Impact	Likelihood
the development, as well as the maintenance being outsourced. This did not end well. Eventually the organization insourced the software development, but by that time the quality of the code had gotten so out-of-hand that the entire codebase for the product had to be systematically rewritten at great additional expense.		
In software engineering, Don't Repeat Yourself (DRY) is a principle formulated by Andy Hunt and Dave Thomas.[100] It is aimed at reducing repetition, replacing it with abstractions. The alternative to DRY is typically referred to as WET, which is commonly taken to stand for either "write everything twice," "we enjoy typing" or "waste everyone's time."[101]	High	Medium
The *broken windows theory*[102] is a criminological theory that visible signs of crime, anti-social behavior and civil disorder create an urban environment that encourages further crime and disorder, including serious crimes. The theory thus suggests that policing methods that target minor crimes such as vandalism, public drinking and fare evasion help to create an atmosphere of order and lawfulness, thereby preventing more serious crimes. Applied to software development, the broken windows theory suggests that writing bad code leads to more bad code and that good code, in proximity to bad code, over the course of time, becomes bad code.	High	Medium
Severity	2	

---

[100] Hunt, Andrew; Thomas, David (1999). The Pragmatic Programmer: From Journeyman to Master (1 ed.). USA: Addison-Wesley. ISBN 978-0201616224.

[101] DRY architecture – See: https://bit.ly/1hQ65ME.

[102] Broken windows theory – See: https://bit.ly/1wl25HA.

CHAPTER **22**

Modular Systems – Golden Rules and Measures

Modularity has many benefits. System assets have well-defined boundaries providing encapsulation. In a loosely-coupled architecture, crossing the encapsulation boundary can only happen via well-defined APIs, which adhere to the rigors of proper versioning, strong type checking, and input sanitization. Loose coupling allows assets to upgrade independently of each other and in any order. A loosely coupled interface cements a contractual relationship between a service provider and a service consumer. This is often called the interface contract (See Chapter 2: Service Interfaces). A Service Level Agreement (SLA) defines the terms of the interface contract (See Chapter 2: System Asset SLA).

Modularity is a key enabling factor for reusability, extensibility, and scalability. Modular assets employ the rule of *Separation of Concerns*. They divide labor among encapsulated components, each of which is loosely-coupled via well-defined interfaces.

An asset is intended to be a complete black box to all callers of its external interfaces. Dependent assets need not know how an API is implemented (not even the language it was written in), and the definition of the API should avoid any coupling to its implementation.

	Golden Rule	Severity
7.1	Expose and consume only well-defined external interfaces.	1
7.2	Manage and version control external interfaces.	1
7.3	Do not couple external interfaces to their implementation.	2
7.4	Handle retries appropriately.	2

Expose and consume only well-defined external interfaces

Modularity forms the basis for loose coupling which makes complex systems simpler to understand, maintain and change. This can be likened to the *single responsibility principle*[103] for Object Oriented (OO) design. Modularity also minimizes redundancy and increases the likelihood of reuse at various levels of abstraction. Failure to enforce the use of well-defined Interfaces generally leads to monolithic systems that are brittle, costly to maintain and costly to extend. Even relatively simple changes to monolithic systems become increasingly complex and error prone over time. These systems are often described as being a *big ball of mud*.[104]

Interfaces that attempt to be all things to all parties by continually adding optional parameters which fundamentally change their behavior rarely deliver as expected.

Poor choice of abstraction often lies at the root of complex interfaces that impede adoption and are error prone to use. In some cases, early abstractions give way under the weight of increasingly complex requirements. A common pitfall is to continually extend the early abstractions until they break, when adding new broader abstractions may have better addressed the growing complexity. In some cases, starting over is the right answer.

Interfaces should be based upon key abstractions (discrete capabilities) from the subject matter domain that make them intuitive, durable, and resistant to major change. These abstractions should appeal to a broad collection of heterogeneous consumers who may make use of them in ways not originally intended. Such serendipitous reuse is often the genesis of innovation.

Golden rule measures

	Golden Rule Measures
7.1.1	Only documented external interfaces from other assets are used. In other words, only use the interfaces exposed by an asset that are intended to be used by other assets.
7.1.2	Raw SQL interfaces are not exposed.
7.1.3	REST on HTTP(S) is used preferentially for external interfaces (that are developed internally).
7.1.4	External interface specifications are documented consistently.
7.1.5	Custom headers and media types are used consistently.
7.1.6	Distributed transactions across external interfaces are not used.

---

[103] Single responsibility principle - https://bit.ly/1mln7mA.

[104] Big ball of mud - https://bit.ly/JuF4g4.

Best practices for interface definition

Define interfaces that describe discrete capabilities modeled upon *domain specific abstractions*.[105] Ensure Interface definitions are not coupled to implementation, neither syntactically nor semantically. When an interface describes a discrete domain specific abstraction, it is more readily understood. Such interfaces become minimal, but complete.

Model interfaces on key domain abstractions, which makes them more durable and naturally fits into a larger programming model. Using abstractions lowers coupling, since abstractions naturally hide implementation.

Keep interfaces at the same level of abstraction consistent by adhering to common conventions, nomenclature, patterns, and standards. Within an interface, the concept of *progressive disclosure*[106] makes it possible to "show a small number of features to the less experienced user, lowering the hurdle of getting started, while also providing a larger number of features available for the expert."

Keep interfaces closed to breaking change and open to extension. Interfaces should be explicit about what cannot change as well as how and where extensions may be added. By constraining extensions, interfaces maintain control while expanding reuse opportunities.

Define external interfaces to be interoperable and adaptable to a variety of clients, devices, and platforms. interfaces also should adapt to new classes of clients who use them over a variety of protocols that may impose network latency and bandwidth constraints.

When updating an API definition, never delete a parameter or attribute and never change the meaning of a parameter or attribute. Update interfaces only by extension, to maintain backwards compatibility (i.e. to not break an existing API consumer when the API is modified).

---

[105] Domain specific modeling – See: https://bit.ly/2t5BuCA.

[106] Progressive disclosure – See: https://bit.ly/1NubzGY.

Body of evidence

Story	Impact	Likelihood
Company A did not instill any rigor across its different development groups. Its philosophy was "Let a thousand flowers bloom." When building a new product, the product development team was forced to learn and integrate numerous inconsistently defined APIs. It took much longer and cost more for both development and testing than initially estimated by a factor of 250%. The development team had naively assumed that there was at least minimum consistency across the various assets it planned to reuse, and this level of reuse was critical to the business case for the product.	High	High
Company B built a new product that used information already part of an existing product. Rather than consume the external APIs from the supporting assets, the new product simply linked to URLs from the existing product. As the organization employed a single sign-on system, this approach initially worked. But the existing product had never intended their URLs to be permanent, so when the product updated, and the URL syntax changed, the new product failed to return much of the data its users depended on.	High	High
Google, Amazon, and others started by providing SOAP[107] based web services. They had very low adoption rates. When they switched to REST interfaces on top of HTTP(S), which could be accessed equally from programs written in JavaScript, Java, C++, et al, they suddenly had a huge increase in adoption rates. Since AJAX[108] style applications relied on JavaScript, Google and others were able to build more sophisticated applications, providing a richer user experience based on RESTful interfaces than they could using SOAP.	Medium	High

---

[107] SOAP – Simple Object Access Protocol – See: https://bit.ly/1Sm62HI.

[108] AJAX – Asynchronous JavaScript and XML - See: https://bit.ly/1dU2F98.

Story	Impact	Likelihood
Company C built a platform composed of a few dozen assets but did not set any specific standards or guidelines for schema definitions. When they expanded the platform, it became extremely complicated to upgrade the schemas because there were no standards guiding the different teams involved in the upgrade, so many large meetings were required to keep the changes coordinated. In the end, the update delivered late and over-budget. No data was lost, but some data became inaccessible to products because the new schema was not compatible with the older one and didn't pick up some of the data. They also wound up inconsistently naming several data attributes resulting in other data being inaccessible.	High	High
Company D moved to the Internet from a purely mainframe-based system in the late-1990s. A new team was stood up to do the Internet migration, since the existing team did not yet have the skills. When the implementation was complete, ownership was transferred back to the original team for regular maintenance and upgrades. The old team did not like the way the new team had defined some of the data structures, so they changed the names of some of the data elements. The new Internet applications broke as a result, requiring additional rework – all because there were no standards for naming data elements and attributes.	High	High
The team that owned asset X decided that the easiest way to integrate with asset Y was to directly access asset Y's back-end database, rather than use the exposed REST interface. Their thinking was "If we use the REST API, we are just going to have to parse the XML and recreate SQL to update our database. Why go through the overhead?" Eventually, asset Y released an update that completely changed the table layout of the back-end database. Even though it took great care to ensure that its new REST APIs were backwards-compatible with the old, asset X immediately crashed when the new version of asset Y was released. Even though asset X was deployed with a fully redundant architecture across multiple availability zones, each instance of asset X crashed, and the service went down. The result was a failure to meet the product's SLA, lost time, increased support effort and missing key delivery milestones (since resource had to be immediately pulled off the new release of asset X to fix the problem).	High	High
Severity		1

Manage and version control External Interfaces

Agility necessitates change. Every new system you build is going to require changes in future that you never anticipated. Those changes will most likely be made by other people. Anticipate what their job will be like and design for it. Draft the email you would like to receive in 5 years thanking you for such a great extensible design and how easy it was to extend. Then do everything needed to ensure that email will be sent.

Proper up-front design can minimize the risks, complexity, and costs of making changes, but cannot eliminate them. Loosely coupled designs accommodate change by extension without breaking existing clients. Failure to anticipate the impact of probable changes to a system as it evolves often leads to frequent piecemeal changes that maintain compatibility but degrade overall design quality or introduce breaking changes that increase cost and complexity.

System assets and the modules of which they are composed should follow naming standards that convey their boundaries and capabilities. Consistent use of nomenclature and common naming conventions make names meaningful. The alternative is akin to a *Tower of Babel*[109].

Golden rule measures

Number	Golden Rule Measures
7.2.1	All exposed external interfaces are registered in the API inventory (See: API inventory in Chapter 8).
7.2.2	A new major version of an external interface will be supported for a minimum of three years.[110]
7.2.3	Incompatible API versions (major versions) do not interfere with one another.
7.2.4	Assets are deployed in a manner that ensures backwards-compatible versions of APIs replace one another.

---

[109] Tower of Babel - https://bit.ly/1TcE2qg.

[110] Why three years? This recommendation is one that comes from experience but is hard to justify. The original thinking went like this: Once you release a non-backwards-compatible API, you will need to give your clients one year to begin the massive migration that is likely required. Then you give them another year to complete the implementation and deploy it. Then you add a year, because one of your clients will probably just plain refuse to make the change because of time or budget constraints and instead will escalate the issue. The politics of sorting this out will take another year. Hence three years. The other side was that asking somebody to support a major version for three years usually outweighed the arguments that it was just cheaper to not worry about it so much and "the heck with backwards compatibility."

Body of evidence

Story	Impact	Likelihood
Asset A exposed an un-versioned interface which was called by asset B and asset C. Asset B required more information (in both the request and the response) than the interface that asset A exposed, so asset A updated the interface to support the new functionality. When the new version of asset A was deployed, it had to be coordinated so that new versions of asset A, asset B, and asset C were deployed at the same time in lock-step. Even though asset C had no need for the new functionality, it was required to upgrade, or it would have crashed when the new version of asset A was released. Since the new functionality was not required by Asset C, the upgrade was not treated as urgent, so asset A and asset B had to wait until asset C was ready before they could upgrade. All future changes to asset A had to be coordinated with all dependent assets since the APIs were not versioned and backwards compatibility could not be guaranteed.	Medium	High
Asset B exposed an external public interface that it intended to be used by an application owned in the same group. The APIs exposed by asset B were not rigorously version controlled, since it was just easier to update the consuming application if any changes were required to the APIs (or so the developers thought). A few years and several reorganizations later, Asset B's external interface was packaged into an API product that was sold to customers. The customer built its system using the API and became dependent on the exact implementation of the API. As luck would have it, the design of the API did not completely hide the implementation. Nor was it versioned. When new business requirements necessitated a change to asset B, they could not easily be accommodated since they would have forced a change to the API that was used by a customer, who simply refused to make the change. The customer's response to the announcement that the API they were using had to be updated and their code required modification was "If you make us make this change, we might as well take the opportunity to cancel your service and go to your competition." Asset B was forced to maintain the existing API and its code implementation *forever*. New functionality could only be accommodated in a brand-new API. When asset B built its new API, it rigorously managed and version controlled the interface definition. They had learned their lesson.	High	High
Severity		1

Do not couple External Interfaces to their implementation

External interfaces (APIs) define how other assets interact with the asset providing the interface. As such they both cement the contract between assets (along with SLAs) and provide a means of preventing a change to one asset necessitating a cascading shower of changes to propagate through all other assets. A properly implemented asset need never change their external interfaces unless changes in the asset are supposed to provide additional and/or changed capabilities for calling assets. Even in these cases properly architected assets only change their external interfaces in a backwards-compatible way so that if a calling asset does not need the enhanced functionality provided by an upgrade, it is not required to change.

Messages form the basis for exchanging information via interfaces. As such, the messages should reflect the durable abstractions chosen by those interfaces. At each level of abstraction messages should form a common canonical data model that can then be expressed in a variety of formats and representations.

The lack of a common data model creates a morass of integration complexity when attempting to exchange, master, or mash-up data spanning different sources. It often requires the use of costly and complex transformations that lack fidelity and that become increasingly difficult to maintain.

- Message implementations should avoid *leaky abstractions* [111] that couple them to implementation. Since messages are a key element of interfaces used by services it is just as important not to allow implementation details to leak into them. A common example of a leaky abstraction is the direct serialization of an implementation object into a message format. Serializations like these change as the underlying object model changes.

- Messages at the same level of abstraction should minimize overlap, redundancy, or the need for complex transformations when used between requests. Messages should streamline and simplify conversations between consumers and providers, not impede them.

- Messages should be consistent and adhere to common conventions, patterns, and standards for a given format. Consistent use of common nomenclature, naming conventions and patterns increases opportunities for reuse and simplifies consumption.

---

[111] Leaky abstractions – See: https://bit.ly/2DgJ9CA.

Golden rule measures

	Golden Rule Measures
7.3.1	External interfaces are built with a layer of indirection so that the asset's internal data structures may change without forcing changes in the interface.
7.3.2	Third-party proprietary, commercial, and platform-specific elements that promote coupling are not used in external interfaces.

Body of evidence

Story	Impact	Likelihood
Consumer A wished to use the interfaces exposed from many systems of Company X. Each interface was exposed over different protocols, used different terminology, and included various levels of documentation and reference materials. Consumer A saw this as a real pain since it took them much longer to use everything they wished. The end result was that Consumer A had a low opinion of Company X, which resulted in lower adoption of the organization's services and lost revenue.	High	Medium
Severity		2

Handle retries appropriately

Bad stuff happens! Servers will fail, databases will get corrupted, dependencies will get overloaded, network glitches will cause requests to get lost. No matter how reliable a component claims to be, it is never 100% reliable. Everything will fail at some point. Part of creating a robust system is handling failures appropriately including appropriately timing-out and retrying any request that does not return. But if a service provider fails to respond quickly because it is overloaded, then having all its dependencies constantly retrying requests only makes things worse. On the other hand, patiently waiting for a response that will never come doesn't help either.

> The *circuit breaker pattern*[112] can be considered a best practice for dependency management (i.e. managing the way you interact with assets whose external interfaces you call). For example, you might be dependent on a service whose SLA reads: "99% of responses returned in under 2 seconds", but through using the service you find that 90% of the responses are returned in 1 second and 0.1% time out after 2 minutes. What should you set your time-out to? If you set it to 2 minutes (and your SLA guarantees 98% of responses in 2.5 seconds), then when the dependent service fails, your service will just be sitting there (and you will fail your SLA). So instead you might want to set your timeout to something like 3 seconds but continue to listen for the response, so you can capture metrics regarding its SLA. If you start to see the average response time creeping up from 0.5 seconds to 1 second to 2 seconds to 3, you might want to treat the dependent service as down long before you've waited 2 minutes for a full time-out. But when you do decide to retry a request that did not respond before the time-out period, be careful to do so in a manner that does not make an already overloaded service worse. For example, use an exponential back-off algorithm.

Golden rule measures

	Golden Rule Measure
7.4.1	Each call to an external interface has an appropriate time-out set, with the ability to retry the request (when that makes sense).
7.4.2	When retrying a request, an exponential back-off algorithm is implemented to avoid exacerbating failure scenarios (e.g. wait 1 minute for the 1st retry, 2 for the second, 4 for the third).

Body of evidence

Story	Impact	Likelihood
Asset A called asset B, though interface B1, to apply a change to some data. Programmatic mechanisms did not exist to allow asset A to know when asset B had successfully completed its processing (e.g. it was a long running process). As such, occurrences existed where either the change wasn't applied, or asset A timed-out and retried the request, applying the change again (and again, multiple times). The net result was that incorrect data was presented to end users.	High	Medium
Severity		2

---

[112] *Architecting for Scale: High Availability for Your Growing Applications*, by Lee Atchison, 2006, ISBN: 9781491943397.

CHAPTER **23**

Maintainable Systems – Golden Rules and Measures

Maintainable solutions are easily supported and easily modified. They can be extended into adjacent functional areas with minimal surgery.

	Golden Rule	**Severity**
8.1	Make interfaces directly callable without a proprietary library.	1
8.2	Trace requests and failures to their source.	2
8.3	Appropriately comment source code and interfaces.	2

Make interfaces directly callable without a proprietary library

This is intended to eliminate the need for client artifacts required to access a system or its services. Any required stub code that must be used by the caller should be generated through a standard.

If a service provider's interfaces are so complicated that it requires the consumer to include a proprietary code library to make the interfaces either simple enough or performant enough to use, that complexity will eventually come back to bite both the provider and consumer.

But the more important issue is that forcing the use of a client-side library increases coupling between assets, hindering agility, by forcing releases with interface changes to be done in lock-step. It also increases the cost of service, especially if the client libraries must be maintained for multiple programming languages and environments.

Golden rule measures

Number	Golden Rule Measure
8.1.1	Clients are not required to include a proprietary library in their code to consume the asset's external interfaces.

Body of evidence

Story	Impact	Likelihood
Asset A used a non-standard protocol to expose its service interfaces. Rather than upgrade the service to use REST over HTTP(s), the team decided it would be simpler just to create a code library that the consumer would compile into their code (just like open source, right?). Their only consumer was written in Java, so they created a library in Java, and all was well. Over the years, several other Java-based assets incorporated the library to access asset A's interfaces. Eventually the organization started writing new assets in python, so a new library had to be created. It started from the same Java code-base, but of course diverged since Python is a different language, with several unique aspects. Eventually a change was required to asset A, which necessitated a change to the interfaces and to the client-side library. Now the team had to track down all the places where the client library was used, several instances of which were in applications that no longer had a support team (but were still in use). In addition, the team was forced to build, maintain, and test every operating System/programming language combination in which all the clients of the service were deployed. That original decision to save a bit of money by writing a library to hide the legacy implementation rather than upgrade the service interfaces to REST on HTTP(s), ended up costing the organization 10x the original estimated cost of doing the upgrade *properly*.	High	High
Severity		1

Trace requests and failures to their source

When an end user uses a feature of an application, it almost invariably results in a call into an asset, which in turn calls other assets, which call other assets, and so on. If one or more calls in the tree fail, it is extremely useful to be able to trace the entire call tree, both forward and backward to determine what happened and why. As such, a unique transaction ID should be attached to the request, as early as possible in the call tree (along with an opaque user ID or session token, if possible) and have these IDs carried through every call/response made to satisfy the initial request.

An asset's response to a failure of one of its dependencies should be both predictable and reasonable. A predictable response could mean an error message. It could be throttling requests to avoid overload. A reasonable response is one which is appropriate for the situation. A service should not fail if a non-critical dependency fails. But if a critical dependency fails (like a database is down), it should fail and do so quickly and predictably, consuming as few resources as possible.

Determining failures can be extremely difficult, even with the best tracing information, logging information and error handling. Potential failures ordered from easiest to detect to hardest to detect include:

- **Failure response** – Response was understandable and indicated a fatal error occurred processing the request.
- **Garbage response** – Response was either unintelligible or in an unrecognized format.
- **Inconsistent response** – Part of the response looks good but other parts are not consistent. For example, the response may contain data and a field with number of bytes returned, where the data looks good, but bytes returned is zero.
- **Partial response** – Received part of the data or only part of the responses in an expected sequence.
- **Out of sequence response** – Responses were expected in an ordered sequence e.g. A, B, C. But instead, responses were received in the order: A, C, B. Alternatively, a client sent two requests that should have been temporally ordered, but the response to request two arrived before the response to request one.
- **Response too early** – The request was supposed to allow some period to gather data but responded earlier than expected.
- **Idempotency failure** – Repeat request fails or returns a different response.

- **Unexpected Response** – The response was understandable, but was either an unexpected value, or out-of-bounds.
- **No response** – The request timed out and no response was received.
- **Slow Response** – The request was processed, and the response was received before timing out, but much later than expected. This often indicates the service is overloaded or the network is overloaded.

Failure explanations returned to the client should ideally have as much information as the server log, but if this is too much information to be returned, then at a minimum, the failure response should include a correlation ID that can then be used to query the logs and get any additional detail required for problem resolution. Solving an end-user problem and performing root cause analysis on a problem becomes nearly impossible without this type of instrumentation.

Golden rule measures

	Golden Rule Measure
8.2.1	The ability is provided for an interface consumer to add a unique *transaction ID* to a request, which is returned as part of the response.
8.2.2	The caller's *transaction ID* is carried in any service interface that is subsequently called in order to satisfy the request.
8.2.3	When generating failure events and log file entries, *transaction ID* and either user ID or *session token* are included. Code module, version, and line number where the condition was detected are also included.

Body of evidence

Story	Impact	Likelihood
An end user reported periodic slow response on the product they were using, expressing that it was a major pain point. Improvements had been made by extending the cache of the product, but response time still did not meet expectations. Continued investigation pointed to one of three possible causes: capacity and performance of servers, application code, or source database size. The lack of sufficient debugging and tracing made it extremely difficult to track down the root cause of the problem and fix it. This created a very frustrated end user who threatened to cancel the product and move to a competitor.	High	Medium

Story	Impact	Likelihood
When application A first processed a request, it was logged in the front-end server. The request then wound its way through multiple systems, which in turn called other systems. Each system did its own logging, but there was no traceability of the requests between systems. At some point, a user's request failed, and the service team was tasked at finding out why and fixing it. They could see the failure logged in the front-end server, but the actual failure was somewhere deep in the call tree. The team was forced to manually pull the log files from each service in the call tree and line up the log files based on timestamp to see if they could figure out what went wrong. This was a long and arduous process exacerbated by the fact that the timestamp in the log files only went down to the second and the servers were processing 10 – 100 requests per second. Eventually the team was able to figure out that the root cause of the problem was a slow response by a database six levels deep in the call tree. The database didn't actually fail, which is why the issue wasn't found quickly. Since there was no traceability and the callers were not logging actual response time vs service SLA, it took weeks to find a problem which should have generated an easily discoverable alarm for a failed service SLA.	Medium	High
Severity		2

Appropriately comment source code and interfaces

You may believe that your code is so well written that it doesn't need any comments, but it is unlikely that new members of your team will agree. Code and schema should be easy to read, but comments help the reader maintain context and understanding of not only what the code does, but why it does what it does and where you made compromises for the sake of time.

Proper documentation of the payload schema associated with an interface is required to understand the content that flows through it. XML documents may be self-describing, but they are not self-documenting, especially when complex structures or semantics are involved.

Lack of understanding of the schema often leads to errors in the content or the interface, leading to failures. These errors may be visible or silent. Often the silent failures lead to data corruption or semantic interface errors leading to wrong answers, including: increased rates of errors in content and/or services, and increased development cost due to unavailable information regarding schema semantics.

If you write good code and/or design good schemas, then they will still be running 20 years from now. That means that the person destined to maintain what you are writing is probably still in diapers. Anticipate all her questions and answer them now in the comments. Comment as if you are teaching the code to another person.

Recall the last time you had to maintain a piece of code you didn't know at all. Recall how angry you were at how inscrutable the code was and the lack of good comments. Now you know what is needed in the new code you are about to write. No one needs a comment that just describes the code syntax (e.g. "increment *n* by one"). Why are you incrementing here? What are the implications? If that is not obvious, then add a comment to explain it.

When you are writing a line of code, it is yours until you hit enter at the end of the line. At that point it belongs to your organization and all the future people who will need to fix and enhance it. Consider them as you decide how to comment.

Golden rule measures

	Golden Rule Measures
8.3.1	Source code is commented to facilitate a new team member, sufficiently trained, to be able to jump in and modify a source code module they did not themselves write.
8.3.2	Interface payload schemas are commented either by direct embedding or by references to external documentation.

Body of evidence

Story	Impact	Likelihood
As part of a project, customer account information was being extracted and exported from a product database and imported into another system. The data schemas for the product were known only through tribal knowledge and at times, that knowledge conflicted. As a result, the amount of effort required to extract the data and map it took four- times longer than estimated.	Medium	High
Severity		2

CHAPTER 24

Mastered Systems – Golden Rules and Measures

Data (including, but not limited to business data, content, and operational data) should be handled rigorously. Data items should be mastered, and their transit through systems and way-points carefully managed. Values, identifiers, classifiers, mnemonics, and other descriptors (i.e. metadata) are handled with the utmost rigor.

Treat data the same way you would treat money. If you were transporting money throughout your organization and to / from customers, you would take great care to keep it safe everywhere it was stored and during transit between storage locations. That is how you should handle data as well.

These golden rules apply to the system assets that house data, rather than the data assets themselves. The rules guiding data assets are handled separately (See Part 4).

	Golden Rule	Severity
9.1	Register the master system asset for every data asset.	1
9.2	Keep data quality high.	1
9.3	Encapsulate data.	1
9.4	Trace data to its source.	1
9.5	Do not connect end-user applications directly to data masters.	1
9.6	Do not lose data.	2

Register the master system asset for every data asset

The Data Asset Host registry relates a system asset master to the data asset(s) that it masters. This registration process assigns a unique PGUID namespace to each mastered data asset. To recap, a PGUID is a permanent, globally unique identifier. The PGUID namespace serves a dual role. It ensures that all PGUIDs are globally unique across the enterprise and it allows a suitably knowledgeable service API to identify the data asset associated with any PGUID.

If a system asset is authorized to redistribute data for which it is not the master (a rare occurrence), then it is registered as a redistribution system. A redistribution system is one that provides a *faithful* representation of the data from one or more master and has been verified as such. This faithful representation may change the data model, but it may not drop data fields and must stay well synchronized with the master, as defined by its SLA. Any change to a master asset that affects the handling of data necessitates the testing of redistribution assets along with the master. If a system asset is a redistributor, then it must not master any data of its own.

Golden rule measures

	Golden Rule Measures
9.1.1	The mastering system asset for every data asset is registered.
9.1.2	Redistribution systems, if they exist are registered.
9.1.3	Data assets and data items are only created or modified by the **one** system registered as their master.
9.1.4	A single asset may be either a master or a redistribution system, but not both.

Body of evidence

Story	Impact	Likelihood
Company B organized its product groups divisionally. Product M needed access to data asset X. But data asset X was owned in a different group in the organization, so the product group decided it would just be easier to use a copy of the data asset, which was already being used in product N, which was owned in their own division. The product development group failed to verify whether the copy they were using was an official re-distribution asset or not, and of course it wasn't. This copy was only synchronized with the master monthly, and it carried only a subset of the master data fields. That suited Product M's needs initially, but as new requirements came in, use of the copy became problematic. In addition, product N was scheduled to be decommissioned and had no assigned development group available to make changes. This exacerbated the problem and eventually, the development group building product M had to rewrite their code to use the proper master, which everyone agreed in retrospect, should have been done the first time.	High	High
A department has been receiving data for some time containing customer addresses. The path by which the data arrived was convoluted, passing through several poorly documented unmaintained systems. When customer addresses were wrong, the department did not know which system to use to correct the data. They had no choice but to correct the addresses every time a new feed file was received.	High	High
Severity		1

Keep data quality high

A data master's primary purpose is to store the **single version of the truth** for a data asset or closely related group of data assets. A data master is a centralized, highly normalized store of data items. It is optimized for truth, not efficient access.

Every data master follows a similar pattern: data is ingested (from one or more sources) and normalized, stored, enriched, and ultimately distributed. This is not to imply a linear process. Data may be enriched multiple times and distributed multiple times as dictated by business requirements.

Each data master is *registered* as the owner of one or more data assets. As such, it is the only system asset allowed to create new data items in the set or modify the official version of a data item. If an asset modifies a data item for which it is not the master, it is an ephemeral change, and the change should be expected to be overwritten on the next update from the master. In other words, if an asset is holding a copy of a data item, even if it is a registered redistribution asset, it may not allow the item to be permanently changed in its store in any way other than by synchronizing with the master.

As the registered owner of a data asset, the master is also the registered owner of the namespace for the PGUIDs used as the primary identifiers for the data items in the set.

Golden rule measures

	Golden Rule Measures
9.2.1	Data is only obtained from authorized sources (i.e. the master or registered redistributor for internal sources).
9.2.2	Data is kept synchronized with its source.
9.2.3	Synchronization mechanism(s) are provided for data that is distributed.
9.2.4	Redistributed data is a faithful copy of the original.
9.2.5	Data properties are only populated in a manner that is consistent with the design and definition of those properties. The defined structure, schema, and validity constraints are adhered to.
9.2.6	Data is validated before it is stored (unless the data comes from a trusted source, that has already done the necessary validation).

Body of evidence

Story	Impact	Likelihood
Company A had a system that used its own set of geographic region definitions, rather than receiving them from the internal master system. When it reported end-of-month sales data to the corporate warehouse, the reference data values didn't join up to the official values, resulting in sales reports that had wrong totals for geographical distribution. This made reports useless – or worse, misleading – for executives, who considered the whole IT operation useless as a result.	High	High
Company B's sales organization wanted to track a new customer status regarding a sales promotion program. Because it was so hard to modify the *customer relationship management* (CRM) system, users adapted what appeared to be an unused field to enter their own status codes. The field chosen was sometimes overwritten by downstream processing, as the field was originally defined for a different purpose. The result was that the sales organization incorrectly credited some customers under the promotion and failed to credit others, leading to lost revenue and unhappy customers.	High	High
Company C modeled their *customer master* database so that each customer had a single divisional or office hierarchical structure for the customer's end users. This divisional hierarchy was controlled by the billing department. In other words, the way company C viewed their customers was completely biased towards the way that company wanted to see their bills broken down, and the addresses used were the billing addresses. For the sales department, this was problematic. Sales people needed the addresses for their contacts to be the office location where they sat, not some billing department that was potentially in another state. After several attempts to get IT to change the customer master to accommodate their needs, they finally gave-up and hired contractors to create their own sales and prospecting database that was fed from the customer master but did not feed data back-to the customer master. It became customary for the sales people to edit the database themselves, entering information about end users, office addresses, people leaving the customer, and new people joining. At some point, the sales database became so out-of-synch with the customer master that it could no longer apply data updates from the customer master. Synchronization became worse, until finally the data in the customer master became so out-of-date with reality, that customers were refusing to pay their bills because they were "just wrong." Complaints went through the sales group to IT, but the IT group would not touch the sales database since they did not build it and it was built against their strong recommendation. In the end a multi-million-dollar project taking 18 months was required to join the two databases into one.	High	High

Story	Impact	Likelihood
A data entry field had only five valid values. However, the data entry form allowed free text entry in the field. Errors were not noticed until the end-of-month report was run, at which point it was very difficult to reconstruct what the field values should have been.	High	High
Company D's data warehouse received a one-time dump of product codes from the *product master* system. No mechanisms were created to keep the warehouse in sync with the product master. Every time a new product was introduced, technical resources had to carefully modify data in the warehouse. This delayed new products and created opportunities for errors.	High	High
Severity		1

Encapsulate data

Data encapsulation, also known as *data hiding* or *information hiding*,[113] is the mechanism whereby the implementation details of a data set are kept hidden from external assets, which only have access to the data through external interfaces. In the case of a data master, this is the publishing interface (aka the distribution interface).

Golden rule measures

	Golden Rule Measures
9.3.1	Data is only created and/or modified for which this asset is the registered master.
9.3.2	The data model for distributed data contains a layer of indirection (from the master data model) so that its structure, keys, enumerations, and other internal details may change without forcing changes to assets consuming the data through an appropriate interface.

Body of evidence

Story	Impact	Likelihood
See story about Company C under rule 9.2: *Keep data quality high*.		

---

[113] Information Hiding – See: https://bit.ly/1UizwFm.

Story	Impact	Likelihood
Company A distributed data between data masters and products using replication technology. As such the data representation seen by the products was exactly the internal representation of the data in the master, complete with table structure, internal keys, and tables intended to be internal to the master and not exposed to product applications. The master and the product application were *tightly coupled*. Exacerbating the problem, there was no versioning of the master data model. When a product required new data or a new data enrichment, it had to be implemented in the data master and the product simultaneously. Testing had to be done in lock-step and both had to release at the same time. As a rule, the data masters released on a 9-month cycle, but the products released quarterly. When a new business requirement necessitated a change to the master data model, it was a huge upheaval since changing both data master and product in lock-step fit neither group's normal process.	High	High
In Company B, three different systems had write-access to the content metadata system, so that each could update its content publication details. The three systems were all tightly coupled to the internal design of the content metadata system. As a result, it was nearly impossible to change the design of the content metadata system because of the complexity of coordinating changes to four systems at once.	High	High
Severity		1

Trace data to its source

A source is simply where the data came from. Data always comes from somewhere even if it is authored internally, in which case the source is internal. Sources may be human or machine, internal or external, original sources or redistributors. Data provenance refers to the original source of the data. In practical terms, this means the source which defines proper usage and rights for the data. Data lineage refers to the direct ancestor(s) of the data. In a properly architected system, data lineage should be traceable through all internal systems back to the initial source of the raw data.

Golden rule measures

Number	Golden Rule Measures
9.4.1	Data is traceable back to the system which distributed it, as well as the master and original source.
9.4.2	Data is only identified using an identifier designated as a preferred by the data's master (i.e. the PGUID).
9.4.3	Data that is derived from other data items is traceable back to the original data from which it was derived.
9.4.4	The source of every data value is preserved (and stored with the data).

Body of evidence

Story	Impact	Likelihood
Company C redistributed content. Many of the content sets in the organization's collection were acquired from smaller companies and integrated into the premier products post-acquisition. Some document collections used PGUIDs (Permanent globally unique identifiers) and some did not (many of which were the sets acquired from smaller companies). One of the premium features of the organization's product was its ability to alert the end user when new content was received that met certain user-defined criteria. But for the content sets that did not use PGUIDS, it was up to the alerting application to decide (using field-by-field comparison), whether the data it received was a new record or just a refresh of an existing record. As such, the algorithm used to decide whether content was new and alert-worthy was hit-or-miss. Customers began to realize that they were receiving duplicate alerts, while other data which should have generated an alert did not.	High	High
Severity		1

Do not connect end-user applications directly to data masters

Data masters should scale proportionally to the amount of data and its rate of growth or update, not based on end-user population. In addition, the data model for keeping a content master as the "single version of the truth" is rarely structured appropriately for the performance needs of end-user applications.

Golden rule measures

	Golden Rule Measures
9.5.1	Data masters do not expose request/response interfaces for data access, only one-way publish-subscribe interfaces.

Body of evidence

Story	Impact	Likelihood
Company A delivered a product whose premiere feature was its ability to search across multiple structured content sets and display search results. To save money, the content curation team and the search engine worked off the same database (implemented on a mainframe). As the customer-base grew, so did load on the database. The organization reached a point, where during peak usage, they ran out of capacity to handle both end-user searches and curator data updates. To maintain their customer SLAs, they were forced to stop all curation updates during peak load. A person would monitor the load on the system and when it reached a certain peak, they would flip a switch that turned on a red light in all the offices. This was the signal for the curators to stop working on the system. During this "wasted" time, they were allowing their competitors to get ahead.	High	High
Company B delivered a product that displayed mashups of multiple structured datasets. They used a single set of databases that were updated both by third-party data-feeds and internal editors. The same databases were used by the product for retrieval and display. The content group wanted the database structure to be highly normalized, so that no data field was ever duplicated and there was no chance of two copies of a data field having different values. The product group, on the other hand, wanted the data to be structured the way they displayed it, i.e. highly denormalized. The conflict between the way the groups wanted the data to be structured could not be resolved using a shared database.	Medium	High
Company C's content master was connected directly to end users over the Internet. When new content was published, the load on the system caused delays in the user experience and sometimes caused outages. The problem couldn't be solved through scheduling, since the system was accessed by users in almost every time zone around the world.	High	High
Severity		1

Do not lose data

Data items are never deleted unless absolutely necessary (i.e. for contractual / legal reasons). Once a data item is created and its PGUID has been minted, it remains forever. If the data item is no longer valid (e.g. maybe it was a duplicate), then the item is marked as such. We call this *sunsetting* the data, to distinguish it from deleting data. The property values for the sunset data item are not deleted either, but they are also marked to indicate that they are no longer valid.

Data received from 3rd party sources is not discarded, even if the data is not currently used by the master. Often the best way to do this is to preserve the raw data file from which the data was received and over time, move old raw data files to cheap storage. We don't overwrite data values either. When we get an update, we create a new data value with a new *creation date* and mark the data value to indicate it has been superseded.

Golden rule measures

	Golden Rule Measures
9.6.1	Data Items are never deleted (unless legally required). If a data item is sunset, the PGUID remains valid, but is marked as no-longer-active.
9.6.2	Data received from third party sources are not discarded.
9.6.3	Data values are neither deleted nor overwritten.

Body of evidence

Story	Impact	Likelihood
Content set A was ingested from a single source. During the ingestion process, data was normalized and any properties not in the master data model were discarded. The original source data was not preserved. After a new requirement was added to include a bit more of the source data, it was discovered that this data no longer existed. The inability to go back to the original data had many costly impacts. Support cost to do the data correction over time was significant.	High	High
When company A first started getting news data for incorporation into its mainframe content repositories, the data came with photographs and other image data. The organization did not at that time have any way to present images to customers, so typically discarded the images, preserving and processing only the text. As systems became more sophisticated with the ability to store and distribute images, the fact that these historical images were never preserved became a real detriment to the organization's news archive product.	High	High

Story	Impact	Likelihood
Company B has been in the data business for a long time. Some of the very first data sets added to its data collection were input in upper case only, even though the original source data was in mixed case. Since the original data with mixed case was never preserved, when the organization eventually supported case-sensitive searching, there were false hits when users searched for uppercase versions of search terms. In addition, documents were missed when customers searched for lower or mixed case terms. Since the original data was not preserved, it was deemed too was expensive to fix.	High	High
Severity		1

CHAPTER 25

Global Systems - Golden Rules and Measures

Global solutions can be easily localized for use in one or more geographic locations and cultures.

Localization is the process of presenting data and accepting user input in a manner that is appropriate to a specific geo-locale, including, but not limited to: language, script, culture, currency, color conventions, iconography,[114] holidays, and sort-order.

The *Global* golden rules apply only to assets that will potentially be localized to other geographies. If an asset is truly and forever intended to serve only the needs of a single locale, the Global rules do not apply. For example, it may be company policy for all employees to speak English now and forever. In such an instance an asset that only faced employees would not need to be global.

Globalization is the process of structuring, organizing, and encoding data and code so that it may be localized to a geography. Globalizing does not require localization, but it is a necessary pre-requisite for doing so. As such, globalizing is a good idea even if there is no existing requirement to support more than a single locality.

If an asset is truly and forever intended to serve only the needs of a single locale, the *global rules* should be scored so there is a record, but no debt should be assessed.

	Golden Rule	Severity
10.1	Handle data in a globalized way.	1
10.2	Distinguish third-party translations from company translations.	1
10.3	Adapt to the user's preferred locale.	2

> Build systems and applications to be global, even if there is no existing need to serve more than one locality.

---

[114] ISO has an official lexicon of internationally recognized symbols: https://bit.ly/2pGH1iE.

Handle data in a globalized way

Global data is defined as data which may be localized to a specific geography or culture. For example, if data is encoded in ASCII (a 7-bit format), it may only carry English. If data is encoded in ISO 8859-1[115] (an 8-bit format) it may carry western European languages, but not Asian languages hence it is not global. Data encoded in Unicode, on the other hand, is global, even if it has not been localized beyond US English. When we refer to data being handled *consistently* in the measures below, what we mean is: *consistently according to a well-defined standard*.

Golden rule measures

	Golden Rule Measures
10.1.1	Text is encoded either in UTF-8, UTF-16, or UTF-32[116].
10.1.2	Text is normalized to a consistent *Unicode normal form*[117] prior to any comparison or sorting operations.
10.1.3	Language, region, and script identification appearing in natural language text is preserved.
10.1.4	Writing direction hints and instructions appearing in natural language text is preserved. Note that text may be bidirectional. For example, right-to-left text may include an English phrase which is left-to-right.
10.1.5	Representations of date, time, currency, and other numbers, including a standard for rounding, are exchanged in a locale-independent manner with an accompanying locale identifier.
10.1.6	Money values are represented as a numeric value (representing the amount of money) plus a specification of the currency.
10.1.7	Money values converted between different currencies, is done consistently across all assets.
10.1.8	Date and time values are represented consistently across all assets.
10.1.9	Time zone values are represented consistently across all assets. Note that some countries change the date they switch back and forth from daylight savings time every year.
10.1.10	Decimal numbers are represented consistently across all assets.
10.1.11	Telephone numbers are represented consistently across all assets.
10.1.12	Street Addresses are represented consistently across all assets.
10.1.13	Email addresses are represented consistently across all assets.

---

[115] ISO 8859-1 – See: https://bit.ly/2B25Ozx.

[116] UTF – See: https://bit.ly/2ULTQ7t.

[117] Unicode normal form – See: https://bit.ly/2n1Gkh3.

Body of evidence

Story	Impact	Likelihood
Company A was building their first CRM (customer relationship management) system. As the system was being architected, designed, and implemented, the project team needed to decide whether the system would be built for global use or just for the US. The incremental cost of building the system for potential global use was estimated at around $800,000 for addition disk space to handle Unicode versus Latin-1-character sets. The decision was made to develop only for US. One year later, one of the international groups in the organization began researching CRM tools for their sales team. They were willing to adopt the sales processes that had been implemented for the US and wanted to move quickly and cheaply but they needed a solution that provided local language support for Japan, China, and Malaysia. The cost of upgrading the existing system to support Asian languages came in at a whopping $12 million, given that almost every code module had to be refactored to handle Unicode as well as needing the additional storage space. The organization ended up with two (and eventually four different CRM systems).	High	High
Company B had a product which served the United States court system. A unique business opportunity arose to become the sole supplier to the UK court system. The product already had 90% of the required functionality, but the software was built solely for the US and the cost to localize to the UK was prohibitive, even though both countries speak English. The business opportunity was lost to a local competitor.	High	High
Severity		1

Distinguish third-party translations from company translations

A data provider has the obligation to reflect data correctly. This includes support for official translations of documents into multiple human languages. For example, many Canadian laws are published by the Canadian government in both an official English and official French versions.

In an increasingly global economy, it is not unusual for important data to be published in a second language, so applications may provide a translated version of the text to the end user. Such translations could even be machine-generated. If the user is not fully informed of the nature and fidelity of the translation, s/he may be misled by potentially embarrassing mis-translations.

It is therefore strongly recommended that any translations of data through a third-party mechanism -- regardless of whether machine-generated or human-generated -- be clearly and unambiguously differentiated from the "official" publication of the data.

Golden rule measures

	Golden Rule Measures
10.2.1	Any third-party translation of text is unambiguously identified as coming from an external source to the end user.
10.2.2	Any third-party translated text provided to an end user also includes access to the original untranslated text.

Body of evidence

Story	Impact	Likelihood
A $3 million lawsuit was filed against the city of Portland, Oregon[118] (and a list of other defendants) due to a faulty Spanish-to-English translation of a 911 call by a third-party translation service. Help was sent to the wrong address as the woman was gasping for breath. By the time the rescue team determined the true location of the person she had already suffered irreversible brain damage, not having breathed for over 14 minutes.	Catastrophic	High
A panic in the world's foreign exchange market led the U.S. dollar to plunge in value after a poor English translation of an article by Guan Xiangdong of the China News Service zoomed around the Internet. The original article was a casual, speculative overview of some financial reports, but the English translation sounded much more authoritative and concrete.	High	High

---

[118] https://bit.ly/1qDG5mI.

Story	Impact	Likelihood
In 1840, the British government made a deal with the Maori chiefs in New Zealand. The Maori wanted protection from marauding convicts, sailors, and traders running roughshod through their villages, and the British wanted to expand their colonial holdings. The *Treaty of Waitangi*[119] was drawn up and both sides signed it. But they were signing different documents. In the English version, the Maori were to "cede to Her Majesty the Queen of England absolutely and without reservation all the rights and powers of Sovereignty." In the Maori translation, composed by a British missionary, they were not to give up sovereignty, but governance. They thought they were getting a legal system but keeping their right to rule themselves. Generations later, the issues around the meaning of this treaty are still being discussed.	High	High
In a paper published in issue 7 of the Journal of Specialized Translation[120], Dr. Jody Byrne documented the serious negative consequences that could result from imprecise language translations. The abstract of the article reads as follows: "At the very heart of translation studies is the issue of translation quality. Yet, while there are numerous methods for assessing the quality of translations, little is known about what happens when a translator produces a bad translation. This paper will show that translation error, as a whole, can have significant consequences for both translator and client and by examining a number of case studies gathered from official reports and communications, court records, newspaper articles and books it will illustrate the diversity of situations which can arise as a result of translation errors. The paper will then examine the issues of liability and negligence to illustrate the legal means by which translators can be held accountable for the quality of their work. By understanding how liability for faulty translations arises, it will be possible to see the implications of laws and directives governing technical translations which are subsequently examined. This paper examines specific legal requirements relating to technical translation and discusses the consequences of translation errors using specific case studies relating to technical translation."	High	High
Severity		1

---

[119] Treaty of Waitangi – See: https://bit.ly/2miUeNx.

[120] Journal of Specialized Translation – See: https://bit.ly/1Nsk3my.

Adapt to the user's preferred locale

A *locale*[121] is a set of parameters that defines the user's language, region, and any special variant preferences that the user wants to see in their user interface. Usually a locale identifier consists of at least a language identifier and a region identifier. For example, French is spoken in 29 countries and almost every country has a unique dialect, many with several sub-dialects.

Golden rule measures

	Golden Rule Measures
10.3.1	When using locales to modify system behavior, two locale values are supported: one for control of language-specific behaviors and one for control of numeric data handling behaviors.
10.3.2	Resource files and bundles are used to supply user-interface text, including (but not limited to) messages, instructions, help information, field headers, button labels, and text-based navigation aids or links.
10.3.3	Resource files and bundles are used to supply user-interface icons and images. Hand and facial gestures are not used in icons (because it's bound to be a curse in some locale).
10.3.4	Resource files and bundles are used to supply all client-side code (e.g. JavaScript) that contains natural language text, time/date values, currency values, or numeric data exposed to an end user.
10.3.5	Resource files and bundles are used to supply all CSS styling that is part of the user interface.
10.3.6	When providing data to the end user, locale-appropriate representations of numeric data (e.g. date, time, and currency) are used.
10.3.7	If human gestures are used as input, they are locale appropriate.

---

[121] Locale - See: https://bit.ly/2griLg0.

Body of evidence

Story	Impact	Likelihood
Company A wanted to build a single application that they could sell in the U.S., the U.K. and across Europe. The design of the application ensured that all data was stored in Unicode and that all textual data that was presented to the end user was separated from the code. That way the string library containing the textual data could be translated and individual "language-specific" libraries would be installed based on the language of the end user. Unfortunately, the separation of language specific functions stopped at the textual strings and did not include resources like dialog boxes and icons. When the team tried to a deliver a product to Germany, they discovered (at great expense) that the text translated into German would not fit into the space allocated by the dialog box. Delivering the German product took an extra year.	Medium	High
Icons may seem like a great way to break the language barrier, but not every symbol means the same thing in every culture, for example:[122] • You may be inclined to say, "rock 'n' roll!" with a set of bullhorns, but in Spain you'd be saying that someone's wife was sleeping around. • Making an inward-facing peace-sign in the U.S. (making a "vee") is giving someone "the finger" in parts of the U.K. or Australia. • "Thumbs up" is a sign of approval in the U.S., but it effectively means "up yours" in Afghanistan, and parts of Italy and Greece.	Medium	High
Severity		2

Best practice for handling locales

Applications should use resource bundles (i.e. files that can be easily swapped out for different language implementations without hunting through source code) for each locale to identify things like:

- The names that appear in buttons on web pages or screens that identifies what those buttons do.
- The descriptive labels associated with form fields that identify what information is to be entered in that field.
- Messages, for example, those that inform the user, and describe errors.
- Icons that appear within the user interface (so that culturally-appropriate icons can be provided in each locale the application supports).
- JavaScript, Flash, or other client-side logic that carries text displayed to the end user.
- CSS style sheets (so that styling can be appropriate to the needs of individual locales).

---

[122] For additional gestures with dual meanings, see: https://bit.ly/2wQNFIj.

When developing an application that will need to support multiple locales:

- **Honor the locale choices of the user -** If a system asset manifests locale-specific behavior, it is usually best to base that behavior on the user's locale settings. There are two such settings: one for language and one for numeric data handling.

- **Leverage platform-provided classes and methods to set the locale -** Any system asset that needs to modify its behavior based on locale will benefit from leveraging the libraries and other facilities made available as part of their software development environments.

- **Avoid the use of icons involving hands or faces -** there is no hand or face representation that is NOT offensive (or at the very least, laden with undesired cultural overtones) to at least some culture![123]

- **Consider using off-the-shelf, pre-internationalized U/I components -** One of the challenges in providing a culturally-friendly user interface is accommodating cultural variations that appear around the world. Fortunately, several vendors provide libraries of globalized web and native UI widgets that can be easily incorporated into a user interface. ISO maintains a lexicon of officially recognized international symbols.

- **Accommodate the space demands of text of varying languages -** Applications must handle local variations in the width needed to accommodate text inputs (and outputs!). German tends to require the most space, so is a good choice to test with. Techniques that support flexibility in text width are generally likely to make adapting to new locales easier. Examples include:
    - Expandable drop-down lists whose width is not limited by the display width of the text field to which they belong
    - Buttons that contract or expand to accommodate labels of varying lengths
    - Text entry boxes whose length can be substituted with an externally-supplied value (rather than hard-coded into the user interface template).

- **Individually test multiple languages -** Test at least the shortest and longest languages supported as well as one language for each alphabet in use.

---

[123] Global guide to hand gestures: See https://bit.ly/2DxPp83.

PART IV

Data Asset Golden Rules and Measures

As with *Part 3: System Asset Golden Rules and Measures*, this section is organized hierarchically: first by principle then by golden rule. The section elaborates the principles and golden rules that apply to data assets. Data assets are the data building blocks of the organization's solutions. Although they "live in the house built by system assets," they are independent assets.

The goal of the *data asset golden rules* is to quantify any business risk associated with the architecture and implementation of the data assets and to quantify the associated technical debt. These rules do not ensure that the actual value placed in a data field is the correct one, or that curation and operational processes are consistent with business needs. These rules are associated with the non-functional requirements of curating quality data – just as the system asset golden rules are associated with the non-functional requirements of building technology. To get quality output, not only do you have to follow the golden rules, but you must execute as well. The two approaches support each other, and don't conflict. One is not a substitute for the other.

Since data assets exist within system assets, there is some duplication between system asset golden rules and data asset golden rules (particularly when applied to data mastering and global data). This is done on purpose. For example, if a system is built that encodes data in 7-bit ASCII, and carrying multiple languages is a business requirement, then not only do we have technical debt associated with the system asset, but we have additional technical debt associated with the data asset as well. Correcting the problem requires remediating both the system and the data.

As with Part 3 of the book, each golden rule is associated with a body-of-evidence and each body-of-evidence story is assigned a *business impact* and a *likelihood-of-happening* if the golden rule is not followed. The combination of impact and likelihood dictates the severity of the rule.

CHAPTER 26

Compliant Data – Golden Rules and Measures

Manage and protect data in compliance with laws, regulations, and corporate policies. This requires that data be classified (known as Data Classification or Information Classification).

	Golden Rule	**Severity**
D1.1	Classify and manage data according to the Data Classification.	1
D1.2	Retain data as required by the business and by legal and regulatory requirements. Destroy[124] thereafter.	2

Classify and manage data according to the data classification

A dataset's classification[125] generally defines the rules for handling data in a compliant manner as well as guidelines for retention.

Golden rule measures

	Golden Rule Measures
D1.1.1	Classify a data asset according to the *data classification* methodology. Record this classification in the *data specification* for the data asset.
D1.1.2	Manage data assets in compliance with applicable regulations as defined by data classification.
D1.1.3	Data whose usage is restricted by its provider regarding intellectual property rights, privacy, or any other aspect must be managed and shared with respect to these restrictions.
D1.1.4	Access to data must not be granted until the terms of access are documented and agreed to by the data owner (or her delegates) and the party or parties receiving access.

---

[124] Most security organizations have policies governing the destruction of data that depends on the data classification. This might include erasing the data multiple times or even destroying the physical disk(s) on which the data was stored.

[125] Refer to Chapter 2 for the definition of Data Classification.

Body of evidence

Story	Impact	Likelihood
Data redistributors have restrictions on replicating certain forms in specific media. For example, they may be able to replicate in print but not online. If specific forms are replicated, they must have the word "draft" stamped across them. Company A did not adhere to these restrictions and violated a contractual agreement, resulting in loss of access to the data and lost revenue.	High	High
Publishers can sue a data redistributor for breach of contract if they don't manage embargoes appropriately. The publishers watch when the data update and they know if the data is loaded too early. Company B received early access to an earnings report with an explicit embargo (i.e. the earnings report was not to be released before 9:00 PM EST). There was a glitch in the organization's network time protocol and the organization accidentally released the report one second early. The SEC got involved and there was a prolonged investigation. In the end it turned out that the story was not released early, but it was time-stamped 8:59 rather than 9:00. But even though there was no legal wrong doing, the organization suffered the expense associated with the investigation as well as bad press.	High	High
Company D did not comply with regulatory and contractual obligations regarding personal or confidential data and suffered legal sanctions, and an expensive lawsuit. The resulting damage to the organization's reputation affected the share price.	Catastrophic	Low
Company E's customer data included personally identifiable information (PII). The data was not managed according to the organization's data classification methodology, thus risking that PII data was divulged inappropriately. Had this happened, it would have violated customers' privacy and regulatory requirements, would have hurt the organization's reputation and revenue, and exposed it to financial liabilities.	Catastrophic	Low
Although redacting Personally Identifiable Information (PII) from data that is provided by a government agency is not by law the responsibility of a data redistributor, Company F suffered poor public relations when they published the social security numbers of military personnel present in the Congressional Record (which the organization redistributed in its products).	Catastrophic	Low
Severity		1

Retain data as required by the business and by legal and regulatory requirements, and destroy thereafter

The legal requirement to retain *records* is covered by various regulations. Depending on the country,[126] the industry and the type of data, the retention periods are different, as is the definition of what exactly constitutes a record.

In the U.S., various regulations (including the Sarbanes-Oxley Act[127]) guide the SEC in enforcing retention periods. These periods may be two, three, four or seven years, depending on the organization and type of record. The Federal Energy Regulatory Commission requires companies to keep certain types of pricing information for five years. The U.S. Department of Labor's Occupational Safety & Health Administration (OSHA) requires that some health-related records be kept for either 30 years or the duration of a person's employment plus 30 years.[128] Employment law enforced by the U.S. Equal Employment Opportunity Commission stipulates that documents about job applicants and personnel records be kept from one to three years. For companies in the health-care industry, things get even trickier. Under the Health Insurance Portability and Accountability Act's (HIPPA)[129] privacy rule, for instance, the Department of Health and Human Services requires that certain records be held for six years.

You get the idea, its complicated, and that's just in the U.S. EU laws can be even stricter. Almost every country has its own laws requiring record retention within its borders.

Golden rule measures

	Golden Rule Measures
D1.2.1	Manage data retention and purging to comply with legal and regulatory requirements, corporate data retention standards, and business requirements.

---

[126] Data Retention in selected countries: https://go.ey.com/2Sjwv07.

[127] Sarbanes-Oxley – See: https://bit.ly/2Dltz8U.

[128] Note that storing data for 30 years almost guarantees that the system which created the data will be retired before the end of the retention period. That needs to be factored into the architecture any system handling this kind of data.

[129] HIPPA – See: https://bit.ly/1PaH2Qr.

Body of evidence

Story	Impact	Likelihood
Company A was a redistributor of content purchased from company B. A business decision was made to stop distributing the content from company B, since usage was relatively low, but the cost of carrying the content carried a fixed fee, regardless of how much usage there was. The content was removed from the production environments but was accidentally not deleted from the test environment. It was standard practice to load new content into the test environment, verify it, then back it up and load it into production. The next time this was done, the content from company B was loaded back into production. When the error was discovered six months later, company A had to pay company B for six months of access, even though there was zero usage.	High	Medium
On 10 May 2006, the U.S. Securities and Exchange Commission filed a civil injunctive action against Morgan Stanley & Co. Inc. alleging in its complaint that Morgan Stanley did not produce responsive e-mails to the SEC's investigation, because it over-wrote back-up tapes. Morgan Stanley agreed to settle the matter by paying a $15 million civil penalty. Morgan Stanley also agreed to adopt and implement policies, procedures and training focused on the preservation and production of e-mail communications. It also hired an independent consultant to review these reforms. The legal fees, the cost of implementing the new policies and the cost of the independent consultant were all borne by Morgan Stanley in addition to the penalty.	High	Medium
The Clinton White House spent more than $10 million to pull records off backup tapes and look at them again in light of subpoenas relating to Whitewater and Monica Lewinsky. Hilary Clinton was involved in that scandal as well as another scandal related to destroying emails during the 2018 presidential election.	High	Medium

Story	Impact	Likelihood
Company B's legal department decided it was just too complicated to understand all the data retention laws, so they issued an edict that every record had to be retained. However, they did not have the budget to pay for the additional storage, or the training necessary to teach people what a record was. Most people just continued doing what they were doing the way they were doing it. As such the organization was not only in breach of various regulations, it was in breach of its own corporate legal policy.	High	Medium
Company C did not remove "Tasini"[130] documents that were identified for removal. The author who had the rights to those documents sued both the Publisher and the redistributor for profiting from their data. Financial penalties were awarded on a per document basis.	High	Medium
Severity		2

---

[130] See NY Times Co. vs. Tasini - https://bit.ly/2RMBAsQ.

CHAPTER 27

Reliable Data - Golden Rules and Measures

Data should be maintained in a well-controlled manner, so that end users can rely on data's structure and values to be confined to those promised.

	Golden Rules	**Severity**
D2.1	Data curation processes are designed and followed.	1
D2.2	Data schemas are defined and adhered to.	1
D2.3	Data is accurate.	1
D2.4	Data is complete.	1
D2.5	Data is timely.	1
D2.6	Data quality control processes are defined and followed.	1

Data curation processes are designed and followed

There should be well-established processes for curating data. *Data curation* [131] is the management of data throughout its lifecycle, from creation and initial storage to the time when it is archived for posterity or becomes obsolete.

---

[131] Data curation – See: See https://bit.ly/2t9qoN0.

Golden rule measures

	Golden Rule Measure
D2.1.1	There are current, documented content curation policies associated with the data asset.
D2.1.2	A process for managing changes to the data asset is defined and followed.
D2.1.3	There are committed resources responsible for maintaining the data to the quality level required for a positive customer experience, as evidenced by a positive operational data quality metric trend.

Body of evidence

Story	Impact	Likelihood
Company A's lack of content curation policies, led to reduced content quality, which led to customer dissatisfaction and competitive weakness.	High	High
Company B had acquired many independent content-sets over time. The organization did not unify the content curation groups, preferring to leave each acquired group relatively autonomous. One specific group decided to insert "XXX" into a customer address field to designate the account as deleted. The policy was not communicated to any other content curation group and was only communicated to the product group acquired from the same company. As the use of "XXX" was meaningless outside of this specific context, it effectively corrupted the data for any shared use.	High	High
Company C collected all the state legal codes and laws and placed the data into a single content set. State codes can have multiple date fields, such as adoption dates, effective dates, revision dates, and publication dates. As such, each date must be fully qualified to properly reflect the meaning of the field. Company C organized its content curation group by state. In other words, there were several independent *content curation* groups, each "owning" a group of states. One of the groups designed its XML schema such that identifying which date each field meant required tacit knowledge. While the meaning of each date field was common knowledge to the editors that had been with the organization for a while, it was not well known among new editors, nor new product developers. This led to incorrect data presented in products and customer dissatisfaction.	High	High

Story	Impact	Likelihood
Company D did not have adequate oversight or awareness of problems that occurred when data was loaded into their content systems. For example, nobody noticed when the number of total documents decreased significantly during one data load; Supplemental data overwrote base data instead of adding to it. For example, 1000 Jury instructions + 100 supplemental documents should have equaled 1100 documents, but instead only 100 documents were collected. On a second occasion, an error in data workflow caused data to appear without references to known, embedded citations over an extended period. This resulted in customer complaints.	High	High
Company E consolidated all their reference data groups together into a single group (e.g. citation recognition rules, person entity data, geographical data, et al). After one particularly large budget cut, the reference data group was nearly eliminated due to a lack of management understanding as to what it did. There was a dashboard of quality metrics for each core dataset. But there were none for reference data. In addition, entity data was only unified with core content by the product groups, so its utility and value were opaque to management of the content group, all of whom had a print publishing background. Over time, the quality of the reference data degraded, leading to inconsistent or missing link behavior in content and products as well as errors in analytical data products.	High	High
Company F collected data on public and private corporations. When a corporation merged or changed names, indexing was updated to reflect the changes in new documents, but older documents were not re-indexed, causing incorrect linking in historical data products.	High	High
Severity		1

Data schemas are designed and adhered to

Data asset and interface schemas that are under the control of the organization should be managed and controlled.

To ensure that data remains of high quality and meets business requirements, the implementation of a data asset must follow its design.

Golden rule measures

	Golden Rule Measure
D2.2.1	Data asset schemas are maintained with version control.
D2.2.2	There is a defined process for maintaining data asset schema that includes communicating changes to stakeholders.
D2.2.3	The process for maintaining data assets schema is followed.
D2.2.4	Data assets encoded in XML identify its controlling schema or DTD.
D2.2.5	Data assets encoded in XML provide the locations of XML schemas that define all the XML elements and attributes in the asset.

Body of evidence

Story	Impact	Likelihood
Content set A's data type definitions (DTDs) were stored on a file system with no version control. Individuals in different teams copied them locally and made changes (some of which were significant). There was little or no coordination between the teams making changes. Downstream systems had to consume very disparate models for very similar data by creating specialized code for each seemingly random variant. Bringing the modified DTDs back together to a single definition for use across multiple products was deemed infeasible, as there was no versioning or history of changes. Each new product and each new enhancement bore the additional cost of dealing with the variants, slowing down the enhancement process and needlessly adding development cost.	High	High
Content set B's schemas were changed in a non-backwards-compatible way without prior notification to product developers and stakeholders. This broke downstream systems and caused a product outage.	High	Medium
Content set C was implemented without modeling and the schema was produced with little design or forethought. Due to the poor quality of the markup implementation, many forms (i.e. structured fill-in-the-blank forms) were not identified properly or had incomplete metadata. As such, they were excluded from the product data collection. A key product was unable to leverage those forms because they were difficult to find and/or not linkable. So, even though this valuable data was created and curated, it was not included in the product and many customers ended up switching to a competitor's product.	High	High

Story	Impact	Likelihood
Content set D had multiple DTDs which were never consolidated. This led to inconsistencies and poor quality in published data. The missing data properties made analytics more difficult to construct and negatively impacted several products which included the content set.	High	High
Severity		1

Data is accurate

Data must be accurate to its original source, its context preserved, and its origin tracked. In this context, "preserve" does not mean "preserve for all time," but rather "preserve for the life of the content revision" or "preserve during processing."

Requirements to preserve the history of changes to data may come from contractual, legal, regulatory, and/or business sources. They should be spelled out in the *data specification*.

Golden rule measures

	Golden Rule Measure
D2.3.1	Enhancements and enrichments applied to a data asset are each identifiable and neither disturbs the integrity and context of original data.
D2.3.2	Data collected from third parties is preserved either in its original format or in a loss-less transformation from the original format to a new format.
D2.3.3	Relationships expressed in original data are preserved throughout processing.
D2.3.4	Derived data is traceable back to the source data items from which it was derived.
D2.3.5	Data assets use permanent globally unique identifiers (PGUIDs) provided by data masters to reference those masters' data items.

Body of evidence

Story	Impact	Likelihood
Content set A was ingested from a single source. During the ingestion process, data was normalized and any properties not in the master data model were discarded. The original source data was not preserved. After a new requirement was added to include a bit more of the source data, it was discovered that this data no longer existed. The inability to go back to the original data had many costly impacts. Support cost to do the data correction over time was significant.	High	High
When company A first started getting news data for incorporation into its	High	High

Story	Impact	Likelihood
mainframe content repositories, the data came with photographs and other image data. The organization did not at that time have any way to present images to customers, so typically discarded the images, preserving and processing only the text. As systems became more sophisticated with the ability to store and distribute images, the fact that these historical images were never preserved became a real detriment to the organization's news archive product.		
Company B has been in the data business for a long time. Some of the very first data sets added to its data collection were input in upper case only, even though the original source data was in mixed case. Since the original data with mixed case was never preserved, when the organization eventually supported case-sensitive searching, there were false hits when users searched for uppercase versions of search terms. In addition, documents were missed when customers searched for lower or mixed case terms. Since the original data was not preserved, it was deemed too was expensive to fix.	High	High
Company C split news stories across newsletters that were put online as separate documents - with no connection to each other. For example, the cover story of a newsletter may have begun on page one and then continued on page four. The full story was unfortunately treated as two documents, one that began on page one and ended abruptly in mid-sentence, and a second one with the text from page four, (which was difficult to understand without the text from page one. This led to a confusing presentation and less than useful search results.	High	High
Company D processed legislation data from the U.S. federal government as well as from state governments. This incoming data was a deeply nested, hierarchical structure, but during ingestion the data was transformed to a flat RTF-based structure. Autogenerating a Table of Contents required restoration of the hierarchy originally provided in the document. It became an expensive cleanup exercise to recover the data and structure that was needlessly discarded.	High	High
Company E accidentally placed valuable content into the wrong product content set, making the content accessible to customers who had not paid for access, and inaccessible to customers who had paid for access. Since all the software involved was operating correctly, the problem was not easily diagnosed, and it was difficult to trace the problem back to its origin. Had the content in question been identified with Permanent Globally Unique Identifiers (PGUIDs) that clearly determined the origins of the content, problem resolution could have been much more rapid and less costly, revenue would not have been put at risk, and customer satisfaction could have been restored more quickly.	High	High
Severity		1

Data is complete

A data asset should be complete as required by and advertised to consumers. Current and prior data values, from each source, are synchronized with their sources. Data completeness includes metadata completeness. Data should neither be discarded nor overwritten.

Golden rule measures

	Golden Rule Measure
D2.4.1	The Data asset contains a complete set of data as defined in its *data specification*.
D2.4.2	Historical data (e.g., archives, prior editions, history of revisions) are preserved as defined in its data specification.
D2.4.3	Original data is kept in sync with its sources, including both current and historical data.
D2.4.4	Data that is derived from original data is recalculated when original data changes.
D2.4.5	Data is traceable back to its master data asset.

Body of evidence

Story	**Impact**	**Likelihood**
Company A collected *court rules* from various court websites around the country and aggregated the rules into a content set that is integrated into its products. The process involved individuals going to each site, scraping the data off the site, and reformatting it. As the organization expanded its coverage to more courts, it eventually hit a limit as to how much data it could handle given the highly manual nature of the process. As such, updates were missed, and the quality of the data began to degrade, resulting in customer complaints.	High	High
In company B, due to the poor quality of the markup implementation, many forms (i.e. structured fill-in-the-blank forms) were missing important metadata. As such, they were excluded from the product data collection and inaccessible to customers using the organization's premier product. Customers complained, and several ended up switching to a competitor's product.	High	High
Severity		1

Data is timely

Data timeliness generally refers to the latency involved in data being ingested, enriched, processed, distributed, included in products and available to end users. Timeliness targets should be defined in the *data SLA*.

Golden rule measures

	Golden Rule Measure
D2.5.1	Product data is synchronized with the master regularly and in a timely manner as defined in the data SLA.
D2.5.2	New and/or updated data is ingested, processed, distributed, and accessible for retrieval in a product application with latency no greater than what is defined as acceptable in the data SLA.
D2.5.3	New and/or updated data is indexed and searchable with latency no greater than what is defined as acceptable in the data SLA.

Body of evidence

Story	Impact	Likelihood
Company A collected data from multiple different sources and consolidated the data into a single record taking some fields from one source and some from another. The process for doing this was *editor discretion*, meaning that each editor decided, based on their own bias, and tribal knowledge, which source had the better data when there was any disagreement between sources. A second editor would then validate the work of the first. If they disagreed, a third editor would get involved to break the tie. As the organization expanded its coverage, it did not expand the content curation staff at the same rate and data updates became increasingly delayed. As customer complaints grew, content curation practice was changed to release the data as soon as the first curator was done. But the root cause was the highly manual process, which was not corrected. Now the data was both delayed and inconsistent. Customer complaints grew.	High	High

Story	Impact	Likelihood
Company B distributed news. It collected news from multiple sources globally as well as employed journalists who wrote their own stories. A new release of the news master was not properly synchronized with the content curation system, and when it found news items with data fields it did not recognize, it "kicked out" the whole story into a queue for a human to process. Since the systems were out of sync, "kicking out" a story was not uncommon; the *reprocessing* queue grew longer and longer. The organization's SLA target from news happening to news availability was two seconds. Some stories were trapped in the queue for days, clearly in contrast to the business' objectives.	High	High
Company C redistributed content. Many of the content sets in the organization's collection were acquired from smaller companies and integrated into the premier products post-acquisition. Some document collections used PGUIDs (Permanent globally unique identifiers) and some did not (many of which were the sets acquired from smaller companies). One of the premium features of the organization's product was its ability to alert the end user when new content was received that met certain user-defined criteria. But for the content sets that did not use PGUIDs, it was up to the alerting application to decide (using field-by-field comparison), whether the data it received was a new record or just a refresh of an existing record. As such, the algorithm used to decide whether content was new and alert-worthy was hit-or-miss. Customers began to realize that they were receiving duplicate alerts, while other data that should have generated an alert did not.	High	High
Severity		1

Data quality control processes are defined and followed

Data assets have a well-established set of operational data quality control processes to ensure the data's value.

Golden rule measures

Number	Golden Rule Measure
D2.6.1	Operational data quality processes include measurements of: timeliness, completeness, and accuracy vs. acceptable levels as defined in the data SLA.
D2.6.2	Operational data quality processes include turnaround time on problem resolution vs. acceptable levels as defined in the data SLA.
D2.6.2	Data quality metrics are updated at a rate appropriate to the data update frequency and importance.
D2.6.3	Data quality metrics trending-over-time is provided to support continuous improvement.

Body of evidence

Story	Impact	Likelihood
Company A spent considerable time and money collecting data from multiple sources, maintaining it, and editorially enhancing the data with annotations. But they failed to measure key data quality characteristics. So, over time, they lost visibility as to the data quality. Maintenance and improvement opportunities were also not tracked. Poor data quality lead to customer dissatisfaction, damage to company reputation, and competitive weakness. It could have led to legal liabilities as well.	High	Medium
Company B was proficient at keeping their primary content at a high-quality level, but for some reason, did not treat metadata with the same rigor. So, they could not properly determine whether data had changed and whether data reloads were successful or not. While the content curation group hit all their (self-defined) quality targets, the products did not. The search capability of the product depended on accurate metadata to achieve complete results and the alerting capability depended on knowing which data changes were the result of actual world events, rather than internal refreshes and corrections. The lack of synchronization between the groups and their internal targets let to poorly performing products and dissatisfied customers.	High	High
Company C rigorously managed the quality of its core content data and metadata but left the management of configuration data up to individual software developers and system operators with little or no oversight. An error in the configuration data in one system caused the enrichment process not to run. This caused missing data for some customers and loss of access for others. Company reputation, revenue, and customer satisfaction were put at risk.	Medium	High
Severity		1

CHAPTER 29

Modular Data – Golden Rules and Measures

Data is structured and managed so that it can be used in many products in different locales, repeatedly enriched for ever-increasing value, mined for analytics, and reformatted for optimal customer experience, at a low cost.

	Golden Rule	Severity
D3.1	Databases and models are designed flexibly to support changing requirements.	1
D3.2	Meaning is defined separately from presentation and not inferred from presentation.	1
D3.3	Master data and product data can evolve independently (i.e. are not tightly coupled).	1

Databases and models are defined flexibly to support changing requirements

The schema used to store a data asset is basically the internal representation of the structure of the data. In contrast, the data schema seen by consumers of the service is a representation of the data known as the data interface schema.

One of the most important principles of an asset-oriented architecture (AOA) is for assets to be loosely coupled. Loose coupling means that assets may be changed independently, and in any order, which implies that a change to a storage schema cannot require a change to an interface schema. Of course, to expose new functionality, interfaces and interfaces schema must change, but the salient point here is that changing a storage schema can be done without necessitating a change, and therefore making changes to the interface schema may be done thoughtfully, in a backwards-compatible manner.

When creating a data interface, the schema is generally flattened. In other words, there aren't lots of individual tables linked with foreign keys, known only by the database. The internal data model for the data master is generally highly-normalized since that data model has been optimized for "truth." The interface schema, on the other hand, should be highly-denormalized presenting a record-oriented or object-oriented view of the data. As such, the only external keys that should be presented through the interface are opaque, permanent keys (i.e. PGUIDs).

NOTE: If the data is exposed through a database-level interface (e.g., JDBC, ODBC), then the data interface schema is typically an SQL view or other DBMS-type view. This approach is not recommended, but if it must be done, it is permissible if and only if, the schema for storing the data does not require the schema used by the exposed view(s) to change.

Golden rule measures

	Golden Rule Measures
D3.1.1	The schemas used for distributing and for mastering a data asset may be modified independently of each other.
D3.1.2	The only keys used in an interface schema to reference other data items are PGUIDs.

Body of evidence

Story	**Impact**	**Likelihood**
Company A's primary revenue stream came from product X, which used the same *database definition* (DBD) for the customer-facing product and for content curation and data management. Modifications and improvements for either product or content curation became too costly and were therefore discouraged because every data change required both product and curation system changes to be released in lock-step. The lack of 'separation of concerns' caused product stagnation, loss of market share and revenue loss.	High	High

Story	Impact	Likelihood
Company B's product used structured database tables that were accessed directly by applications exposed to its customers. To compete in the market, the organization's product group defined an enhancement to the product that required a change to the table structure. This was infeasible to implement because of the number of applications that would have to be changed to conform to the new structure. The revenue that was associated with the new feature did not justify making the change, so the product stagnated. Frustration grew in the product group with the inability to justify enhancements until they eventually acquired a competing company and its products. The two product groups were then consolidated resulting in many layoffs in the technology group. Had applications been insulated from the table structure by a layer of views, the table structure could have been changed while keeping the views stable.	High	High
Company C built a product with a database, that used human readable labels as keys. A product manager requested a simple change to a field name on a report. The change could not be made, because it would have destroyed referential integrity in the database.	Medium	High
Severity		1

Meaning is defined separately from presentation and not inferred from presentation

Each field of each data item should have a well-defined simple data type (e.g. a string, an integer, a date) or compound data type (a combination of simple types). In addition, every field should be self-describing, such that the field name or field identifier tells you specifically what the field means. For example, while the field may be *address-compound-type*, its meaning might be *shipping address*, or *billing address*. Data presentation, on the other hand, has to do with how a data item is displayed and may include attributes such as font, foreground color, and spacing.

Golden rule measures

	Golden Rule Measure
D3.2.1	Presentation markup is not used to express semantics. Presentation markup, e.g. line breaks, needed to mimic the original presentation should not also be communicating semantics.

Body of evidence

Story	Impact	Likelihood
See the story about Company E for Data Asset Rule D3.1: Master data assets are modeled.	High	High
Company A supplied large structured documents to its end users (in XML), each of which had a table-of-contents that was used to navigate the document. The XML markup that was designed to be used for the Table of Contents, specified certain formatting rules such as centering and spacing. This markup was incorrectly used in other parts of the document to take advantage of the formatting rules. But when the product application reconstructed the table-of-contents from the markup, the result was incorrect and confusing. The attempted reuse of markup that carried semantic meaning for display formatting had significant unintended consequences.	Medium	High
Company B distributed two types of structured lists in its content: simple lists and checklists. Checklists, as presented in the organization's product allowed end users to edit and print, while simple lists did not. Many of the lists were misclassified (due to incorrect metadata). The net result was customer complaints resulting in a costly project to remediate the incorrectly tagged lists.	High	High
Company C was a small company delivering content to the legal industry. Newly hired editors, poorly trained in content curation practices, used product display characteristics to determine what markup they used. In other words, if it looked right in the product, that was good enough. Given they did not understand semantic markup, things that look like case citations were treated as cases, and hierarchical citations were sometimes treated as statutes, no matter what they really were. Business items were misclassified as news items; executive orders were misclassified as news items. Dates were sometimes keyed as alpha characters and sometimes keyed as numeric values. Tables-of-contents were frequently missing from content, which created a confusing navigational experience for the end user.	Medium	High
Company D distributed medical reference data. One of the content-sets they distributed were journal articles. Their primary journal article master could only handle formatted text, so when an article included an equation or an image, they were replaced with "See Equation in Original" and "See Figure in Original," making the online version of the article of limited use.	Medium	Medium

Story	Impact	Likelihood
Published Supreme Court opinions indicate the names of justices sitting at the time of the opinion using small capitals. This allows the reader to see if the statement comes from someone on the court at the time without having to look up the composition of the court on a particular date. Company F stripped out the small capitals and instead put all the names in mixed case. They also did not capture the semantic meaning of the small caps in metadata (which would have been the proper thing to do). By removing the information from the formatting and not capturing it elsewhere, they made the content less useful to the end users of their products. This especially applied to those end users who had switched from the organization's print product to their on-line product.	Medium	Medium
Severity		1

Master data and product data evolve separately

Loose coupling is defined as the manner of integrating two systems (across an interface boundary) in such a way that each can upgrade independently of the other. This definition applies equally well to both system assets and data assets. Loosely coupled assets can be developed and tested independently, reducing the total amount of integration testing required since each asset's impact on the other can be determined completely based on changes to the interface(s) between them.

To facilitate loose-coupling, well versioned interfaces (and data models) default to making all changes in a backwards-compatible manner. Backwards compatibility means that the data provider can upgrade and enhance the interface in such a way that assets which use the interface do not break.

The general rules of backwards compatibility are:

- Use the *major.minor.revision* versioning scheme (anything but a major version change must have backwards compatibility).
- Never change the meaning of a data field.
- Never delete a data field.
- Do not let internal implementation details "leak" through the interface.

- Data model changes are done solely by adding new fields. The interface contract requires that interface consumers do not *choke* when seeing a new field. They just ignore it.

Golden rule measures

	Golden Rule Measure
D3.3.1	Product data (i.e. data directly accessed in a request/response manner from product applications) is distinct from master data.
D3.3.2	A backwards-compatible change to either the master data schema or the master interface schema does not force a change to the product schema (and vice-versa).

Body of evidence

Story	Impact	Likelihood
See the story about company D under Data Asset Rule D3.2: Master Data Assets are modeled.	High	High
In company B, a product used the same database definition (DBD) for the end-user-facing product and for content curation. Modifications and improvement for either product or content curation were discouraged because of the high cost of one impacting the other. The lack of "separation of concerns" caused product stagnation.	High	High
Severity		1

CHAPTER 30

Mastered Data - Golden Rules and Measures

Master data declares an authoritative "single source of truth" that avoids data redundancy. Since it is meant to displace lower quality sources of the same data and can be used in many places, standards for master data are set to a high bar.

	Golden Rule	Severity
D4.1	Each data asset is mastered by one and only one system asset.	1
D4.2	Master data assets are modeled.	1
D4.3	Data enrichments are mastered.	1

Each data asset is mastered by one and only one system asset

The purpose of a data master is to hold "the single version of the truth" and be the authoritative source for a data asset.

Golden rule measures

	Golden Rule Measure
D4.1.1	Data assets and data items are only created or modified in the **one** system registered as their master.
D4.1.2	Data item properties are stored exactly once in the data master. If a valid reason is presented to duplicate the storage of a data item property, then rigorous methods are applied to ensure the two instances always agree.
D4.1.3	Data assets that are partly comprised of data from other masters obtain that data either directly from the data asset master or from a registered distribution system for the data asset master that provides a faithful copy.

Body of evidence

Story	Impact	Likelihood
In company A, a group building an internal administrative application required access to employee data. The process for getting access to the official database of employee data required filling out a request that justified exactly which fields were needed and why. It also required the names of every individual who would have access to the employee data and the signature of each of those individuals on a document that defined "appropriate use." Once the request was submitted to the human resources department and reviewed, password protected access would be granted (or not) to a specific table in the HR database which was purpose generated to have only the fields for which access was granted. Even though the process was arduous and bureaucratic, it was justified by the fact that company A was global, operating in over 20 countries, each of which had unique laws and regulations regarding data privacy. One of the developers in the group, frustrated by the apparent bureaucracy, started searching around the company intranet and discovered a "copy" of the employee data, which was not controlled by HR and had none of the bureaucratic restrictions. Of course, this data was not the master and unbeknownst to the development group, was neither maintained nor updated frequently. It was also missing key employee attributes as well as any data for retired employees or employees on extended leave. As such, the application was missing key data that was only discovered shortly after its release. The team had to "go back to the drawing board" and recreate the application from the proper HR database, which of course, had a completely different data model that the one they were using.	High	Medium
See story about company B, under *System Asset Golden Rule 9.1*: Register the master system asset for every data asset.	High	High
See story about company C, under *System Asset Golden Rule 9.2*: Keep data quality high.	High	High
Severity		1

Master data assets are modeled

Given the central role that data masters serve in any data-oriented system, it is imperative that not only the software be properly architected, but the data is as well. This data architecture process is also known as data modeling.

Golden rule measures

	Golden Rule Measure
D4.2.1	Master data assets are described by a conceptual data model.
D4.2.2	Master data assets are described by a logical model.
D4.2.3	Data models are maintained in an approved repository with version control.
D4.2.4	Data model changes are communicated to stakeholders.
D4.2.5	A data asset's master data interface has a physical data model and/or schema (or other design artifact) and its implementation is in strict conformance to it.
D4.2.6	Structured data fields are defined with reference to a type, foreign key, or list of values that limits the field contents to legitimate values only.
D4.2.7	The implementation of a master data asset conforms to the intent of its Data Specification.

Body of evidence

Story	Impact	Likelihood
Company A maintained data in a legacy, display-driven, proprietary format that did not provide the semantics and structure necessary for optimizing the data. As such, widely available COTS tools for editing and validating data, semantics, and structure could not be used and all editing and modeling tools had to be written internally. This led to additional cost for maintaining the proprietary systems and tools that were built over the years.	Medium	Medium
Company B maintained data in *rich text format* (RTF), a proprietary Microsoft format, which is optimized for word processing and not for the data manipulation, mining, and content curation processing. The organization had limited flexibility with master data because they couldn't use the plethora of content curation and validation tools on the market that were written to support industry standard data formats such as XML or JSON.	Medium	Medium

Story	Impact	Likelihood
Company C had a central data modeling and data architecture group, and a central group that owned all content masters. Products, on the other hand, were organized and owned by individual business units, who had complete authority to do what they needed for their products. Multiple products used the same content sets, but each product group took the central data model and modified it to suit their own needs (in a product schema). Over a two-year period, one single master data model had 27 schema versions released. Over the same two-year period, the product schema (which did not have formal models), required 59 data-schema releases. Since the product schema had neither conceptual nor logical data models, it ended up releasing over twice the number of versions, with more impact to end users than should have been necessary. The lack of models led to discovery and correction of defects later in the implementation phase.	Medium	Medium
See story about company A, under *System Asset Golden Rule 9.3: Encapsulate data*.	High	High

Story	Impact	Likelihood
Company E built all its data in logical models with structured fields, each of which had a well-defined meaning. In addition, the way the data was displayed in products was via a template, which was a data model that defined which data fields went where on the screen as well as labels and formatting and highlighting attributes. The architecture of the data was extremely well-thought-through from a distribution point of view but did not extend to the end-user product. The product application, which was installed onto end-user desktops, had to compile the templates into code for the data to display quickly enough. This dependency meant that a data change could take 18 months to deploy by the time the new data was available through the masters and distribution systems, new display templates were produced and incorporated into a product release, and the product update was distributed to end users and installed. This caused product managers to design "clever" ways of getting new data out more quickly, such as using a 24-character name field to carry two data items, a 14-character truncated name that was left justified in the field and a 7-character field that was right justified in the name field (but had nothing at all to do with a name). This became common practice. Rather than define new templates, product managers would search through existing templates for fields not currently in use and would then "squish" the new data field they needed into that format. Sometimes, the previously unused field would later need to be used for its original logical purpose; but as the field was now occupied by illogical data, more illogical data was the result. As the organization focused increasingly on data analytics, all the illogical data quickly became useless. The original logical architecture became perverted, because the architects only thought about the data mastering and distribution, without thinking about how value ultimately was delivered to the end user.	High	High
Severity		1

Data Enrichments are mastered

All data should be mastered, by which we mean there is a single, authoritative version. This includes data enrichment or derived data. Often the data enrichment is done in the master so is, by definition, mastered. But some data is simply calculated "on the fly" by products. In this case, what needs to be mastered is the process (or formula), by which the data is calculated. PBEA does not mean to imply that somehow a formula is distributed from a data master in some transportable fashion and interpreted by products (although that certainly would satisfy the golden rule). Instead PBEA simply suggests that there should be a clear mechanism to prevent two different products calculating the same value using different approaches, potentially yielding different results.

Golden rule measures

	Golden Rule Measure
D4.3.1	Decisions regarding what enrichments are applied to a given data asset are documented.
D4.3.2	Data enrichments are applied within the data asset master (system asset).
D4.3.3	Enrichments considered high value for this data asset maintain metrics that demonstrate the quality of the enrichments and the trend in that quality over time.
D4.3.4	There are committed resources responsible for maintaining enrichment to the quality level required for a positive customer experience, as evidenced by a positive enrichment quality metric trend.

Body of evidence

Story	Impact	Likelihood
Company A delivered legal data, such as federal and state statutes, cases, and judicial opinions. One of the premium features of company A's product was its ability to identify attorney and judge names in the case data and resolve those names to a specific entity in their attorney/judge master, thus providing a link from the name referenced in the case to the profile of the individual. The individual's profile would then link to other cases they had been involved in as well as case outcomes. Initially, name resolution was only done for law firms, not for government agencies. In addition, the data from some states were processed and some were not, depending on whether that data was available at the time the enrichment process ran. When a salesperson demonstrated the product to a prominent decision maker at one of the agencies, that individual immediately asked to look himself up. When he found himself missing from the database, he was unimpressed with the product, telling the salesperson "Come back when you have a product that works."	High	High
Company B was organized with a central content team, that built all its content masters, and product development teams organized by business unit. It was common practice for product managers to work only with their product development partners, while content curation staff worked only with the content team. It was not common practice for the content curation group and the product groups to coordinate their requirements and product groups tended to only involve content curation when absolutely necessary (such as when they needed to incorporate new data from a new source). If a product development group could produce some analytical algorithm to derive the data they needed from data already available from the content master, they generally did so. It was also not typical for product managers of different products to coordinate business requirements amongst themselves, so it was very common for two different products to derive the exact same logical data item using two completely different algorithms, ending up with different results. When it happened that a single end user purchased two different products from Company B, it was common for the end user to see what they believed was the exact same data field displayed with different values in each of the two products reducing confidence that either value was correct.	High	High
Severity		1

CHAPTER 31

Global Data – Golden Rules and Measures

To support the rich diversity of global business and to enable sharing data for optimization and directly for customers, data assets should follow the globalization and localization rules.

Globalization is the process of structuring, organizing, and encoding data so that it may be localized to a geography. Globalizing does not require that data subsequently be localized, but it is a necessary pre-requisite for doing so.

As such, globalizing is a good idea even if there is no existing requirement to support more than a single locality.

Please note that there is overlap between the globalization rules for data and the globalization rules for systems. This is not an accident. Most of the actual work required for globalizing is system work, but both systems and data must be globalized to actual be global.

	Golden Rule	Severity
D5.1	Number-centric data is stored in a globalized way.	3
D5.2	Textual data is stored in a globalized way.	2

Number-centric data is stored in a globalized way

Number-centric data, including time, date, and currency, is stored in a global manner, such that it may be localized to a specific geography.

Golden rule measures

	Golden Rule Measure
D5.1.1	Date, time, currency, or other numbers that may be used in calculations are stored in locale-independent representations, and optionally, additionally, in locale-specific representations.
D5.1.2	Money values that may be used in calculations are stored such that the numeric value is separated from the currency identifier. The currency identifier is compliant with the organization's *standard for the representation of currency values* (e.g. ISO 4217).[132]
D5.1.3	When money values are converted to different currencies, the original money representation is preserved.
D5.1.4	Time of day values not accompanied by a date are stored either in a DBMS-specific time type field, or in a string format compliant with the organization's *standard for the representation of date and time values*.
D5.1.5	Date/Time is stored in Coordinated Universal Time (UTC) as a single value.

Body of evidence

Story	Impact	Likelihood
Company A operated globally across 20 countries. One of the content sets that was developed in the U.S. was needed for products that were delivered to customers in Great Britain and Australia. Unfortunately, the content set encoded all monetary values in text without a currency identifier. As such, they could not be converted to local use and therefore could not be incorporated into the British and Australian products, making them inferior to local competition.	Medium	Medium
Company B delivered a product that focused on medical malpractice litigation. Part of the product's content coverage included the outcome of cases that were litigated where the amount awarded was disclosed. Unfortunately, the monetary awards were stored as text rather than as a data field, so the amounts could not be converted to "today's value." The competitor's product could do this and was thus considered superior.	Medium	Medium

---

[132] ISO 4217 – See: https://bit.ly/2E4hwv6.

Story	Impact	Likelihood
Company C stored time values in local time rather than UTC. All the organization's data centers were in the Midwest USA, so this meant central time. Products "knew" that the data centers were all in central time, so where necessary they converted to local time. As the organization expanded, it built data centers in other geographies, which also adopted the convention of using local time. Now the products had to know which geography the data came from, to convert the times correctly. When the Midwest data centers were decommissioned, and the systems migrated to the cloud, they had to artificially maintain CST to avoid product impact, even though the data centers were no longer in the Midwest.	Medium	Medium
Company D had a content set which had multiple date fields and multiple time fields. When the content set was modeled, each date/time was defined as a separate field (since that was how the data would be displayed), with no connection between dates and times. When an application using the content then converted the time (which was stored in UTC) to local time, it had no knowledge of which date field was associated with the time field, so if the local time conversion crossed midnight, the data presented to the end-user was now off by one.	Medium	Medium
Company E stored dates sometimes as alpha and sometimes as numeric. Dates related to content were not handled in a consistent way. The organization's product did not consistently interpret dates correctly in search queries and results.	Medium	Medium
Severity		3

Textual data is stored in a globalized way

Text should be represented in databases and documents using an encoding format that allows carriage of multiple languages. When text is stored or transmitted, the language of the text should be carried as well.

This is not to imply that if 90% of the content is written in English, that every data item must redundantly carry an additional field that says the data is in English. But it is to say that for the 10% which is not in English, there should be a way of carrying the language with the data.

It is important to note that the character set and encoding of the text never carries enough context to know the language of the text that was encoded. But for search engines, et al to work properly, knowing the actual language of the text is required.

Golden rule measures

Number	Golden Rule Measure
D5.2.1	Text is represented using UTF-8, UTF-16 or UTF-32 when persisted to a repository.
D5.2.2	Textual data conveys the language in which it is written.

Body of evidence

Story	Impact	Likelihood
Product M could not display special characters. As such, foreign names and terms were not reproduced faithfully and could not be searched.	Medium	High
Product N provided a common search capability across multiple content sets. Even content sets that were predominantly English had some foreign language documents, but the language of the data was not specified. As such, the product presented incomplete search results.	Medium	High
Severity		2

PART V

Technology Ownership and Operational Readiness

The role of *technology owner* was introduced in Chapter 4. It is elaborated here.

For all the technology supporting the business, explicitly defining ownership eliminates finger-pointing and prevents critical functions from 'falling through the cracks.' Defining clear responsibility and ownership helps to ensure that the technology supporting end users and employees do not become orphaned as people change jobs and the organization shifts. To this end, PBEA defines the roles of *Technology Owner* and a handful of supporting functions and provides a checklist of ownership and operational readiness.

What does a technology owner own?

A technology owner owns the process for creating software (including the systems and tools used to create it), the quality and functionality of the end result, and the system's adherence to SLAs during live operations. This includes (but is not limited to):

- **Product and asset development and operations**
    - **Architecture** - Asset inventory, technical debt management
    - **Software Development** -Source code quality control
    - **Testing** – Functional testing, performance testing, integration testing
    - **Build-to-Deploy** – Continuous integration, continuous deployment
    - **Hosting & Operations** - Account management, SLAs, reliability, availability, performance, incident response, licensing
    - **Security** - Application security, infrastructure (or environment) security, platform security, secure practices, data compliance

- **End User Computing Environments**
    - Desktops, laptops, lab machines, desktop software, software licensing, shared applications

In most large organizations, the various roles of the technology owner are delegated to individuals in the same organization as the technology owner and in some cases into other organizations. But even when responsibility is delegated, ultimate responsibility lies with the technology owner and not with any delegated person or organization. No organization is perfect, but for the sake of discussion, we will use the following typical structure, which assumes that the technology owner is responsible for the development and deployment of a group of assets as well as their hosting and live operation.

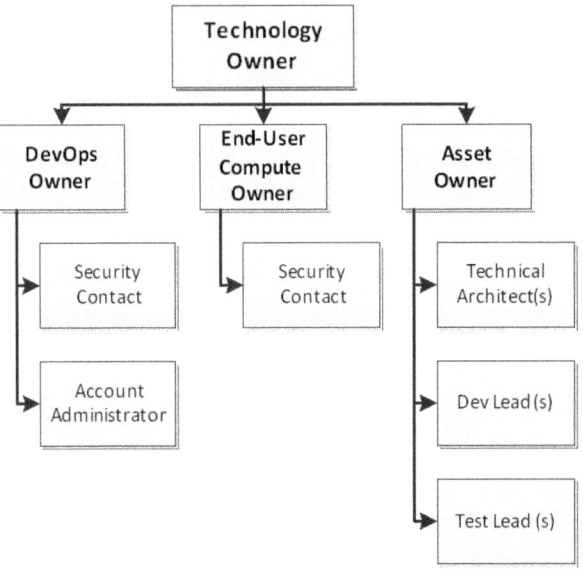

Following is a typical decomposition of roles:

- **DevOps Owner** – Responsible for hosting and operations, continuous integration, and deployment.

- **End-User Compute Owner** – Responsible for desktops, laptops, test servers, lab equipment, and all software and tools which support the process. This function is often centralized in an organization, but even though often true, the technology owner is still responsible for their own environment. This includes often ignored functions like license compliance.

- **Asset Owner** – There is a golden rule: "One Asset – One Owner." This is not to imply that a single individual cannot own multiple assets but is meant to imply that ownership of a single asset (from cradle to grave) may not be split across individuals.

Depending on the size and/or complexity of the organization, there could be an individual in each box, or every role may be performed by the technology owner herself, or anywhere in between. This is not the only way to organize roles, but it is common; as such it provides a useful model to use as the backdrop for the discussion on ownership and operational readiness. As long as the role/responsibility matrix is clearly defined, and ownership is assigned to individuals (rather than faceless organizations), the requirements of the PBEA technology ownership model are satisfied. To recap, by ownership we mean accountability and responsibility.

The following sections describe these responsibilities in more detail. Each section also lists a set of standard artifacts that should be produced by the group that owns those specific responsibilities. Where responsibilities are specific to operating in the cloud vs. an internal data center, these are broken out separately.

Asset Ownership

Asset owners are primarily responsible for the development, and deployment of assets and/or products. In a true DevOps organization, the asset owner also leads the DevOps functions covering her assets.

In larger organizations this may not be true and there may be a single DevOps function that covers assets owned by multiple asset owners. Regardless of this possibility and even if the DevOps lead is more senior than the asset owner, in the PBEA model, the asset owner is ultimately responsible for all aspects of the asset starting with requirements, through architecture and design through development, testing, deployment to live operations.

Even if hosting and operations are delegated to a separate team, the asset owner is accountable and responsible. Hence the term 'owner.'

CHAPTER 33

Architecture Responsibilities

In addition to producing the architecture and high-level design of individual assets, architecture responsibilities include working with enterprise architects to fill out the asset checklists, assessing risk, defining corrective actions., and estimating technical debt.

These responsibilities include ensuring:

1. **All assets are registered** – Each asset is represented in the asset registry and has an assigned AssetID and asset owner. Assets are the named, tangible building blocks of a technology platform.

2. **All third-party technology is registered** – PBEA strongly recommends maintaining a registry of all third-party technologies that are in use across systems. Each technology solution is associated with one or more specific technological problems and has a status (e.g. Standard, Deprecated, Prohibited). *Technology owners* are responsible for ensuring all third-party technology in use (regardless of whether it is purchased or open source) is registered and that none of this technology is *prohibited*.

3. **All assets are under architecture governance** - Architecture golden rules defining non-functional requirements have been established and the governance checklist provides a score for how each asset complies with the rules.

4. **All assets are at least *safe*** - This score indicates that the assets are secure and compliant.

CHAPTER 34

Software Development Responsibilities

Software Development Responsibilities include:

1. All source code is protected, so that it is only accessible by individuals bound by company intellectual property policy.

2. All source code is backed up according to company policy. That usually means being able to recover it even in the event of a disaster, where all the servers and potentially all the buildings become unavailable.[133]

3. Developed software meets all functional requirements defined by the business and agreed to be in the release.

4. Developed software follows the defined architecture and adheres to golden rules.

5. Developed software meets the minimum set of non-functional requirements including reliability, availability, and performance. Non-functional requirements which are not met are accounted for by the technical debt associated with the asset.

6. Developed software has sufficient hooks and debugging capabilities so that in the case of a failure or SLA violation, service may be quickly restored, and the root cause can be determined and ultimately fixed.

---

[133] I know of at least one set of products whose main servers were in tower one of the World Trade Center. Their backup servers were in tower two. They had no off-site backups. After 9/11, those products could not be updated or rebuilt. They had to be rewritten from scratch.

Testing Responsibilities

Testing responsibilities include:

1. **Functional Testing** – Ensuring each asset delivers its portion of business requirements as defined by placement-of-function.

2. **Performance Testing** – Ensuring each asset meets or exceeds its performance SLA as well as determining how far above the SLA the software is capable of handling before failing.

3. **Reliability Testing** – Ensuring each asset has no internal failures and gracefully handles the failure of assets it depends on.

4. **Security Testing** – Ensuring each asset is resilient to most known attacks and has a minimal 'attack surface.'

CHAPTER 36

Build-to-Deploy Responsibilities

This is the process of building software and deploying it to servers, as well as moving through the stages of development to testing to production. Most Agile development organizations adopt the *continuous integration (CI)*[134] model, which automates system build and deployments through development and test environments. This is often done multiple times per day and as often as every time new code is 'checked-in.'

Truly advanced organizations have so automated the continuous integration process that they have achieved *continuous delivery and deployment (CD)*[135] which extends CI through functional testing, integration testing and final deployment to the production environment.

---

[134] Continuous integration – See: https://thght.works/1khpAOV.

[135] Continuous deployment - https://bit.ly/1FtNPBw.

CHAPTER 37

Hosting & Operations Responsibilities

Hosting and Operations responsibilities include:

- **Maintaining a Resource Inventory (Compute Inventory):** Hardware inventory management processes are followed in order to ensure a central inventory of all virtual, physical or cloud-based systems used to deploy the asset is kept up-to-date. This applies both to technology deployed internally as well as that provided to customers. All physical or virtual systems are inventoried and traceable back to the assets they support and the individual(s) responsible for meeting SLAs.

- **Maintaining a Software Inventory (for License Compliance):** In order to be compliant with software licensing, each **technology owner** is responsible for ensuring that all deployed software is tracked according to software asset management. In particular:
    - Each instance is logged onto with a domain account to ensure ownership. Local accounts are *not* used.
    - All major contracts and license terms *are* in a centralized repository.

- **Providing Reliability, Availability, and Performance Reporting:** Every customer-facing product and every system asset supporting it should report regularly on reliability, availability and performance (vs SLA commitments). The DevOps team should see an SLA violation before the customers do.

- **Incident Management:** Every customer-facing product and every system asset supporting it has named individuals responsible for restoring service in the case of an outage consistent with the SLA for the product or asset. In other words, for a product that runs 24x7x365, Individual(s) responsible for Incident response are available 24x7x365.

Artifacts needed:

- **Reliability, Availability, and Performance Report** – This report tracks whether the asset is meeting is health, latency, response-time, error-rates, up-time, et al vs the defined SLA and over time. There should follow organizational standards defined for these reports so that the reports from multiple assets from multiple asset owners and technology owners may be amalgamated into a single report for a product.

- **Resource Inventory** – This report lists all compute, network, storage, and software-as-a-service (SAAS) resources supporting each asset. In the cloud, this is essentially what gets billed, so if resources are tagged with the AssetID, this report becomes easy to produce.

- **Software Inventory** – This report lists all licensed software (including open source) installed on every compute instance supporting each individual asset. The software inventory report may then be used to verify software license compliance.

CHAPTER **38**

Hosting Security Responsibilities

Each **Technology owner** needs to have a designated *security point of contact* (which could be the technology owner herself).

A security point of contact understands how the group or unit uses technology along with the efficacy of local security controls. In working with leadership, they balance the need to secure the business with the need to run the business effectively.

These security points of contact form a virtual team that may be called to respond to security incidents affecting the entire company. Have a process for convening the team and dealing with company-wide security emergencies. Who owns managing an emergency of that scope? How is it handled if that person is on vacation? What is the internal SLA for responses from each security contact? Rehearse this at least annually.

As asset and project teams create, set up, and/or manage technology, they need to ensure that they continue to meet and/or exceed company policy and standards as well as adhere to the PBEA golden rules.

Security processes

The following processes are recommended:

- **Security Assessments:** There are two security assessments required when deploying technology to a hosting provider.

- o Ensure that a Third-Party Security Assessment[136] is completed and up to date for the hosting provider. This ensures that the hosting provider has sufficient capabilities (if correctly implemented) to meet company security requirements.

- o Ensure that a VPC Security Assessment[137] is completed for each environment. This ensures that the design and implementation of the Virtual Private Cloud (VPC) for each environment meets security requirements. This includes:
    - IP Address ranges in use properly allocated
    - VPC Flow logs are enabled
    - Access logs are enabled for all load balancers
    - Any DNS name in use is properly registered
    - Firewalls between the VPC and the data center and between the VPC and the end users are properly configured.

- **Asset Stack:**
    - o Use an approved machine image that has been properly hardened and patched.
    - o Rotate images at least every 90 days to ensure latest patches are applied but be prepared to apply patches immediately when a *zero-day exploit*[138] is discovered.
    - o Refresh images with critical patches within the 90-day window.
    - o Ensure access controls between services (security groups) are defined.
    - o Regular Security Testing includes specific scans:
        - Perimeter scans
        - Vulnerability scan
        - Configuration Scans
        - Source code scans are optional. Peer code review is recommended instead.

---

[136] A Third-Party Security Assessment is a placeholder for whatever process the organization uses to determine that the Cloud or Hosting provider has sufficient capabilities (with external certification) that a properly implemented technology stack is secure.

[137] A VPC Security assessment is a placeholder for whatever process the organization uses to determine that a VPC design has sufficient controls.

[138] A zero-day exploit is a cyber-attack that occurs on the same day a weakness is discovered in software. See https://bit.ly/2DiIMrj.

- **Access Privileges:**
    - The privileges granted to an individual *should* adhere to the principle of least-privilege. More on the IAM user account access, below. If the individual leaves the organization or changes jobs, access privilege is quickly revoked. Internal attacks from malicious employees or ex-employees are a significant source of security exposure.
    - Regularly review whether everyone who has access privileges still requires it to perform their job.

Artifacts Needed:

- **Third Party Security Assessment** - Ensures that the hosting provider or service provider has sufficient capabilities (if correctly implemented) to meet company security requirements.

- **VPC Security Assessment** - Ensures that the design and implementation of the Virtual Private Cloud (VPC) for each environment meets security requirements.

- **Security Scan Report** – Details whether perimeter scans, security scans, configuration scans and peer review of source code has been performed, how recently and the results.

Cloud account management

Having administrative access to cloud accounts allows an individual to stand up resources and services in a VPC and therefore potentially run up large bills. As such, delegating that responsibility requires review and governance by the technology owner. This includes responsibility for running the systems in the account, and ensuring the bills get paid.

The *account administrator* is the individual with delegated authority from the *account owner* or *technology owner* to administer the account and is also the person who generally has root credentials. The administrator may then delegate certain responsibilities to other members of the team according to the principle of least privilege.

The following processes and controls are recommended:
- **Use the Company Master Account:** There should be a master account for the organization, where billing, invoicing and volume discounts are handled. Cloud Accounts *are* provisioned under this master account. Employees should never open

Cloud Accounts using personal or corporate credit cards (unless the organization does not have a master account). The master billing account is also referred to as the 'payer account' or 'consolidated billing account' depending upon the context of the discussion.

- **Provision Cloud Accounts only to organizations that operate assets** - Accounts should not be provisioned for individuals or projects. This implies that the account (and the associated credentials and billing responsibilities) are associated with products, platforms, or assets.

- **Each account should have a single 'root account' identity with unrestricted control over the account.** – The root account acts as the account 'super user' and is used to provision user accounts. This 'root account' identity *must not* be used for console Access or API access under normal circumstances. Root account identity access keys *must* be disabled. This prevents using the root account for API access. Root account console sign-in credentials *should* be stored in a secure repository with access for the primary and secondary owner.

- **In each account, specific IAM[139] user accounts are provisioned.** The privileges granted should adhere to least privileges appropriate to the type of account (dev, test, and prod). IAM user accounts with administrative or escalated privileges makes use of two-factor (multi-factor) authentication. When available, IAM user accounts should be federated to the appropriate individual's enterprise credentials to provide account lifecycle management (i.e. if the individual leaves the organization or changes jobs so that they no longer play a role requiring access, this access is quickly revoked).

- **The account owner will have general administration duties or oversight of their account and usage within -** The account owner is *accountable* for attending periodic business reviews to assess account usage and potential security and cost optimization opportunities.

- **Billing alarms should be created and set to the thresholds of the monthly anticipated spend** - The account owner is accountable for responding to those billing alarms and adjusting resource usage accordingly.

- The account owner is the primary contact for the cloud vendor technical account manager (TAM) and will be sent notifications and information.

- Each account should enable CloudTrail on their account (for AWS).

---

[139] IAM = Identity and Access Management.

End-User Computing Environment Responsibilities

End-user compute responsibilities include the allocation of desktops, laptops, servers, lab equipment and all software, tools, and configuration which support the process. This function is often centralized in an organization, but even though often true, the technology owner is still responsible for their own environment. This includes often ignored functions like license compliance.

Appendices

- **Appendix 1** – provides a checklist for technology ownership and operational readiness. This is where we capture "rules" that apply to groups of assets, organizations, processes, and environments.

- **Appendix 2** – provides an additional checklist for technology ownership and operational readiness for environments that are deployed in the cloud environment rather than a private data center.

- **Appendix 3** – provides a quick reference for the golden rules for systems.

- **Appendix 4** – provides a quick reference for the golden rules for data.

APPENDIX 1

Technology Owner Checklist

Below is a checklist of responsibilities of a **Technology Owner**. Further descriptions of each of the checklist items are in the sections above.

Asset Ownership	
☐	All source code is protected, so that it is only accessible by individuals bound by company policy.
☐	All source code is backed up according to company policy.
Architecture	
☐	Every asset is defined in the asset inventory.
☐	All third-party technologies are registered. No technology in-use is prohibited.
☐	An asset checklist has been completed (to the appropriate governance level) for each deployed asset.
☐	Every asset is *safe* (i.e. security and compliance is low-risk).
Hosting & Operations	
☐	All resources (compute, network, and storage) are inventoried and traceable back to the asset.
☐	All software deployed on any server (or infrastructure) is appropriately licensed and maintains security updates.
☐	Access to hosted resources is constrained to properly provisioned authenticated individuals within the account following the *rules of least privilege*.
☐	A report or dashboard is available (and produced on a regular basis) for all products and systems (whether internal or customer-facing) detailing Reliability, Availability and Performance (as per company standard metrics).
☐	A report or dashboard is available (and produced on a regular basis) for all products and systems (whether internal or customer-facing) detailing all SLAs (as per company standard metrics).
☐	There is a documented process for resolving incidents and outages including identified ownership and escalation.
☐	Disaster recovery is periodically and regularly tested, and the results are published.
Hosting Security	

☐	Company security standards and policy statements that apply to your environment are fully understood and complied with.
☐	There is a designated security point of contact for every product or system and this individual is known to the CISO.
☐	The contractual security, privacy, and compliance addendums for all third-party services are complied with.
☐	Each deployment has completed (and passed) a security assessment (either directly or indirectly by deploying using a pre-approved VPC template).
End-User Computing	
☐	All desktops, email and network access are protected according to company policy.
☐	All software deployed on any desktop is appropriately licensed.
☐	All individuals (employee or contractor) using company equipment or company licensed software have a company ID assigned. When an individual exits the organization, their credentials and privileges are revoked quickly (e.g. within 24 hours).
Environment Security	
☐	Company security standards and policy statements that apply to the environment are fully understood and complied with.
☐	There is a designated security point of contact for every environment (end-user-computing and/or lab machines) and this individual is known to the CISO.
☐	Computers that are used for browsing the Internet do not have transparent write access to data masters or production systems.
☐	Computers that are used for browsing the Internet do not have access to sensitive administrative interfaces.
☐	All changes to either the software installed in production environments, as well as the configuration of those systems and connecting network are recorded.
☐	All increases and decreases in capacity are recorded.
☐	All recorded changes to production environments are performed by individuals with appropriate authority and reviewed and approved by individuals of appropriate authority.
☐	Auditable records of all changes, who made the changes, and who approved them are retained according to the organization's retention policy.
☐	All code destined for production undergoes a code review by at least one other qualified individual <u>before</u> being installed in production. The review results are retained.
☐	A security defect analysis on all source code is performed at least annually.

APPENDIX 2

Additional Checklist for the Cloud

Account Management	
☐	Accounts are provisioned under the Company Master Account.
☐	Account contact information for billing and invoicing, security, and operations is populated, defaulting to the DevOps team lead.
☐	CloudTrail logging is enabled (in AWS). The ability to delete or tamper with logs is disabled.
☐	Billing alarms are set up and handled.
☐	Periodic business reviews are scheduled with the cloud provider to ensure resources are being used efficiently.
Identity and Access Management	
☐	The *root account keys* are disabled.
☐	The *root account console credentials* (username/password) are stored in a secure repository.
☐	IAM accounts are provisioned such that each individual granted access is granted only the minimum access necessary to perform their job.
☐	Any individual with IAM credentials is tracked to ensure they are an employee or contractor of the organization and remain so. Credentials and access privileges are withdrawn quickly after an individual leave the organization (e.g. 24 hours).
☐	End-user passwords meet the minimum standard for complexity, so they are hard to guess.
☐	Multi-factor authentication (MFA) is used for external access to administrative interfaces. (e.g. password plus IP address).
Configuration	
☐	Rules are set up to ensure all compute instances are associated with known VPCs.
☐	Rules are set up to ensure all IP addresses in use are attached to compute instances (e.g. EC2 for AWS) or network interfaces (e.g. ENI for AWS).
☐	All resources follow the tagging standard to ensure they are properly associated with, assets, environments, products, and billing.
Logging	
☐	CloudTrail logs for AWS, or the equivalent, have been enabled for every region in each account.

☐	VPC flow logs for AWS, or the equivalent, have been enabled for all VPCs.
☐	Standard naming conventions have been applied to organize and access log files.
☐	CloudTrail logs, for AWS, or the equivalent, have been collected into a centralized bucket in the object store (S3, for AWS) accessible only by authorized teams.
☐	Config logs, for AWS, or the equivalent have been collected into a centralized bucket in the object store (S3, for AWS) accessible only by authorized teams.
☐	VPC flow logs, for AWS, or the equivalent have been collected in a centralized bucket in the object store (S3, for AWS) accessible only by authorized teams.
Security	
☐	A *security assessment* has been completed achieving a minimum of level of trust for each environment.
☐	There exists an approved security evaluation for the hosting provider.
☐	IP address ranges in use have been allocated by a central authority to ensure there are no conflicts.
☐	An approved VPC pattern has been followed.
☐	Compute instances only reside in a non-default VPC (which has been assessed).
☐	A standard "locked-down" machine image is in use.

APPENDIX 3

Golden Rules for Systems Quick Reference

1	**Secure Systems (*Safe* Solutions)**	Severity
1.1	Protect end-user authentication secrets.	1
1.2	Control access to important systems and data.	1
1.3	Keep web traffic private.	1
1.4	Sanitize inputs from untrusted sources before use.	1
1.5	Do not let data become code.	1
1.6	Minimize access to regulated data and protect it when used.	1
1.7	Do not place sensitive data in a URL.	2
1.8	Use third-party software safely.	1
1.9	Catch internet-facing security exposures before they are exploited.	1
1.10	Record and report on important security related events.	1
1.11	Use standard authentication implementations.	2
1.12	Use standard encryption implementations.	3
1.13	Architect system assets to degrade gracefully when attacked.	1
1.14	Deploy system assets only into known safe environments.	1
2	**Compliant Systems (*Safe* Solutions)**	
2.1	Protect the organization's intellectual property (IP).	3
2.2	Use third-party intellectual property (IP) in accordance with its license.	1
2.3	Store source code in a secure and managed repository.	2
2.4	Ensure end-user interfaces are accessible.	1
3	**Scalable Systems (*Responsive* Solutions)**	
3.1	Deliver acceptable performance under anticipated load. Degrade gracefully when load exceeds capacity.	2

3.2	Optimize the cost of capacity.		2
3.3	Set appropriate limits on auto-scaling.		1
4	**Manageable Systems (*Responsive* Solutions)**		
4.1	Respond to standard control commands dynamically.		1
4.2	Publish appropriate operational events and error messages.		2
4.3	Publish Performance and Capacity data.		1
4.5	Maintain a complete inventory of all operational resources.		1
5	**Reliable Systems (*Responsive* Solutions)**		
5.1	Record all requests and measure adherence to your SLA.		1
5.2	Record all requests made to other assets and measure the dependent assets' adherence to their SLA.		2
5.3	Continue to meet SLA obligations in the event of a single resource failure.		1
5.4	Continue to meet SLA obligations in the event of a site failure.		2
5.5	Ensure that functional testing of the solution, includes at least one test case covering each of the capabilities or features supported (as defined by placement-of-function).		2
5.6	Handle hard failures (unrecoverable) and soft failures (recoverable) appropriately.		2
5.7	Ensure all production changes are repeatable and auditable.		1
6	**Simple Systems (*Effective* Solutions)**		
6.1	Do not use unmaintained assets or deprecated APIs.		1
6.2	Do not couple an asset to an environment.		2
6.2	One asset, one team.		1
6.3	Follow placement-of-function (PoF).		2
6.4	Package code to facilitate independent releases.		2
6.5	Minimize code duplication.		2
7	**Modular Systems (*Effective* Solutions)**		
7.1	Expose and consume only well-defined external interfaces.		1
7.2	Manage and version control external interfaces.		1
7.3	Do not couple external interfaces to their implementation.		2

7.4	Handle retries appropriately.	2
8	**Maintainable Systems (*Effective* Solutions)**	
8.1	Make interfaces directly callable without requiring a proprietary library.	1
8.2	Trace requests and failures to their source.	2
8.3	Appropriately comment source code, schemas, and interfaces.	2
9	**Mastered Systems (*Effective* Solutions)**	
9.1	Register the master system asset for every data asset.	1
9.2	Keep data quality high.	1
9.3	Encapsulate data.	1
9.4	Trace data to its source.	1
9.5	Do not connect end-user applications directly to content masters.	1
9.6	Do not lose data.	2
10	**Global Systems (*Effective* Solutions)**	
10.1	Handle data in a globalized way.	1
10.2	Distinguish third-party translations from company translations.	1
10.3	Adapt to the user's preferred locale.	2

APPENDIX 4

Golden Rules for Data Quick Reference

		Severity
D1	**Compliant Data (*Safe* Solutions)**	
D1.1	Classify and manage data according to the data classification.	1
D1.2	Retain data as required by the business and by legal and regulatory requirements. Destroy thereafter.	2
D2	**Reliable Data (*Responsive* Solutions)**	
D2.1	Data curation processes are designed and followed.	1
D2.2	Data schemas are defined and adhered to.	1
D2.3	Data is accurate.	1
D2.4	Data is complete.	1
D2.5	Data is timely.	1
D2.6	Data quality control processes are defined and followed.	1
D3	**Modular Data (*Effective* Solutions)**	
D3.1	Databases and models are designed flexibly to support changing requirements.	1
D3.2	Meaning is defined separately from presentation and not inferred from presentation.	1
D3.3	Master data and product data can evolve independently (i.e. are not tightly coupled).	1
D4	**Mastered Data (*Effective* Solutions)**	
D4.1	Each data asset or data item is mastered by one and only one system asset.	1
D4.2	Master data assets are modeled.	1
D4.3	Data enrichments are mastered.	1

D5	**Global Data (*Effective* Solutions)**	
D5.1	Number-centric data is stored in a globalized way.	3
D5.2	Textual data is stored in a globalized way.	2

Index

access controls, 131
access privileges, 287
agility, 52
Amazon S3, 181
Amazon Web Services (AWS), 23
amplified attacks, social engineering, 77
anticipated load, performance under, 160–61
Apache Struts library, 139
API governance, 51–53
API inventory, 65, 66
API review, 49
application asset, 21
application programming interfaces (APIs), 21, 24, 49
architect system assets, and denial-of-service attack, 150
architects, 37
    enterprise (EAs), 41
    solution, 41
    solution (SAs), 93
    technical, 41, 93
architectural approach, 2
architecture, 39
    definition of, 1
    enterprise, 1, 2–3
    enterprise, definition of, 1
    physical, 49
architecture debt, 57, 60, 61–62, 104
architecture diagramming, 69
architecture golden rules, 105, 275
architecture governance, 47–54
    PBEA method for, 61
architecture metrics, 55
    asset checklist and, 55–59
architecture objectives, for systems, 107–9
architecture patterns, 69
architecture principles, 55, 56
    of PBEA, 103
architecture responsibilities, 275
architecture review process, 49
architecture roles, 37
asset
    application, 21
    service, 21
asset behaviors, 58
asset checklist, 55–59
asset governance, 47–49
    purpose of, 57
    triggers, 51
asset governance process, and architecture debt, 61
asset instance failure, 81
asset inventory, 65, 66
asset owners, 20, 40, 190, 273
asset scores, 56
asset stack, 286
asset team, leader of, 20
asset-oriented architecture (AOA), 19, 47, 251
assets, 3, 15, 19–20
    coupling and environments, 189–90
    data, 3
    independent, 20
    loose coupling of, 255
    ownership of, 190–91
    software, 21
    system, 3, 20–23
    types of, 19
    unmaintained, 187–89
authentication solutions, 147
auto-scaling group, 159
auto-scaling process, limits on, 164–65
availability, measuring of, 80
best practice, definition of, 65
blackouts, 82
body-of-evidence, 63, 105
broken windows theory, 195
brownouts, 82
build-to-deploy responsibilities, 281
business benefits, and enterprise architecture, 47
business capability, 14–15
business capability owner, 38
business continuity, 82
capacity, 171
capacity cost, optimization of, 161–63
catastrophic impact, 11
change management, 87

circuit breaker pattern, 206
cloud account management, 287–88
cloud checklist, 295–96
code complexity, 194
code duplication, 194–95
code path analysis, 71
code, packaging of, 192
commercial off-the-shelf (COTS) packages, 21
commercial-off-the-shelf software (or COTS), 30
compliance architecture, 75
compliance exercise, 75, 76
compliance failure, 107
compliant data, 111, 235–39
compliant solutions, 153
compliant systems, 115–16
   and intellectual property, 153
component, 3
component behavior, definition of, 1
component, definition of, 1
configuration management database (CMDB), 68
consume-ability, 52
continuous delivery and deployment (CD), 281
continuous integration (CI), 281
contract, service interface, 26
Cookbook, 69
corporate standards, enforcing, 53
cryptolocker, 76
data
   accuracy of, 245–46
   and code, 136–37
   and company translations, 227–29
   and compliant systems, 115–16
   and modular systems, 197–206
   and reliable systems, 119
   architecture objectives for, 111–12
   mastering of, 213–23
   modular, 251–56
   nature of, 27
   regulated, 137–39
   reliable, 241–50
   sunsetting, 222–23
   textual, 267
   third party translation and, 227–29
   timeliness of, 248–49
   translation of, 227–29
data architecture process, 259
data asset golden rules, goal of, 233
data asset host inventory, 65, 67
Data Asset Host registry, 214
data asset owner, 40
data asset, completeness of, 247
data assets, 3, 14, 19, 27–30, 59, 233
   authoritative source for, 257–58
   debt and, 60
data assets schemas, 251
Data Breach Prevention and Compensation Act, 139
data classification, 28, 235–36
data curation, 241–43
data encapsulation, 218–19
data enrichments, 262–63
data interface schemas, 252
data interfaces, 252
data masters, 214–15
   and end-user applications, 220–21
data modeling process, 259
data presentation, 253–55
data protection, 28
Data Protection Regulation 2016/679 (GDPR), 28
data provenance, 219
data provider, 227
data quality, 216–18
   control processes for, 249–50
data quality control processes, 249–50
data quick reference, golden rules for, 301–2
data retention, 28, 237–39
data sanitization, 133–36
data schemas, 243–45, 251
Data Service Level Agreement (SLA), 29
data source, 219–20
data specification, 29–30
data storage, 27
data type, 253
databases, and changing requirements, 251–53
dataset classification, 235
debt, 56, 59, 63
   and commercil decision, 62
   and financial planning and analysis function, 63
   and IT planning and execution decisions, 63
   architecture, 57, 60, 61–62
   calculating, 60–61
   maintenance, 63
   technical, 61–62, 62
decomposition of roles, 270

denial-of-service attack, 150, 160
Department of Health and Human Services, 237
dependent assets, 177–78
deprecated APIs, 187–89
design, definition of, 1
destructive test, 72
development environment, 17
disaster recovery, 81
domains, 19
effective solutions, 14, 123
   and architecture objectives for data, 112
   and architecture objectives for systems, 108–9
employee authentication, 147
encapsulation, 121
encryption implementations, 149
end-user authentication, 147
end-user authentication secrets, 129–31
end-user computing responsibilities, 289
end-user interfaces, accessibility of, 157
enterprise architects (EAs), 37, 41, 56, 59, 93
   and the governance process, 48
enterprise architecture, 2–3
   metric based approach to, 3
   purpose of, 13
enterprise architecture (EA)
   component of, 63
enterprise architecture (EAs), 1, 41
   and PBEA approach, 93–99
enterprise architecture governance, 55
enterprise architecture, definition of, 1
enterprise environment, 17
environments, 16–17
Equifax, 139
error messages, publishing, 169–71
errors, handling, 184
evidence, body of, 63, 130–31
   and access control, 132
   and and web traffic, 133
   and assets coupling, 189–90
   and auto-scaling, 165
   and calleable interfaces, 208
   and capacity cost, 162–63
   and code duplication, 194
   and code packaging, 193
   and data, 137
   and data accuracy, 245–46
   and data classification, 236
   and data completeness, 245–46
   and data curation, 242–43
   and data encapsulation, 218–19
   and data enrichments, 262–63
   and data masters, 221
   and data presentation, 254–55
   and data quality, 217–18
   and data quality processes, 250
   and data retention, 238–39
   and data sanitization, 135
   and data schemas, 244–45
   and data source, 220
   and data timeliness, 248–49
   and data translation, 228–29
   and databases and models, 252
   and dependent systems' SLAs, 178–79
   and deprecated APIs, 188
   and end-user accessibility of, 157
   and external interfaces, 199–201, 203, 205
   and failures, 210–11
   and functional testing process, 183
   and global data, 227
   and handling errors, 184
   and intellectual property (IP), 154
   and internet-facing security exposures, 144
   and master data assets, 214–15, 259
   and number centric data, 266–67
   and operational events, 170–71
   and operational resources inventory, 172–74
   and performance and capacity data, 172
   and placement-of-function, 192
   and product and master data, 256
   and production changes, 185
   and regulated data access, 138
   and retries, 206
   and security event reporting, 145–47
   and sensitive data, 140
   and site failure, 181–82
   and SLA adherence, 176
   and source code storage, 157
   and source codes, 212
   and standard authentication, 148–49
   and standard encryption, 150
   and sunsetting data, 222
   and system assets, 150
   and textual data, 268
   and third party intellectual property, 155–56
   and third party software, 142–43
   and unmaintained assets, 187–89
   and user's preferred locale, 230–31
asset ownership and, 191

    authoritative source for data assets, 258
    standard control commands, 169
    system assets, 151
    under anticipated load, 161
external interfaces, 198–201
    and version control, 202–3
external interfaces (APIs), 204–5
failure scenarios, 80–82
failures, and its source, 209–11
Federal Energy Regulatory Commission, 237
financial planning and analysis function
    and debt, 63
functional specification, 29
functional testing process, 182
functional tests, 279
funding envelopes, 35
Gartner TIME model, 21
GDPR (General Data Protection Regulation), 28
global data, 112, 226–27, 265–68
global solutions, 225
globalization, 225, 265
golden rule, 87–89
    and data globalization, 225
    and global data, 265
    and maintainabe systems, 207
    and manageable systems, 168
    and modular data, 251
    and modular systems, 197
    and reliable systems, 175
    and simple systems, 187
    for data protection, 235
    for master data, 257
    for reliable data, 241
    of data handling, 213
    of PBEA, 105
golden rule measures, 127–28, 130
    ad master data assets, 214
    and access control, 131
    and asset ownership, 191
    and assets coupling, 189
    and auto-scaling, 164
    and callable interfaces, 208
    and capacity cost, 161
    and code duplication, 194
    and data, 136
    and data accuracy, 245
    and data classification, 235
    and data completeness, 247
    and data curation, 242
    and data encapsulation, 218
    and data enrichments, 262
    and data masters, 221
    and data presentation, 253
    and data quality, 216
    and data quality processes, 250
    and data retention, 237
    and data sanitization, 134
    and data schemas, 244
    and data source, 220
    and data timeliness, 248
    and databases and models, 252
    and dependent systems' SLAs, 177
    and deprecated APIs, 188
    and end-user accessibility of, 157
    and external interfaces, 198, 202, 205
    and failures, 210
    and functional testing process, 183
    and global data, 226
    and handling errors, 184
    and handling retries, 206
    and intellectual property (IP), 153
    and internet-facing security exposures, 144
    and master data assets, 259
    and master system asset, 214
    and number centric data, 266
    and operational events, 170
    and operational resources inventory, 172
    and performance and capacity data, 171
    and placement-of-function, 192
    and product and master data, 256
    and production changes, 185
    and regulated data access, 138
    and sensitive data, 140
    and site filures, 181
    and SLA adherence, 176
    and source code storage, 156
    and source codes, 212
    and standard authentication, 148
    and standard control commands, 168
    and standard encryption, 149
    and sunsetting data, 222
    and system asset deployment, 151
    and system assets, 150
    and textual data, 268
    and third party intellectual property, 155
    and third party software, 142

and translation of data, 228
and unmaintained assets, 188
and user's preferred locale, 230
and web traffic, 132
authoritative source for data assets, 257
for code packaging, 193
security events reporting, 145
under anticipated load, 160
golden rules
for data quick reference, 301–2
for systems quick reference, 297–99
of PBEA, 101, 103
Google CDN, 141
governance, challenges of, 50
Health Insurance Portability and Accountability Act's (HIPPA), 237
high impact, 11
hosting and operations, 39
hosting responsibilities, 283–84
houses, 3
human interfaces, 21
impact
catastrophic, 11
high, 11
medium, 11
implementation patterns, 69
incident management, 283
independent assets, 20
independent releases, 192
Infrastructure as Code (IaC), 122
infrastructure asset, 31
initial build cost, 60
integration test, 72
intellectual property (IP)
protection of, 153
third party, 154–56
intellectual property protection, 115
interface contract, 197
interface definition, 26, 199
interface schemas, 243
interface version, 26
interface, definition of, 1
interfaces
and commenting on, 211–12
making callable, 207–8
internet-facing security exposures, 144
inventories, 65–66
inventory, definition of, 66
IT planning and execution decisions

and technical debt, 63
JavaScript library, 141
jQuery, 141
legacy technology, 22
Lemme, Peter, 180
licensing risk, 141–42
licensing terms and conditions, definition of, 30
lifecycle, system's, 21
limits, 26
Lion Air, 180
locale, user's preferred, 230–32
locales, best practices for handling, 231–32
localization, 225
localization rules, 265
loose coupled assets, 255
loosely coupled modules, 121
maintainable solutions, 207–12
maintainable systems, 123, 207–12
maintenance, 63, 123
maintenance debt, 61, 63
manageable solutions, 167–74
manageable systems, 117–18, 167–74
master data, 257–63
and product data, 255–56
master data assets, 259–61
master system asset, registering, 214–15
mastered data, 112
medium impact, 11
message implementations, 204
microservice, 21
modification rights, definition of, 31
modular data, 112, 251–56
modular systems, 197–206
and data, 197–206
modularity, 121, 197, 198
monitoring practice, 83–84
Murphy's Law, 179
negative outcomes, 64, 103
Netflix, 181
non-functional requirements, 13
Nu News, 43–45
number-centric data, 265–67
on-premises hardware, 31
operational characteristics, 26
operational events, publishing, 169–71
Operational Expense (OpEx), 23, 68, 161
operational governance, 59
operational instance inventory, 66, 68–69
operational practice, 82

operational resources, inventory of, 172–74
outcomes, negative, 64
outcomes, positive, 64
owner
   asset, 40
   business capability, 38
   data asset, 40
   product, 37–38
   technology, 38–40
ownership, definition of, 30
parameterized queries, 136
patterns, 69
PBEA approach, implementation of, 93–99
PBEA Architecture principles, 14
PBEA golden rules, 74
PBEA governance processes, 53–54
PBEA method, 11–12
   and architecture governance, 61
   business objectives of, 14
PBEA Objectives
   governance levels and, 49
PBEA processes, 17
PCI regulations, 137
penetration tests, 73
performance, 171
performance and capacity data, publishing, 171–72
performance measurement, 79–80
performance reports, 283, 284
performance tests, 279
personally identifiable information (PII), 236
PGUID namespace, 214
PGUIDs (Permanent globally unique identifiers), 220, 222, 249
physical architecture, 49
physical assets, and infrastructure assets, 31
placement-of-function (PoF)
   follow, 192
placement-of-function (PoF), 15–16
   artifacts, 16
   process of, 15
placement-of-function (PoF) inventory, 65, 66
platform, 19
positive outcomes, 64, 103
Principle Based Enterprise Architecture (PBEA) Method, 3, 11–12, 65
problem resolution process, 32
product data, and master data, 255–56

product owner, 37–38
production changes, 185–86
production environment, 16
products, example of Nu News, 43–45
profiles, of assets, 57
program increments, 35–36, 48
proprietary library, 207–8
public APIs, 52
public interfaces, 30
records, legal requirements and, 237
recoverable failures, handling, 184
recovery point (RPO), 73
recovery time (RTO), 73
redistribution rights, definition of, 31
region failure, 81
registries, 65
registry, definition of, 66
regulated data, access to, 137–39
reliability tests, 279
reliability, measuring of, 80
reliable data, 112, 241–50
reliable solutions, 175–86, 175–86
reliable systems, 175–86
   and data, 119
Representational State Transfer (REST), 24
requests, and its source, 209–11
resource inventory, 284
resource inventory, maintaining, 283
responsive solutions, 14, 111
   and architecture objectives for systems, 108
   and Service Level Agreements, 78–79
responsive solutions, 117
responsive solutions, 117–18
responsive solutions, 119
retries, handling, 205–6
reuse, 51
risks
   abstract, 141
   managing, 74
   mitigating, 74
root cause analysis, 90
safe solutions, 14, 129–31
   and architecture objectives for data, 111
   and architecture objectives for systems, 107
safe solutions, 115–16
sanitization, data of, 133–36
Sarbanes-Oxley Act, 237
scalable architecture, 117

scalable solutions, 159–60
scalable systems, 117, 159–65
Schaeffer, Dwight, 180
secure solutions, 129
secure systems, 129–31
    and measures, 129–31
    golden rules and, 129–31
security, 39
security architecture, 74–75
security breach, 107
security compliance, 75–76
security events, reporting, 145–47
security exercises, 75
security function, placement of, 76
security incidents, 76–78
security organization, 76
security processes, 285–87
security related events, reporting, 145–47
security scan report, 287
security testing tools, 73–74
security tests, 279
sensitive data, 140
Separation of Concerns, 197
servers, poorly managed, 77
service asset, 21
service interface contract, 26
Service Interfaces (APIs), 24–26
Service Level Agreements (SLAs)
    adherence to, 176–77
    and responsive solutions, 78–79
    for a system, 23–24
    guarantees for, 24
service, definition of, 1
service-oriented architecture (SOA), 19
services, 19
    degradation of, 84–85
    provided by a system asset, 24
simple solutions, 187–95
simple systems, 187–95, 187–95
single asset, 19, 20
single resource failure, 80
    and SLA obligations, 179–80
Single Team Owned Service Architecture (STOSA), 20
site failure, 81
    and SLA obligations, 181–82
Smith, Richard, 139
social engineering amplified attacks, 77
Software as a Service (SaaS), 49

software asset governance, 53–54
software asset governance process, 53–54
    business benefits of, 53
Software Asset Management (SAM), 30, 53, 141
software assets, 21, 30–31
software development, 39
software development lifecycle (SDLC), 48, 51
software development responsibilities, 277
software inventory, 284
    maintaining, 283
software license compliance, 116, 141
solution architects (EAs), 93
solution architects (SAs), 37, 41, 56
    and the governance process, 48
solutions, 14–15, 15
    and business capabilities, 15
    testability of, 70–71
source, 219
source code
    commenting on, 211–12
    storing of, 156
source code control system, 32
standard authentication, implementation of, 147–49
standard control commands, response to, 168–69
standard encryption, implementation of, 149
system
    migration of, 21–23
    retirement of, 21–23
system asset governance process, 51
System Asset SLA (Service-Level Agreement), 23–24
system assets, 3, 19, 20–23, 48
    and API review, 49
    and measures, 127–28
    and software assets, 30
    architect, 150
    degradation of, 160
    deployment of, 151
    encapsulation, 197
    golden rules of, 127–28
    master, 214–15
    services provided by, 24
    unit testing of, 71–72
system images, 32
systems and data
    global, 125–26
    mastered, 124–25

systems assets, governance levels for, 49–50
systems quick reference, golden rules for, 297–99
systems, and loose coupling, 121
systems, architecture objectives for, 107–9
team, ownership of, 190–91
technical architects (TAs), 37, 41, 56, 57, 93
   and the governance process, 48
technical architecture, 41
technical debt, 47, 61, 62
Technology Health and Business Risk
   dashboard, 56
technology owner, 38–40, 269, 285
   checklist, 293–94
technology ownership, 269–71
technology problems, 147
Technology Solution Classification
   Methodology, 92
technology standards, 90–92
technology standards registry, 65, 67
technology war stories, 11
test environment, 16
test harness, 71
testability, 70
testable solutions, 70–74
testing responsibilities, 279
textual data, 267

third party security assessment, 287
third-party repository, 141
third-party software, safety and use of, 140–43
third-party technology, 275
threats and attack vectors, 76
total cost of ownership (TCO), 108
true cost, 35, 60–61
trusted code repositories, 141
U.S. Department of Labor's Occupational Safety
   & Health Administration (OSHA), 237
U.S. Equal Employment Opportunity
   Commission, 237
U.S. Securities and Exchange Commission, 238
unit test, 71–72
unmaintained assets, 187–89
unrecoverable failures, handling, 184
URL, and sensitive data, 140
usage rights, definition of, 31
version change, 31–33
version, interface of, 26
versioned interfaces, and loose coupling, 255
versioning. See version change
VPC security assessment, 287
waterfall delivery model, 35
web traffic, private, 132

www.ingramcontent.com/pod-product-compliance
Lightning Source LLC
LaVergne TN
LVHW081529060526
838200LV00049B/2263